THE KOREAN ECONOMIC DEVELOPMENTAL PATH

The Korean Economic Developmental Path

Confucian Tradition, Affective Network

Seok-Choon Lew

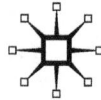

THE KOREAN ECONOMIC DEVELOPMENTAL PATH
Copyright © Seok-Choon Lew, 2013.
All rights reserved.

First published in 2013 by
PALGRAVE MACMILLAN®
in the United States—a division of St. Martin's Press LLC,
175 Fifth Avenue, New York, NY 10010.

Where this book is distributed in the UK, Europe and the rest of the world, this is by Palgrave Macmillan, a division of Macmillan Publishers Limited, registered in England, company number 785998, of Houndmills, Basingstoke, Hampshire RG21 6XS.

Palgrave Macmillan is the global academic imprint of the above companies and has companies and representatives throughout the world.

Palgrave® and Macmillan® are registered trademarks in the United States, the United Kingdom, Europe and other countries.

ISBN: 978–1–137–35972–8

Library of Congress Cataloging-in-Publication Data

Lew, Seok-Choon, 1955–
    The Korean economic developmental path : Confucian tradition, affective network / Seok-Choon Lew.
        pages cm
    Includes bibliographical references and index.
    ISBN 978–1–137–35972–8 (hardback : alk. paper)
    1. Economic development—Korea (South) 2. Korea (South)—Economic policy. 3. Korea (South)—Social policy. 4. Confucianism and state. 5. Korea (South)—Civilization—Confucian influences. I. Title.
HC467.96.L49 2013
338.95195—dc23   2013025075

A catalogue record of the book is available from the British Library.

Design by Newgen Knowledge Works (P) Ltd., Chennai, India.

First edition: December 2013

10 9 8 7 6 5 4 3 2 1

*To my wife,
Young-Kyung Ko,
with love and friendship forever.*

Contents

List of Figures and Tables	ix
Preface and Acknowledgments	xi
List of Contributing Coauthors	xv
Notes on Korean and Chinese Letters, Names, and References	xvii
List of Chinese Letters (Classic, not Simplified)	xix

Introduction

Chapter 1
Missing Links in Understanding Korean Development   3

Part I   The Cultural Dimension: Confucian Tradition

Chapter 2
Confucian Ethics and the Spirit of Capitalism in Korea:
The Significance of Filial Piety
with Woo-Young Choi and Hye Suk Wang   25

Part II   The Social Dimension: Affective Networks

Chapter 3
Affective Networks, Social Capital, and Modernity in Korea
with Mi-Hye Chang and Tae-Eun Kim   49

Chapter 4
Historical Development of Affective Networks in Korea:
The Nongovernmental Sector and Confucian Tradition
with Mi-Hye Chang   75

Part III The Political Dimension: State–Society Relations

Chapter 5
Confucian Capitalism of Park Chung Hee:
Possibilities and Limits   95

Chapter 6
Generalized Reciprocity between Strong State
and Strong Society: Park Chung Hee and the
Korean Developmental Path
with Hye Suk Wang   119

Chapter 7
Did the 1997 Financial Crisis Transform the
S. Korean Developmental State? Focused on
the Public Fund
with Hye Suk Wang   141

Conclusion

Chapter 8
Moral Economy of Growth   173

References in English Language   183

References in Korean Language   197

Index   205

Figures and Tables

Figures

1.1 The articulation of formal and informal sectors in the Korean development model: economic, political, and sociocultural dimensions   18

6.1 Synergy between strong state and strong society   123

7.1 Arrangement of bureaucratic agencies, before the enactment of the Public Fund Oversight Special Act, 2000   161

7.2 Arrangement of bureaucratic agencies, after the enactment of the Public Fund Oversight Special Act, 2000   163

Tables

1.1 Economic policies of the Korean development model: support and discipline   6

2.1 Practice of ancestor rites by religion, 2000   41

2.2 Youth's opinion on future practice of ancestor rites, 2008   42

2.3 Housewives' opinion on ancestor rites, 2003   43

3.1 Classification of groups   52

3.2 Institutionalization of affective networks in East Asian business organizations   54

5.1 Survival of 100 largest firms in Korea, 10-year intervals, 1965–1985   105

5.2 List of top 10 *chaebols*, three time points   106

6.1 Types of developing countries   121

6.2	Forms of social capital	122
6.3	Financial resources of the *Saemaeul Undong* (New Community Movement)	130
7.1	Mobilization of the public fund by financial resources (Nov. 1997–Jun. 2006)	145
7.2	Government expenditure and the public fund, 1998–2006	147
7.3	Changes in number of financial institutions, 1997 and 2006	148
7.4	Distribution of the public fund by injection type and financial institutions	149
7.5	Government ownership change among commercial and local banks	150
7.6	Composition of top 30 *chaebols'* borrowings by year, 1991–2000	154
7.7	Corporate sector's financial liabilities outstanding, 1997–2002	157
7.8	Assets and sales of top 50 and 200 companies	158
7.9	Public fund recovery by types (Nov. 1997–Jun. 2006)	166

Preface and Acknowledgments

Ever since I started teaching at Yonsei University in 1987, there have been many people who still teach me to become a real "scholar" sensitive to Korean context. Colleagues in social science, on and off campus, as well as journal editors, popular and academic, used to ask me if conceptual schemes adopted and empirical evidences provided are applicable and relevant to Korean setting. Among many, however, believe it or not, the most demanding group is the students, and it is for sure that this book is an output of such pressures from the students.

A convincing proof would be the fact that contributing coauthors of chapters included in this book are all my former graduate students: Mi-Hye Chang (chapters 3 and 4), Woo-Young Choi (chapter 2), Tae-Eun Kim (chapter 3), and Hye-Suk Wang (chapters 2, 6, and 7). I have to confess that we had so many occasions to argue against and even "yelling" to each other to carry on almost every chapter draft. Coworking with students is not as comfortable as some would imagine. Students are the most critical reference you can have, because they know what you have been preaching and writing which means, in turn, you cannot cheat them at all. In this sense, they as well as I went through the same thorny path. This is precisely the reason why I appreciate pressures from their passion, intelligence, and partnership.

It goes back to the late 1990s when I first work on affective network and Confucianism. It was at an international conference held in *Andong*, a spiritual capital of Korean Confucianism located at a hilly and isolated town of southeastern part of Korea. Chaibong Hahm, Gilbert Rozman, Daniel Bell, Yun-Shik Chang, and Geir Helgeson were among the many I met there and they offered tremendous challenging ideas on Confucian legacy of Korea or East Asia. This book is a collection of my endeavors with graduate students thereafter until 2012.

This book defines the Korean development as the moral economy of growth derived from a synergy between a strong state and a strong society and argues that Confucian cultural orientation has played a critical role in the process. In the Introduction (chapter 1), shortcomings of conventional political or economic explanation are critically reviewed and a new integrated multidimensional perspective to articulate the interplay of cultural, social, and political dimensions of Korean development is offered. Then the text is divided into three parts.

Part 1, made of one single chapter (chapter 2), starts with an explanation on the cultural dimension of Korean development focusing on filial piety. The Confucian imperative of filial piety, which demands remembering and representing one's ancestors, acts as an important spiritual ethos for Koreans to become economically competitive by providing a self-sacrificing work ethic and zeal for education. It argues that filial piety did not stop at being a simple ethical standard: it was the fundamental moral basis for a macro-social dynamic closely linked to the development of capitalism and democracy in Korea.

Part 2, made of two chapters (chapter 3 and 4), is devoted to describing the institutionalization of Confucian value into a unique social arrangement in which "affective networks" formed along traditional ties are contributing positively to the development of "strong society" in Korea. Chapter 3 asserts that affective networks based on traditional human relations are forms of social capital that enrich trust and generalized reciprocity in modern Korea. Chapter 4 traces the historical development of affective networks in modern Korean civil society, particularly in nongovernment and nonprofit sectors.

Part 3, made of three chapters (chapter 5, 6, and 7), shifts the focus to political dimension: state–society relations. Chapter 5 highlights "Confucian capitalism" in which state bureaucrats organized capitalism in a way that policy decisions of the state superseded decision-makings of businesses, and the private sector was mobilized around the needs and plans of the state through traditional Confucian affective networks. Chapter 6 challenges conventional assumption that Korean development was achieved by "strong state and weak society" and illustrates how Korea during the Park Chung Hee era was a showcase of synergy between a strong state and a strong society. This combination evinces the mutual embeddedness of the state and society under Confucian culture. Chapter 7 examines the path that the Korean developmental state took after the 1997 crisis by focusing on the "public fund" used for restructuring the economy. It deplores the missing disciplinary role: the state's incapacity in disciplining the society. Chapter 8 concludes the book with a brief discussion on the theoretical underpinning of affective network on trust and social capital to establish the significance of moral economy.

This book traces back the origins of Korean development from the cultural and moral dimension, and argues that the source of weakened autonomy and capacity of the state after the 1997 crisis also should be traced from the loss of fundamental ethos. It elucidates the positive effect of cultural inheritance that has been most blamed in the earlier studies as hampering economic growth and democratization of Korean society: Confucianism, affective networks, and state intervention. As such institutional characteristics have undeniably formed the historical path of Korean development, the future of Korean development cannot be alienated from this path as well.

Institutional supports that enabled me to complete this book should be acknowledged. One year leave from Yonsei with the University Research Grant in 2009 allowed me to concentrate on completing the whole work. A visiting fellowship at the Korea Institute, Research School of Pacific and Asian Studies, the Australian National University, for the period of March to July 2009, offered me a perfect environment to continue the work. Professor Hyung-A Kim and Jim Fox were great intellectual partners to work with. The Korean-American Educational Commission offered a Fulbright Senior Research Grant for the period of September 2009 to January 2010 to be a visiting fellow at the Graduate School of International Relations and Pacific Studies, University of California, San Diego to carry out the work. Professor Stephan Haggard and Jong-Sung Yoo, as well as Jihyeon Jeong, then PhD student, were, big or small, inspiring partners working there. Also, this work was supported by the Academy of Korean Studies (KSPS) Grant (AKS-2007-CB-2001) funded by the Korean Government (Ministry of Education).

In preparing the final draft including tables, figures, and references, I have the fortune to have Min-Woo Ji, Minyong Lee, and Kyu-Eun Kim to provide a quick proof sorting and reading. In addition, I have to express sincere gratitude to Gilbert Rozman, Princeton University, who suggested me to submit the manuscript to Palgrave Macmillan so that I can work with Koohi-Kamali Farideh and Isabella Yeager to edit and publish. Lastly, I want to make a note that Professor Hattori Tamio of Tokyo University has been a continuous source of intellectual stimulus in writing this book.

Chapter 1 is largely from a book chapter, "The Korean Development Model: Lessons for Southeast Asia," pp. 176–204, in David I. Steinberg (ed.), 2010. *Korea's Changing Role in Southeast Asia: Expanding Influence and Relations.* Singapore: Institute of Southeast

Asian Studies (ISEAS). Chapter 2 has appeared in "Confucian Ethics and the Spirit of Capitalism in Korea: The Significance of Filial Piety." *Journal of East Asian Studies*, Volume 11 Number 2 (2011), pp. 171–196. About half of chapter 3 is from a book chapter, "Affective Networks and Modernity: The Case of Korea," pp. 201–217, in Daniel A. Bell and Hahm Chaibong (eds.), 2003, *Confucianism for the Modern World*. Cambridge: Cambridge University Press.

Contributing Coauthors

Woo-Young Choi is an associate professor of sociology at *Chonbuk* National University in Korea and completed a doctoral dissertation at *Yonsei* University in 2002, entitled "The Public Spirit of *Sarim* Politics in the Middle *Chosun* Period: Ideology, Structure, and Change." Since the summer of 2013 he is on leave for a year at the University of Washington, Seattle, to carry out a team project on East Asian welfare regime.

Hye-Suk Wang is a research professor of Institute of East and West Studies, *Yonsei* University in Korea and stayed for two years at the National Taiwan University to complete a doctoral dissertation at *Yonsei* University in 2013, entitled "Familial Foundations of the State Welfare: A Comparative Approach to the National Health Insurance Program in S. Korea and Taiwan."

Mi-Hye Chang is a senior researcher at the Korean Women's Development Institute and completed a doctoral dissertation at *Yonsei* University in 2001, entitled "Relative Effects of Cultural and Economic Capital on Mode of Consumption: Survey Findings on Seoul Residents." Her recent research works focus on multiculturalism in Korea.

Tae-Eun Kim is an MA graduate in sociology from *Yonsei* University in 2000, and her MA thesis was entitled "Formative Principles of Pre-Modern Korean State: Local Governance System in Centralized *Koryo* Dynasty."

Notes on Korean and Chinese Letters, Names, and References

Korean letters including names of people and places are romanized following the McCune-Reischauer system, except for already established customs such as Syngman Rhee, Park Chung Hee, Seoul, or *chaebol*. Frequently appearing Korean terms such as *Yŏn'go* are followed by the Chinese letters and English translation in parentheses. The names of Korean authors are romanized, using the spelling that appears in their publications. If they appear in the main text or in chapter endnotes, family names with first name initials, usually separated two capital letters, are suggested, for example, Ahn C. Y. If their references (articles or books) are in Korean language, the separated two capital letters of their first name initials are connected with a hyphen, for example, Choi B.-Y. Full names are listed in the bibliography with McCune-Reischauer Romanization in parenthesis, for example, Choi, Bong-young (Ch'oe, Pong-yŏng) and Ahn, Chung Young. For Chinese terms, the Pinyin system is adopted, except for already established ones such as Chang Kai-shek or Lee Kuan Yew.

Chinese Letters (Classic, not Simplified)

Chapter 1

Confucian tradition (儒敎傳統)

affective networks or alternatively "*Yŏn'go Kwan-kye*" (緣故關係)

blood relations (血緣)

school ties (學緣)

acquaintanceship by locality (地緣)

dongchanghoi (同窓會, alumni association of a school)

hyangwuhoi (鄕友會, social gatherings of people from the same home town)

sarim (士林)

state–business collusion (政經癒着)

Yŏn'go (緣故)

Guanxi (關係)

Chapter 2

filial piety (孝, *xiao* in Chinese, *hyo* in Korean, and *kou* in Japanese)

the Way (*Dao*, 道)

the Principle (Li, 理)

the Supreme Ultimate (*Tai Ji*, 太極)

the Five Cardinal Relationships (*Wu-Lun*, 五倫)

affection between father and son (父子有親)

ancestor worship (祖上崇拜)

CHINESE LETTERS (CLASSIC, NOT SIMPLIFIED)

coming-of-age (冠)

marriage (婚)

funeral (喪)

ancestor memorial (祭)

four previous generations (四代奉祀)

rising in the world and achieving fame (立身揚名)

father and son (父子)

ruler and subject (君臣)

husband and wife (夫婦)

elder and younger brother (兄弟)

friend and friend (朋友)

Fung Yu-lan (馮友蘭)

the Heavenly Principle (天理)

Chapter 3

affective networks (緣故關係, *yŏn'go kwankye* in Korean)

group egoism (集團利己主義)

guanxi (關係, relation)

chaebol (財閥, conglomerate)

keiretsu (系列, line or sub-contract relation)

xiangzhen enterprise (鄉鎮企業)

jiazu enterprise (家族企業, family enterprise)

family (家 *jia* in Chinese)

blood ties (血緣)

school ties (學緣)

regional or locality ties (地緣)

kye (契, a traditional way of saving among close friends, or, micro-credit rotating) *hyangwuhoi* (鄉友會, social gatherings of people from the same hometown)

chongchinhoi (宗親會, an extended family reunion)

the *Song* (宋) dynasty in China

Zhu Xi (朱熹)

xing-li-xue (性理學)

public (公)

the virtue (德)

exemplary persons (君子)

authoritative conduct (仁)

private (私)

self-cultivation (修身)

The *Great Learning* (大學)

irrationalism (無理)

Rejection and Defeat Campaign (落薦落選運動)

New Democratic Party (新民黨)

Democratic Reunification Party (統一民主黨)

New Korea Democratic Party (新韓民主黨)

Peace and Democratic Party (平和民主黨)

New Democratic Union (新民主聯合)

Democratic Party (民主黨)

New Political National Congress (新政治國民會議)

New Millennium Democratic Party (新千年民主黨)

Chapter 4

promoting friendship (親睦圖謀)

mutual help (相互扶助)

ye (禮, the highest moral value)

xxii   CHINESE LETTERS (CLASSIC, NOT SIMPLIFIED)

sarim (士林, literati out of state office)

hyang'yak (鄉約, village pact)

appeals directly to the king (上疏, presenting memorials to the King)

exemplary person (君子)

commoner (小人)

ruling by virtue (德治)

Chapter 5

Categorizing vocations into high and low classes and ranks social order in a hierarchical manner (士農工商, literati, farmers, artisans, and traders in descending order)

The philosophy of practical learning (實學, *shilhak*)

The institution of civil service examinations (科學制度)

affective networks (緣故)

ties based on blood (血緣)

ties based on locality (地緣)

ties based on school (學緣)

state–business collusion (政經癒着)

searching for fish in trees (緣木求魚)

National Security Legislature Council (國保委)

Social Purification Committee (社會淨化委員會)

guanxi (關係)

Chapter 6

diligence (勤勉)

self-help (自助)

corporation (協同)

serve the nation through enterprise (企業報國)

Order of Industrial Service Merit (產業勳章)

National Restoration (民族中興)

Modernization of the Fatherland (祖國近代化)

Chapter 7

the principle of separation of industrial and financial capital (金産分離)

The Government Funds Management Fund (*Kong'gong cha'gŭm kwalli kigŭm*, 公共資金管理基金)

Introduction

Chapter 1

Missing Links in Understanding Korean Development*

Introduction

The 1990s and 2000s exhibited an explosion of work on the fast-growing economies of East Asia, by individual scholars as well as international development institutions. Several influential books such as Johnson (1982), Amsden (1989), and Wade (1990) have explored the distinctive nature of the East Asian developmental state, especially the role of government in determining the allocation of resources to particular industries, in building industrial infrastructures through public firms, and in developing the educational system. A widely discussed report published by the World Bank (1993) on the East Asian "miracle" endeavored to draw lessons, not just from the experience of Japan, South Korea, and Taiwan but also from four fast-growing economies in Southeast Asia—Singapore, Indonesia, Malaysia, and Thailand. They all pointed out that high-performing Asian economies are the only economies that achieve high growth and diminish inequality at the same time.

Most of this literature considers the region to be economically integrated, coherent, and homogeneous. Terms such as the "Asia-Pacific," "Pacific Asia," "East Asia," "Asian Miracle," "Yen Bloc," "flying geese," "tigers," "dragons," and so on have tended to reflect and encourage this perception (Jomo, 2001). However, this perception is far from the truth: the countries of the region have little in common in terms of the nature, quality, and effectiveness of their developmental paths. To be sure, the World Bank differentiates first-tier newly industrializing countries, such as Taiwan and South Korea, from second-tier newly industrializing countries, including Indonesia, Malaysia, and Thailand. The World Bank stresses that despite differences in their initial conditions and periods of industrialization, the miracle of rapid development in both tiers would not have been possible but for market forces and government intervention with market-friendly industrial policies.

However, even the little dragons, as the first group is called, show varied degrees of state intervention, industrial policies, and strategies for catch-up to follow divergent paths (Feenstra and Hamilton, 2006). Shin J. S. and Chang H. J. (2003) insist that states in Japan and South Korea pursued market-substituting strategies, whereas other dragons, Singapore and Hong Kong, pursued market-complementing ones. Regarding the role of government, they also insist that even the Korean experience can be differentiated from the Japanese case. In the midst of this lack of agreement about how economic development in the region came about, this book tries to spell out the crucial aspects of Korean economic development. Existing literature on the Korean developmental state shows its limits by overfocusing on economic institutions and policies. This perspective falls short in explaining why some underdeveloped countries, in pursuing a development strategy similar to the Korean one, could not catch up.

This book highlights a different aspect of Korean development—behind the scenes, at the level where the sociocultural milieu comes into effect (Platteau, 1994a, 1994b). In particular, this book focuses on the relationship between the strong state and strong society to explain how generalized reciprocity was created and resulted in a synergy of benefiting development (Evans, 1995; Woolcock, 1998). This is not to say that initial conditions such as economic and political institutions do not matter, but institutional arrangements can be the result of cooperation between the state and society (Putnam, 1993a; Evans, 1996). Sound strategic prescriptions may be copied, but they cannot work properly in alienation from their social and cultural contexts (Chang H. J., 2007; Rodrik, 2007).

Understanding how the Korean developmental model functioned is one thing; claiming that developing economies should follow and emulate the Korean model is another. Too many differences exist between Korea and other developing countries. With regard to the viability and replicability of the Korean developmental model, this book emphasizes on the sociocultural resources that every country inherited from history that might be utilized as a positive factor for the developmental recipe (Rodrik, 2007). Of course, these are Confucian traditions (儒教傳統) and affective networks (緣故關係) that characterized the Korean path of development.

The Korean Developmental Model and Its Missing Links

The Economic Dimension

Many studies deal with the question of whether the economic policies that Korea selected and pursued were economically rational or technically expedient (Johnson, 1982; Amsden, 1989; Wade, 1990; World Bank, 1993; Woo-Cumings, 1999; Haggard et al., 2003; Shin J. S. and Chang H. J., 2003). They stress the important role of government's strategic industrial policies and state intervention with financial support and discipline. However, characterizations of the role of the state and the industrial policies taken by the Korean government vary from market enhancing and market friendly to market substituting.

Some take the Korean case as a textbook study of economic development through strategic participation in the international economy with free-market and free-trade policies, namely, the kinds of policies and institutions that constitute the Anglo-Saxon model. This represents the market-enhancing or market-friendly view (Balassa, 1981; World Bank, 1991, 1993; Aoki, Kim H. K. and Okuno-Fujiwara, 1997). If this interpretation is adopted, there is no point in talking about the Korean development model, because it would essentially be the same as the Anglo-Saxon model (Chang H. J., 2006). Others insist that Korea's rapid growth was possible because of the strategic violation of neoclassical economic rules: they represent the market-substituting view. Further, they charge that the World Bank's *East Asian Miracle* study of 1993 misjudged the Asian miracle as the result of reliance on market forces and "getting prices right" (Amsden, 1989; Wade, 1990; Shin J. S. and Chang H. J., 2003; Chang H. J. and Grabel, 2004; Chang H. J., 2006). For them, Korean development was the result of "getting prices wrong" and the distortion of market prices.

To evaluate these two contrasting views, the main institutional features of the Korean developmental state must be scrutinized. The most widely recognized characteristics of the Korean developmental state model may be "financial support with discipline" (Davis, 2004) as discussed in chapters 5, 6, and 7. However, this feature also exists, more or less, in the market-oriented model, which has never existed in the history of capitalism in pure form (Chang H. J., 2002; Polanyi, 2001[1944]; Fligstein, 1996, 2001). If that is the case, what makes the support and discipline of the Korean development model so particularly effective and efficient that it can outperform the Anglo-Saxon one? The following examination of three arenas—investment, industrial, and trade policies—will offer clues, scrutinizing how and for whom the state extended financial support and, finally, how it disciplined recipients of its support (see Table 1.1).

In trade policy, the export success of Korea is often touted as exemplifying the doctrine of comparative advantage and free trade. However, this view underestimates the historical fact that informational and financial aid from the government was crucial in helping firms export. It is impossible for firms in newly developing countries to compete with already well-established firms from developed countries in the international market. In the face of such competition, it is necessary for the newly developing country to deliberately violate the principle of comparative advantage and protect the new, or "infant," industry before it attains internationally competitive levels of productivity (Lin and Chang H. J., 2009).

In order to help exporting firms, the government provided export subsidies (Amsden, 1989). These subsidies were in the form of loans for exporters, tariff rebates on export inputs, or a generous "wastage allowance" to exporters using domestically scarce inputs (Chang H. J., 2006). The government also provided information on foreign markets, usually through the government trading agency (KOTRA: Korea Trade Agency) but sometimes even through the diplomatic service. There were also efforts to promote the development of private sector organizations that could perform some of these functions (such as exporters' associations, industry-based associations, or general trading companies).

However, such support was not for every sector or every firm. The government offered this support only to targeted industrial sectors, which were anticipated to be competitive in the international market. This included organizing mergers and negotiated market segmentation in industries with too many producers and of suboptimal

Table 1.1 Economic policies of the Korean development model: support and discipline

Policy	Support	Discipline
Industrial policy	Selective support for infant but to-be-competitive industry	Periodical screening of rent recipients
Investment policy	Financial support through nationalized banks	Capital outflow control
Trade policy	Informational and financial support for exports	Heavy tariffs or bans on unnecessary imports

Source: Lew S. C. and Wang H. S. (2010: 179).

scale: subsidizing capital equipment upgrading through "rationalization" or "modernization" programs aimed at specific industries; directly or indirectly subsidizing research and development (R&D) or training in specific industries through the operation of public research or training institutes; and spreading information on best-practice technologies in particular industries through various public or semipublic agencies. As a result, it fostered more favorable conditions for domestic firms to fully realize economies of scale.

Those who are skeptical about state intervention argue that such "selective" industrial policies that target specific sectors or even firms do not work because they often "distort" market signals, are technically difficult to manage, and are liable to capture and corruption by interest groups. However, in a world of limited financial resources and administrative capabilities, there are always some degrees of "selectivity" involved in the execution of industrial policy. Moreover, in developing countries with the weak administrative capacities, policies that are more precisely targeted may in fact have a better chance of success because they save administrative resources.

However, government support is only half of the story. Singapore and Taiwan also used similar financial support for private capital (Jomo, 2003; Shin J. S. and Chang H. J., 2003; Shin J. S., 2005a, 2005b). The important characteristic that differentiates the Korean case from these countries is the disciplinary intervention of the state. The Korean developmental state exerted strict control over private capital to encourage it to be invested and used in a productive way (Davis, 2004).

In any country, especially in the early stages of development, capital flight has to be prevented in order to ensure that whatever investible surplus is generated in the economy at least stays in the country. Korea was not an exception and maintained very strict regimes of capital control until the early 1990s. Every economic transaction involving foreign exchange had to be made through the banks under government ownership and/or control, and those who attempted major capital flight faced heavy punishments, including the death penalty.

The state also controlled the investible capital surplus of *chaebols* so that it could be appropriated in productive investment rather than in consumption. The state imposed heavy tariffs and domestic taxes on—and sometimes even banned the domestic production as well as the import of—certain "luxury" products, especially in the early stages of development. Of course, control over luxurious consumption goods was motivated by political as well as economic concerns.

The disciplining of the privileged class consumption created and enhanced the sense of a national community that shared burdens and fruits equally (Chang H. J., 2006: 28). This concept of sharing contributed to political stability and led to an increase in investment.

More importantly, the state periodically screened the recipients of its support, mostly *chaebols*, on the basis of individual performance to maintain a minimum, if not maximum, level of productivity and competitiveness in the market. *Chaebols* that failed to achieve such levels of performance were expelled from the market. This competition under the governance of the state was harsher and even more ruthless than market competition, as reflected by the volatility in rankings of the top ten *chaebols* in the 1960s and 1970s (chapter 5).

The picture of the Korean developmental state, suggested above, is far from what the World Bank called "free trade" and "getting basic things right." The state deliberately created oligopolistic or even monopolistic market conditions. Neoclassical economists charge that the absence of market competition results in inefficiency, waste of resources, and moral hazard. However, the market is not the only mechanism for the allocation of limited resources. In fact, if there is a failure of coordination, the market causes more tragic social waste, as witnessed by the recent crisis stemming from Wall Street. In the case of Korea, state governance prevented excessive and destructive competition among rational fools from causing allocation inefficiency and social waste. As a result, the competition mechanism created by the state outperformed the market mechanism (Amsden, 1989; Chibber, 1999).

The Political Dimension

Effective intervention in the market through support and discipline requires a strong state equipped with high levels of autonomy and capacity. No matter how proper and perfect economic institutions and policies may be, they must still be successfully imposed on society. This is why other developing countries have failed in achieving economic growth and social development despite following industrial policies similar to those used in Korea. At one extreme, some dismiss the importance of economically rational or technically expedient policies in Korean economic development. They insist that historical serendipity rather than strategic calculation made by autonomous state elites was at play here (Chibber, 2003), and scholars would later classify its result as strategically rational and expedient (Davis, 2004: 151–152). Support and discipline cannot work properly to extract visible results without a strong state capable of pushing capitalists to cooperate with its developmental strategy. Especially regarding the relationship between the state and capitalists, many studies stress the importance of state autonomy in the development process and assume that the Korean state was sufficiently autonomous from its capitalist class that it could simply impose a new developmental strategy with little regard to how firms would react (Chibber, 2003: 52). However, these studies never clearly explain how the state could aggressively orchestrate the big firms' growth and the activities, sometimes even assigning individual firms specific projects to carry out. Some refer to the absence of domestic bourgeoisie (Hamilton, 1986; Amsden, 1989, 2000), while others point to the beneficial legacy of colonialism (Kohli, 2004) or Confucian culture (Berger, 1988; Clegg, Higgins, and Spybey, 1990; Appelbaum and Henderson, 1992; Shin D. C., 2012). These perspectives fail to explain why the same continuity or legacy cannot be applied to the Syngman Rhee administration (1948–1960). Chronological continuity may not always result in structural continuity (Lynn, 2005).

Any account of the developmental state must therefore explain how states acquire power and autonomy, that is, how they originate. To answer this question, this book focuses on state capacity. Two dimensions of state capacity can be suggested: internal and external dimensions of state bureaucracy (Chibber, 2002, 2003). The internal dimension refers to cohesion among intra-state agencies and the external dimension to the state's disciplinary hold on the dominant extra-state agencies, especially capitalists. In other words, state capacity refers to the state's ability to formulate and implement policies in a coherent fashion and to impose discipline on private firms as well as across governmental agencies.

The most critical factor in enhancing state capacity is internal cohesiveness across governmental agencies.[1] Internal cohesiveness is generally supplied by the presence of a robust and rule-following disciplined corps with a "bureaucratic rationality" (Johnson, 1982; Evans, 1995). However, in order for a developmental state to be effective, bureaucratic rationality must also be structured along with the appropriate appointment of power among state policy agencies. In this respect, the existence of technocrats during Korean economic development can be a stereotype of bureaucrats with internal cohesion (Chibber, 1999; Kim H. A., 2004).

The convincing evidence of enhanced internal capacity would be the launching of the new government organization, the Economic Planning Board (EPB) in 1961 at the top of the state bureaucracy to take charge of the entire process of economic development. While economic policy-making had previously been dispersed across a number of agencies,[2] it came to be centralized in the EPB. The EPB quickly became the apex body for economic policy and planning. That was possible because the arrangement of intra-state power relations was transformed to accommodate the mandate given to this new agency. Not only did the EPB exercise direct control over critical elements in the policy process, it was also able to command authority over the functioning of other ministries so that they were answerable to it on an ongoing basis (Chibber, 2002; Kim E. M., 1997).[3] This ensured that Korean state leaders were able to monitor the performance of other agencies and, hence, more effectively oversee the formulation and implementation of policies (Shin J. S. and Chang H. J., 2003). The series of Five-Year Economic Development Plans are just one well-known product of this unit among numerous contributions it made in the subsequent process of Korean development.

The external dimension of state capacity was structured by another major step taken to firmly institutionalize the state's control over the economy, namely, the so-called Illicit Wealth Accumulation Charges (Kim H. A., 2004). It aimed to confiscate illegally amassed fortunes and prosecute related profiteers. Businessmen, especially the *chaebol* leaders, who had made their money under the favors of the past Rhee regime, were arrested and later released in return for their public commitment to "serve the country through enterprise" (企業報國). Although the charges ended in compromise and appeared to be a political ritual without substance, an important consequence ensued. The majority share of the ownership of private banks was nationalized and state-owned banks were subsequently created to give the government rigid regulatory power and dominance over the capitalists (Woo-Cumings, 1999; Kim H. A., 2004; Davis, 2004). In the absence of an alternative route to financial resource mobilization, it gave the state an effective stick to wield against particular firms once the strategy was in place (Chibber, 2003: 58).

Herein lie two key elements of political institutionalization: the creation of coherent bureaucratic agencies that can discipline business and the monopolization of financial resources as their instrument of discipline. With these institutional innovations, Park's government quickly gained firm control over the economy and effectively forced business decisions to follow policy recommendations geared for rapid growth. In the process, of course, those who were obedient to state initiatives were rewarded and those who were against state initiatives were brutally penalized (Chang H. J., 2006). The state did not hesitate to use noneconomic means to achieve compliance with policy directives. However, this explanation, limited to political institutions, fails in answering the following question: why did state bureaucrats not seek their private interests through rent seeking like other strong states did in those times and what made them head straightforwardly for development (Kim H. A., 2004)? In fact, many strong states in underdeveloped countries, based on their high level of autonomy compared to their weak societies, extract the resources of society for private interests and thereby degenerate into "predatory" states (Evans, 1995). The high level of state autonomy itself can be the necessary condition for a predatory state as well. Two factors determine a state's path. One is the intra-state factor, that is, a disciplinary ethos. The other is the extra-state factor, the presence of strong society endowed with a diverse stock of social capital and networks (Putnam, 1993a; Woolcock and Narayan, 2000).

As mentioned above, the main character of Korean state intervention can be summarized as "support with discipline." Here, the word "discipline" can be extended to a more comprehensive discourse on "disciplinary ethos." A disciplinary ethos is "a conception that assumes a certain degree of austerity, self-regulation, and self-imposed personal restraint marshaled in the service of an individual producer's output or productivity" (Davis, 2004: 11). The important point is how and why the state was charged with a disciplinary ethos. Davis (2004: 13) finds the source of this ethos in the "rural-middle-class embeddedness of the state." The inauguration of Park's regime meant that, for the first time in Korean history, political leaders from the rural middle class held state power. Unlike the former president Rhee, Park's regime was supported by the military forces—most of which, including Park himself, were from the rural middle class.

Park considered the "natural diligence and disciplined life of small peasants" ideal and compared it with "lavishness, excessive consumption, and corruption of the landlords and capitalists" (Davis, 2004: 104). He thought that the rural middle class was "industrious, self-disciplined, and capable of restraining consumption" (Davis, 2004: 105)—core elements of an ethic for developing the economy through savings. Park shared the perception of the rural middle class that most rural problems were caused by the usurious and import-substituting class (Kim H. A., 2004). To amend the behavior of amoral capitalists, Park thought the state should have more direct control over resources and redistribute these resources to the rural middle class (Davis, 2004: 99). "Imposing a rural-based, disciplinary orientation onto a capitalist class" was the most important way to establish sound state ethics and to achieve the economic development (Davis, 2004: 108). Furthermore, Park extended the disciplinary ethos to the whole society, including the emerging working class as well as landed proprietors and urban capitalists. In particular, this ethos was most strictly imposed on state bureaucrats (Davis, 2004: 103).

State discipline on bureaucrats was practiced in various ways. In particular, Park stressed capacity and efficiency in public administration and service. For him, inefficiency reflected the absence of discipline and commitment to the state, which was morally reproved and harshly punished. At the same time, he employed diverse disciplinary tools to enhance bureaucrats' administrative efficiency and distribute rewards based on their performance. With these tools and rewards, the Park regime continued "administrative reformation on bureaucratic organization and recruiting" (Davis, 2004: 106). His endless commitment to the disciplinary ethos caused bureaucrats to internalize this ethos as a viable norm.

The bureaucrats could not but discipline themselves for the development of the state and the national community. However, this discipline came not only by the state leader's coercion but also from bureaucrats' own conviction that their commitment to self-discipline would increase productivity, which in turn would contribute to the interest of the public as well as the private individual. Underlying this conviction was the belief that the increase in public interest as a whole would enhance their personal interest and their families' interest as well. They all shared the statist view that the prosperity of the state would extend to that of individuals (Kim H. A., 2004). Based on this shared, normative ethos, bureaucrats could maintain a high level of internal cohesiveness and autonomy in order to discipline the capitalist outside the state (Chibber, 1999, 2003).

Therefore, Park Chung Hee's regime was able to enhance its autonomy and capacity rather than be captured by the urban, import-substituting capitalists' interests in state favoritism and protection (Evans, 1995). Their orientation toward the rural middle class and the resulting support from the majority of the people offered the administration leverage to control and govern the rent-seeking activities of industrial and financial capitalists. It paved the way for economic development under the guidance and governance of the state. Moreover, it created an articulation between rural and urban economies. This characteristic explains how Korea maintained social integration through a low level of inequality despite rapid industrialization.

The Sociocultural Dimension

Many studies on Korea only highlight the institutional and formal sector, that is, economic and political dimensions, which are conducive to economic growth. However, without the critical role played by the informal sector behind the scenes, that is, sociocultural context inherited from the history, the developmental strategy transplanted from above would have failed (Leys, 1996). This book will reveal how the actors in informal sectors responded actively and applied themselves to national development projects. It will explicitly show the synergy brought about by the state and (civil) society (chapter 6). Formal institutions and policies are not enough to depict the whole story of development. Increasing interest in the concept of "social capital" reaffirms the importance of the informal sector, or sociocultural context, behind the institutional and formal sector (Putnam, 1993a; Platteau, 1994a, 1994b; Portes, 1998; Woolcock, 1998).

From the viewpoint of Western civil society, Korea is categorized as a combination of a "weak society" and a "strong state" (Migdal, 1988). This characteristic has been mainly employed to explain the existence of authoritarian regimes and how the strong state can control and extract resources from society in a coercive way without disastrous resistance. Korean society is depicted as premodern and under-organized, without any internal and autonomous mechanism for self-organization for the purpose of capitalist production.

However, from the viewpoint of social capital, the picture of Korean society becomes drastically different. Putnam (1993a: 167) refers to social capital to explain "features of social organization, such as trust, norms, and networks that can improve the efficiency of society by facilitating coordinated actions." Further, he argues that "voluntary cooperation is easier in a community that has inherited a substantial stock of social capital, in the form of norms of reciprocity and networks of civic engagement." He goes on to explain that "as with conventional capital, those who have social capital tend to accumulate more" and most forms of social capital, such as trust, have an attribute of "what Albert Hirschman has called 'moral resources'—that is, resources whose supply increases rather than decreases through use and which become depleted if not used" (Putnam, 1993a: 169).

In his view, this feature of social capital is crucial for economic and political development. It is social capital that makes democracy and markets work. Without social capital in society, economic and political institutions cannot work properly because these institutions need active participation and cooperation from society at large (Woolcock,

1998; Woolcock and Narayan, 2000). In other words, a society with rich social capital is a strong society that can create developmental synergy when combined with the strong state.

The importance of social capital is widely accepted in economics and institutional studies. For instance, the argument by Coleman (1988) is directly linked to the new institutional economics that focuses on "transaction costs" within the market (Williamson, 1989). He explains that because those who do not share social capital always face problems of trust, that is, the problem of opportunistic behavior, it is necessary to introduce reliable safeguards (e.g., insurance or official endorsements). However, if trust exists between two parties in a transaction, safeguards merely become cumbersome formalities that increase transaction costs in accordance with the contract. Consequently, social capital is an important mechanism for reducing transaction costs (Granovetter, 1985).

From the viewpoint of social capital, Korean society has abundant resources for cooperation and development. One of the notable characteristics of Korean society is the intricately webbed nexus among state/nonstate and official/nonofficial sectors. These networks are mainly woven through blood relations (血緣), school ties (學緣), or acquaintanceship by locality (地緣). We may call these "affective networks" (Hahm C. and Bell, 2004) or, alternatively, *Yŏn'go Kwankye* (緣故關係).[4] The affective network is firmly rooted in Korean society: it is the key to understanding the contemporary Korean society.

Most studies on the affective networks of Korea, inspired by the modernization theory, which claims that traditional community is weakened by the industrialization process that causes social mobility among different social strata, simply assume that affective networks would wither away with the advance of modernization (Lee J.-H., 1999a). At the most extreme, they insist that affective networks should be dismantled because they represent underdevelopment or under-modernization.[5]

The most problematic aspect of affective networks, as many previous studies have pointed out, is that they block outsiders from accessing resources on a fair basis. As a reciprocity and personal trust created by cliquish connection is accumulated exclusively, trust in "others in general" outside the group or "the rules of the game" that should be applied generally can be damaged. "Such a condition may injure the fairness of competition, diminish the possibility of productive transactions, and eventually bring about inefficiency of distribution of resources" (Lee J.-H., 1999a: 49).

Others, admitting the prevalence of affective networks, note their positive effect in the process of economic development. According to studies adopting rational choice theory, trust in private networks rather than in law or institutions made positive contributions to rapid industrialization. It argues that an individual's reliance on an affective network is his or her rationally calculated choice in the sense that it reduces uncertainty and transaction costs in a sociopolitical environment of instability and uncertainty (Kim Y.-H., 1996: 106). The preference for affective networks, then, was the result of strategic choices made by rational individuals under particular environmental constraints. Affective networks based on traditional ties can provide the sense of trust essential for the exchange of various kinds of political and economic resources when other institutions are underdeveloped. During periods of social upheaval, the social cost of establishing trust can rise to such levels that the cost of official constraints is higher than that incurred by transactions based on personal trust. Accordingly, people are able to gain access to scarce resources more effectively and efficiently by conducting their transactions through affective networks.

However, this perspective also has limits because it assumes that in an environment of firmly established institutions such as advanced democracy and sound market capitalism, affective networks will not function any longer in the formal sector and will disappear into the informal and private realm. This perspective cannot explain the seeming anomaly: the coexistence of rapid and apparently thorough transition to democracy and capitalism with the continued presence of strong affective networks. Contrary to the common assumption, the affective network does not exist only in a premodern primary group. In the case of East Asia and especially of Korea, extensively intertwined traditional affective networks can easily be found not only in the economic sector but also in the bureaucracy of the state or various voluntary groups in civil society.

In this respect, it is the Western point of view that identifies "the state and market" or "the state and civil society" as dichotomous entities and places them in conflicting relations. In the market relations of Western society, where individualism developed through the Reformation and various civil revolutions and has become a basis for free contracts, noneconomic factors such as human relations or familism in particular do not play an important role. However, in East Asia where Confucian tradition is prevalent, personal relations such as networks based on blood (family), region (locality), and school associations (alumni associations) are closely linked to functions of the market where economic exchanges take place. Accordingly, more emphasis needs to be placed on how affective networks permeate the market or the state bureaucracy, where competition and achievement are the rules of the game.

A clarification on how family ties, the most representative type of affective network, could contribute to the economic development is offered in this book (chapter 2). It argues that family ties bounded by filial piety offer an internal mechanism for economic development and cooperation. This mechanism has three dimensions for economic achievement: developmental, successive, and collective pressures. The first type of pressure shows how Korean families internalize the economic motives among family members as a norm and discipline themselves to enhance their efficiency and productivity for the familial community. The second type of pressure effects how families invest their resources in human capital such as education in the long term and try to appropriate the limited resources not in a myopic but in a long and stable way. The third type of pressure explains how the benefits of economic development and enhancement can be shared among family members providing welfare in the absence of public welfare. This mechanism helps understand the modernization and industrialization processes in Korea.

For example, Korean businesses are famous for the way in which they organize their production and corporate governance (Granovetter, 2005). Most of the largest *chaebols*, including the most internationally competitive, such as Samsung, Hyundai, and LG, are controlled by the founder's family members, usually brothers, sons, nephews, and grandsons. The importance of family ties is even greater for smaller companies. Whereas the largest *chaebols* try to adopt global standards incompatible with familial governance, the smaller companies feel free from such compunction. In these cases, the most important motivation for building and developing their business is to pass it on to their children as part of their "patrimony."

This mechanism can be applied to the various affective groups such as *dongchanghoi* (同窓會, alumni association of a school) and *hyangwuhoi* (鄉友會, social gatherings of people from the same hometown) at the same time. Affective networks based on school ties are especially important in government and politics. The graduates of elite schools and universities dominate the political and economic realms to a degree rarely witnessed in other societies. The highest echelons of the Korean bureaucracy have traditionally been occupied by members of the "KS"[6] that refers to graduates of a particular elite high school and university.

Moreover, regional sentiment based on regional ties has played an increasingly important role in Korean politics. In fact, it can be argued that regional sentiments enabled the first peaceful "turnover" of government to the opposition in the presidential election in 1997, when Kim Dae Jung was elected. If such a regime change is the essence of democratic consolidation, as it clearly is, then regionalism was a major force behind democratization in Korea (Kang, 2003). From this perspective, the social capital of affective networks is the backbone of Korean economic and political development. In this context, affective networks should continuously be highlighted as a positive factor for Korea's success.

As seen in examples above, the mechanism of an affective network facilitates cooperation among members so that individuals can be integrated into the production of public goods. It also prevents the destructive results and social waste that rational fools in pursuit of short-term and private interest can cause. This is how the affective network becomes social capital. The norms that the affective network groups share in common prevent selfish and maleficent behavior of group members and induce them to contribute to the creation of public good. Trust among group members solves the problem of the prisoner's dilemma and enhances collective action for economic development. Last, networks help to mobilize resources and channel effective communication.

Development projects alienated from the informal sector, or decontextualized from history, cannot work properly. Likewise, formal institutions do not function in a vacuum but interact with the given historical as well as sociocultural context. For Korean development, the most fundamental core was the articulated match of a strong state and strong society. The state was able to discipline society not for its private rent seeking but for the goal of development, and society was able to respond actively to the state's project by mobilizing its resources and organizing cooperation through social capital. Figure 1.1 offers the articulation or embeddedness of each sector in the Korean development process. Each chapter of this book provides in-depth discussions on the missing links in understanding the Korean development path.

Book Organization and Chapter Arguments

This book is divided into three parts. Part 1 is made up of a single chapter (chapter 2) that deals with the cultural dimension of Korean development. With the title of "Confucian Ethics and the Spirit of

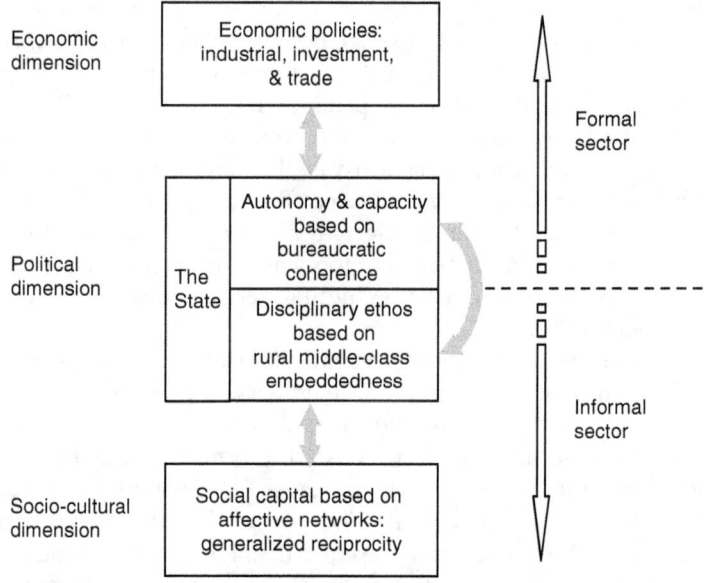

Figure 1.1 The articulation of formal and informal sectors in the Korean development model: economic, political, and sociocultural dimensions
Source: Lew S. C. and Wang H. S. (2010: 191).

Capitalism in Korea: the Significance of Filial Piety," this chapter focuses on the economic effects of Confucian tradition in Korea. Confucianism has primarily been considered to be a negative influence on capitalist development since Weber's work. However, there have been opposing claims that Confucianism played a positive role in capitalist development in Northeast Asia in general. What, indeed, was the positive role of Confucianism?

To answer this question, this chapter examines the religious significance inherent in the Confucian value of filial piety and illustrates how the value came to be a powerful economic motive among Koreans. The religious imperative of filial piety, which calls for remembering and representing one's ancestors, acts as an important spiritual ethos for Koreans to become economically competitive by providing a self-sacrificing work ethic and zeal for education. Three pressures are of importance in remembering and representing ancestors in the modern context: developmental, successive, and collective pressures. It emerges that filial piety did not stop at being a simple ethical standard; it was the fundamental basis for a macro-social dynamic closely linked to the development of capitalism in Korea.

Part 2 consists of two chapters on affective networks that deal with the social dimension of Korean development. They explain how affective networks contributed to the development of "strong society" in Korea. In chapter 3, under the title of "Affective Networks, Social Capital, and Modernity in Korea," existing research trends regarding affective networks (familial, school-based, and regional ties) are examined critically. Here it is argued that affective network groups in Korea are not simply remnants of the past that helped Korea at the "developmental state" stage of industrialization but are fully extant and relevant organizations that will continue to have a role in the process of modernization and democratization. Affective networks are neither closed inner-groups nor do they necessarily lower social efficiency, and are not antagonistic with civil society. Further evidence is given to explain historic-cultural factors involved in the continuing proliferation of affective networks in modern Korea. In particular, it is emphasized that the Confucian worldview supporting affective networks has shown a strong tendency to condemn cronyism and corruption. Through this work, this chapter asserts that the affective network based on human relations is a form of social capital that enriches trust and reciprocity, and can become a useful resource in the coming postmodern era where atomized individuals, commodified by the market, are supposed to find meaningful relations with each other, that is, inter-subjectivity and community (Hahm C., 2000).

Chapter 4, "Historical Development of Affective Networks in Korea: The Nongovernmental Sector and Confucian Tradition," makes clear that affective networks, into which characteristics of Confucian culture have strongly infiltrated, are deeply rooted in the nonprofit and nongovernmental sector in Korea. Strong attachment and devotion to affective networks on the basis of kinship, regional identity, and alumni relationships among Koreans can only be understood when historic-cultural factors are taken into account. Affective networks are influential because they are able to maintain spontaneous reciprocity, especially "generalized reciprocity" that mutually benefits members and their families in times of need. In addition, although affective networks exist officially in the nonprofit/nongovernmental sector, it is found that their roles and functions are extended to penetrate deeply into the state and market sector. Finally, this chapter goes back to history to clarify that the *sarim* (士林) networks, traditional intellectual affective networks in *Chosŭn* Korea, are not incompatible with modern civil society because the networks, especially those formed by *literati* outside state office, assumed the role of a check upon state power.

Part 3 is made up of three chapters designated to the issue of "state–society relations," which constitute the political dimension of Korean development. Chapter 5, "Confucian Capitalism of Park Chung Hee: Possibilities and Limits," highlights that "Confucian capitalism," which exemplified state-led industrialization in East Asia, emerged from a historical context entirely different from that of the West. Civil society and free markets in the Western mode were unnecessary for the development of Confucian capitalism. Instead, state bureaucrats organized capitalism in such a way that policy decisions of state bureaucrats superseded decision-makings of businesses and the private sector was mobilized around the needs and plans of the state through traditional Confucian affective networks. "State–business collusion" (政經癒着) is a term that describes this structural characteristic of Confucian capitalism. However, the collusion has been constantly monitored by media and intellectuals who are the structural heirs of former Confucian *literati*. These "checks and balances" are found to be efficient and effective in minimizing negative consequences of collusion.

Chapter 6, entitled "Generalized Reciprocity between Strong State and Strong Society: Park Chung Hee and Korean Developmental Path," offers a critical challenge to the existing literature that has generally attributed the economic success of South Korea to the role of the strong state. The fact that, in contrast to the state, South Korean society was weak and passive and was simply mobilized by a strong state has been taken for granted. A challenge to this interpretation is made on the basis that the developmental state that is supposed to be autonomous and embedded cannot be fully explained by the simple dichotomy of "strong state and weak society." It is true that planning and carrying out a developmental strategy requires a high level of state autonomy and capacity to counter possible resistance from society. In order to materialize the plan, however, the society in which the state is embedded also needs to be capable of adopting the state's strategy, as well as be an active participant. This is particularly true because a strong state paired with a weak society can readily become a predatory state. This chapter explains how South Korea during the Park era was a showcase of synergy between a strong state and a strong society. We argue that the norm of generalized reciprocity, found at both the macro- and micro-level, played a critical role in preventing free riding, or the tragedy of the commons, and helped individuals participate in the state's plan on a voluntary basis. The leader's value orientation at the macro-level and the responses of villages and business groups at the micro-level are investigated to illustrate these interactions. The conclusion argues that Korean society remains as strong as ever and may have become even stronger. The problem today is that there is no longer a strong state to match a strong society.

Chapter 7 aims to answer the more concrete question: "Did the 1997 Asian Financial Crisis Transform the S. Korean Developmental State?" by examining the path that the Korean developmental state took after the 1997 crisis. It focuses on the "public fund policy" and the critical role of the state in overcoming the financial crisis. Backed on findings, the argument is that failures in the restructuring process were not caused by state intervention in and of itself but by improper state intervention. In this regard, globalization does not shrink the role of the nation state. Rather, globalization demands proper intervention by the state with more and better autonomy and capacity along the developmental path the state has followed.

Finally, chapter 8 concludes the book and offers some implications on the theoretical underpinning of affective network on trust and social capital. The economic success of Korea suggests the importance of informal sociocultural dimensions of development. Traditional culture as well as social networks may make both the market and democracy work better. In Korea, the state and market have been organized and mobilized according to moral economy and thereby it has achieved miraculous success.

Notes

* Chapter 1 is largely from a book chapter, coauthored with Hye Suk Wang, "The Korean Development Model: Lessons for Southeast Asia," pp. 176–190, in David I. Steinberg (ed.), 2010, *Korea's Changing Role in Southeast Asia: Expanding Influence and Relations*, Singapore: Institute of Southeast Asian Studies.

1. This agency is conceptualized as a "nodal agency" or "pilot agency" (Wade, 1990; Chibber, 2002).
2. Under the rule of Rhee, authority over economic policy was shared between the US representatives in Seoul on the one hand and the local government on the other: within the latter, policy decisions were subject to negotiations among several agencies. Chief among these were Rhee himself, the finance ministry, the Central Bank, the monetary board, and the legislature (Chibber, 2002).
3. The EPB not only was the fount of industrial policy but also enjoyed supreme control over the annual budgetary process and allocation of credit. This meant that the same agency that made annual plans also made the annual budget without having to receive parliamentary permission or the agreement of the Finance Ministry. In fact, the

Finance Ministry had no power to override the decisions of the EPB. The nodal agency also had supreme power over the allocation of credit and foreign aid (Woo-Cumings, 1999). Ministries were made responsible for implementing the Board's decision, submitting their spending estimates to it for approval, and also reporting regularly on project implementation. The upshot of this setup was that different strands of industrial policies were effectively coordinated through the establishment of an agency whose task was to render them consistent and then to enforce them. The key was not that all relevant tasks were the sole provenance of the EPB—that would have most likely been beyond the ability of any bureaucratic agency. The key was that the various units working in the overall field were compelled to submit to its authority and to conform to the overall direction of priorities (Chibber, 2002: 75–76).
4. *Yŏn'go* (緣故) refers to interpersonal relations similar to *Guanxi* (關係) in China, which means relationship.
5. The policy recommendations that have been undertaken since the crisis of 1997 have for the most part focused on dismantling cronyism, another name for the affective network that permeates society. The assumption, explicit or otherwise, is that cronyism is not only inefficient but also characteristic of a premodern agrarian society and as such will disappear as modernization and rationalization in society continue (see chapter 3 of this book).
6. "KS" is the initial of *Kyung'gi* High School and Seoul National University, the most distinguished elite schools in Korea. Their graduates are regarded as elites in the social, political, and economic fields.

Part I

The Cultural Dimension: Confucian Tradition

Chapter 2

Confucian Ethics and the Spirit of Capitalism in Korea: The Significance of Filial Piety*

with Woo-Young Choi and Hye Suk Wang

Introduction

Max Weber (1930[1920]) presented a remarkable analysis of the social effects of religious values. In this sociological canon, Weber indicated that value orientation in Protestant Christianity contributed to the formation of a "diligent" work ethic, which characterized modern Western capitalism. However, Weber went on to say that the spontaneous development of capitalism could not be found in non-Western societies for the reason that religious values imbuing economic motives for development were missing (Bellah, 1957). A typical example cited was Confucian culture in China (Weber, 1951[1920]), but Korean society was not an exception (Tu, 1991; Cha S.-H., 1992; Park S.-H., 1994).

This raises questions on Weber's perspective of Confucianism and seeks theoretical foundations for an alternative argument involving the Confucian value of filial piety (孝, *xiao* in Chinese, *hyo* in Korean, and *kou* in Japanese). The point of the argument is not criticism of Weber's theory of capitalism but his interpretation of Confucianism. We suggest that the developmental significance of traditional values may be found by exploring the psychocultural effects of filial piety on the economic orientation of the people. Some may criticize that it is difficult to find economic impetus in filial piety—the former being the crystallization of instrumental rationality and the latter a purely normative virtue. Moreover, others would be skeptical about such efforts since the mere existence of an economic impetus in filial piety never guarantees spontaneous capitalistic development.

Paradoxically, however, support for this work is found in Weber's discussion on Western Europe. Although it is admitted that "Weber's last theory of capitalism" (Collins, 1980) is predominantly institutional and involves a sequence of causal conditions, the emphasis on religious ideas and motivations that are specific to Western Europe is central. We do not deny that the development of capitalism is contingent not only on psychocultural orientations but also on various structural conditions and sociopolitical institutions. Nonetheless, within the context of these macro-social determinants, there is still ample room for a causal relationship between cultural beliefs, work ethic, educational achievement, and—through those mechanisms—economic growth.

In this context, we explore the "religious" aspect of filial piety to demonstrate the economic effects of this value orientation. In particular, filial piety is assumed to have a distinct and far-reaching religious significance that cannot be found in any other Confucian values (Taylor, 1990). Filial piety is a mechanism specific to Confucianism that deals with the issue of death and immortality. In the process, filial piety presents itself as a latent but powerful link to economic motives by putting into practice characteristic rituals of "remembrance and representation" of ancestors. The economic motive concomitant with filial piety is also manifested in the formation of "familism" in Confucian culture. Filial piety generates strong normative pressures offering sociocultural grounds for "developmental," "successive," and "collective" representation and remembrance among family members. The ultimate intention of this work is to establish filial piety as a fundamental basis of the spirit of capitalism in Korea leading to a psychological mechanism, from religious ethos to personal predisposition toward work and education.

Filial Piety: from Mortality to Eternity

Filial Piety as a Religion

It is generally known that religion is the most basic and fundamental mechanism of consciousness confirming human existence. Although confirmation of existence has many dimensions, only religion extends human existence to immortality. The religious assurance of eternal life inevitably collides with the issue of death, because the death of a physical body is not only something to fear in itself but also an obstacle to eternal existence. In this sense, religion, which attempts to guarantee eternal life, must make the interpretation and handling of death its "hardcore" (Eliade, 1985: 9–11).

The fact that Weber hesitated to categorize Confucianism as a religion carries important implications for this study. Weber noticed the absence of religious features in Confucianism such as the transcendent Absolute, messages of redemption, and "the Kingdom of a thousand years" (or Heaven). It was therefore natural for him to perceive Confucianism as nothing more than a secular ethic or as a colossal code of law, political principle, and social protocol for the cultured class (Weber, 1951[1920]: 225). To Weber, Confucianism was devoid of religion's hardcore—that is, the need to extend existence into eternity by handling death in an appropriate manner. The only alternative left to Confucians whose existence failed to extend to eternity was an adamant attachment to this world. This is why Weber designated "the secular adaptation to this world" as a characteristic of Confucianism (Weber, 1951[1920]: 350).

The problem with this is that Weber ultimately failed to grasp the religious nature of Confucianism, which can be found in the norm of filial piety. How does Confucianism, as a religion, deal with the issue of death and eternity? Let us examine the case of Christianity before answering this question. How Christianity deals with death and hence guarantees eternal life is well explained in the work of Weber (1930[1920]). Christianity presupposes the flawless will and action of the Absolute, which are manifested in evident objects. The "Kingdom of a thousand years," Heaven, is a spatial and temporal manifestation of eternal life, and this space and time is de-historicized from a human perspective (Troeltsch, 1958[1912]). Human beings can extend their existence into eternity in the Kingdom of a thousand years by entering the gate to salvation, because the Kingdom is the ultimate refuge that the Absolute designed for humankind at the beginning of the world.

However, the problem of salvation—all important to Christians—was solely the territory of priests of the Catholic Church before the Reformation. During the Middle Ages, under absolute church power and resulting corruption, some Christians began to protest the church's doctrine of salvation. They argued that the main criterion for salvation lay in faithfully following God's (or the Bible's) teachings in one's life. This new doctrine argued that anyone could gain salvation by leading a sinless life and diligently working in one's own calling. Thus, Protestants worked diligently to become rich in this life, in part, due to anxiety over uncertainty about gaining access to heaven and eternal life after death. Finally, after the Reformation, the goal of Protestantism became the accumulation of worldly goods through hard work and frugality—a sign that one is of the "saved." By means of working toward salvation—gaining eternal life—Europe was able to construct a diligent work ethic that became the "spirit of capitalism" (Weber, 1930[1920]).

However, unlike Christianity, Confucianism does not presuppose a priori teleology or divine will (Ching, 1977). Instead, Confucians believe that the abstract universal principle that operates in nature and in the normative world constitutes and governs the real world (Keum J.-T., 1992: 215). The fundamental principles of Confucianism such as the Way (*Dao*, 道), the Principle (Li, 裡), and the Supreme Ultimate (*Tai Ji*, 太極) are basically depersonalized and there is no divine plan for the afterlife. These fundamental principles are omnipresent in the cosmos, in nature, and in human beings as exemplars that constitute and normalize the world. They are external and transcendental—and at the same time immanent and internal—to humans (de Bary, 1998: 40–41). It is humankind's natural and normative obligation to realize these principles by achieving a state of supreme good (Lee K. K., 1998: 262). Discussion on Confucianism thus far has revealed only the ethical or metaphysical aspect; its religious features have not been manifested yet.

The fundamental principle of *Li* retains the immortal essence that governs birth, extinction, and rebirth of nature and the universe (Hahm C.-B., 1998: 262–266). Therefore, the determination of *Li* is not confined to the present world but rather extends to eternity. Indeed, the end of existence cannot stop *Li*'s governance; rather, extinction is a natural manifestation of and an eternal return to *Li*. Thus, death is "relativized" here from the perspective of religious ontology. Biological death does not terminate a person's existence but makes it possible for that person to return to immortal and fundamental principles. Of course, this implies the following condition: human beings should make themselves one with *Li* through practices in the present world (Metzger, 1977). Death is not the critical point that terminates human's existence as long as this conditional imperative is fulfilled; rather, death is the beginning of eternal existence. From this we can comprehend the religious logic of Confucianism in the context of death and eternal existence.

Still, a simple but important question remains: the problem of abstraction and elitism of Confucianism in the context of the practice. As discussed earlier, there are only a constrained few who can overcome death and achieve everlasting existence. *Li*, *Dao*, or *Tai Ji* is available to the religious *virtuosi*; the masses can only meet more minimal religious requirements (Hill, 1973).[1] This minimal religious requirement sheds light on the importance of the practical norms of Confucianism, which prescribe standards for everyday life. It is this very context in which the Five Cardinal Relationships (*Wu-Lun*, 五倫) are highlighted for commoners. However, among the Five Relationships, the practice of filial piety in the form of "affection between father and son" (父子有親) precedes all other relationships.[2] In particular, filial piety after the death of parents is the zenith of a religious solution of Confucianism on the issue of death.

In Confucianism, filial piety is not merely a secular norm but a sublime religious imperative, and its essence is in "remembering" and "representing" one's ancestors, including one's parents. What then is the rationale for remembering and representing? Here lies the clue to the Confucian solution to death. Although this solution involves a rational return to one's nature in principle, as mentioned previously, it needs to be materialized in a tangible way so that commoners can follow and practice. That is, eternal existence of ancestors should be practically confirmed. Confucianism acquires religious persuasive power only when this demand is satisfied, and Confucianism finds the solution to this religious demand in remembrance and representation of ancestors. In other words, remembering and representing ancestors is a mean to guarantee eternal existence.

Consequently, Confucianism places high emphasis on "ancestor worship" (祖上崇拜). The eternal existence of ancestors is confirmed as long as their descendants remember and represent them. Conversely, eternal existence cannot be guaranteed without the descendants' remembrance and representation of their ancestors. As a result, lack of ancestor worship becomes a heretical act against the religious imperative of Confucianism. This explains why filial piety is so highly appreciated while filial impiety is so harshly reviled.

In effect, the biological constraint on existence is supplemented in Confucianism through remembrance and vicarious representation by one's descendants. One can be lifted up to eternal existence through remembrance and representation by one's children, their children, and successive descendants. Every human being without exception belongs somewhere in this ceaseless chain of memories and representations, thereby playing an important role that guarantees eternal existence. This is designated by Confucianism as the natural principle and categorically religious imperative. In this context, remembering and representing ancestors are the core practices of *Li* in Confucian metaphysics, and their execution takes the form of filial piety.

Through remembrance and representation of descendants, death is transformed into immortal life. Hence, Confucianism places more emphasis on filial piety toward the deceased over the living. Filial piety from this perspective is a pressing religious imperative that transcends mere secular norms; thus, it is placed first among the Five Cardinal Relationships. In such a way, Confucianism does have a religious hardcore that manages death and guarantees eternal life. Rather, the hardcore is handled quite practically and rationally through the practice of filial piety. Not by relying solely on divine will but by appealing to humane voluntary practices does filial piety present a rational solution to the religious demand to address the issue of death.

Economic Motives in Filial Piety

All historical religions have relativized reality in principle, but they have also intervened in it directly or indirectly. Confucianism is not an exception. This is especially true in the Confucian world where the sacred and the secular are highly amalgamated (Park Y.-S., 1983) and where religion and politics are unified as well.[3] Confucianism made forceful demands to reflect its religious orientation through the practice of filial piety (Sung K. T., 2005; Lee K. K., 1997; Hsu, 1967). The practice of filial piety had to be "objectified" by a verifiable method, internally as well as externally. It is for this contextual reason that the demand to ritualize important events of life related to filial piety carries so much importance in Confucianism. These events are "coming-of-age" (冠), "marriage" (婚), "funeral" (喪), and "ancestor memorial" (祭) ceremonies (Keum J.-T., 2000; Kim D.-G., 2004). Of course, no culture or religion can deny the importance of these ceremonies in general. However, it is only Confucianism that lends religious meaning to these rituals or institutionalized events. In other words, these ceremonies are concrete processes that deal with the religious hardcore of death and eternity in Confucianism.

The "coming-of-age ceremony" is a religious recognition of a new subject who will remember and represent. The "marriage ceremony" is a religious recognition of a biological union necessary for producing new subjects who will continue remembrance and representation. The "funeral rites" permit humans to overcome sorrow and allow the biological death of ancestors to be sublimated to eternity. Last, the "ancestor memorial ceremony" is a process of religious verification through which the descendants' imperatives of remembrance and representation are confirmed by periodic recall of ancestors who have entered eternity.

There is no question that these ceremonies or rituals are performed so that others can watch and see descendents performing the religious imperative conveyed in filial piety. Indeed, they are Confucian-specific institutionalized methods that confirm and verify the eternal lives of ancestors. As such, the practice of filial piety is connected directly to the assurance of religious citizenship, in terms of not just internal confidence but also external recognition of others. In this respect, there are powerful motives to objectify one's practice of filial piety in the Confucian world,[4] which in turn depends on the practical cost of these ceremonies. As is generally known, this cost is formidable and requires considerable economic means. Especially costly are the memorial ceremonies for ancestors that are repeated annually throughout one's life, unlike once-in-a-lifetime ceremonies, such as coming-of-age, marriage, and funeral ceremonies (Jeon S.-I., 2008). Moreover, given that Confucian memorial rituals must be held in honor of four previous generations (四代奉祀), the economic cost is considerable.

However, regardless of the high cost, the imperative of ancestor memorials cannot be defied nor ritual costs curtailed at will, because it is the most central religious ritual among all ceremonies that ensure ancestors' existence. In fact, the duty of "serving memorial ceremony" is so emphasized in *Chosŭn-era* Korea for this reason (Miyajima, 1996). As such, the objectification of filial piety has become closely related to the assurance of an economic foundation. Practicing filial piety depends heavily on economic ability. Without a worldly fortune, commoners face a serious threat to the eternal life of their ancestors. Furthermore, expression of religious sincerity through "objectified rituals" is directly connected with heightened political as well as ideological justification, a unique phenomenon in Confucian society (Cho H.-I., 1993). In this context, filial piety moves beyond the realm of "verification" to that of "competition." The focus is on who can better commemorate their ancestors and who can better represent their ancestors.[5]

Remembrance and representation therefore go beyond the mere religious dimension into the economic dimension by generating a desire to intensify the material foundations of a superior remembering and representing. In reality, the level of remembrance and representation cannot but differ among individuals and families, and the primary source of this differentiation is, of course, wealth. This competitive remembrance and representation strongly stimulates economic motives. By requiring economic competitiveness for better remembrance and representation of ancestors, filial piety rationalizes one's pursuit of economic wealth with the import of modernization and secularization. In return, the outcome of sincere economic activities resolves anxiety concerned with the question of "who can better represent their ancestors." One's secular success provides visual evidence of one's filial piety for ancestors.

This process is very similar to how the Protestant ethic stimulates its believers to engage in secular activities for the glory of God. It can be said that Confucianism in Korean society has been functionally equivalent to Protestantism in Western societies. Although their functions are equivalent, their forms of practicing religious ethics are not the same. Protestants organized individualistic and atomized patterns of economic pursuit, as the emergence of modern market itself reveals, whereas Confucianism took the form of collective responses to the need for wealth and thus generated different patterns of economic organization as well. In particular, the family became the primary agent of this rational and economic organization of filial piety.

Filial Piety and Confucian Familism

Family in Confucianism

It is difficult to say that familism is a phenomenon unique to Confucian culture or Korea. In all traditional societies, family functions as an absolute entity above individuals and other groups. When society is relatively undifferentiated, family is the most natural group that an individual depends on. Even today, familism is not a unique phenomenon, though perceptions and behavioral principles on familism vary across regions and cultures. In many Third World countries, familism still functions as an important social phenomenon.[6]

We therefore need to examine the uniquely differentiating characteristics of Confucian familism (Hsu, 1967). Although the general meaning of familism—that is family-oriented perceptions and behavior—can be shared, its origin and historical context can differ among societies. This issue cannot be resolved until the mechanism that imbues Confucian familism with importance is articulated. In the end, this comes down to the formation of Confucian familism and its significance; the clue to its formation also lies in filial piety.

As discussed earlier, the religious function of filial piety lies in the subjugation of death and the assurance of eternal existence, and its practice is manifested in remembrance and representation. It is only natural that "family" assumes the role of the subject in this practice; the inclination to remember and represent ancestors is a natural response of those who are extensions of their ancestors. In fact, the phenomenon of remembrance and representation of ancestors occurs universally, including in Christian societies.

However, remembrance and representation in Christian society does not transcend the subjective dimension nor does it unite with religious orientation. In this sense, the meaning and status of family in Christian society is different from that of Confucian society. Rather, as Weber (1961[1923]: 335) appropriately pointed out, the motives for familial remembrance and representation seem to have been relativized by the religious program specific to Christianity. As a result, the meaning of family is reduced in Christianity, whereas in Confucian society, the meaning of family is extended beyond the socioeconomic dimension to the religious dimension.[7] Specifically, family is the religious locus that guarantees eternal existence after death. Thus, in the Confucian world, family takes the place of church, or shrine, in remembering and representing ancestors. No other culture or religion puts more meaning on family than Confucianism, because the Confucian family carries the religious meaning of eternal life (DeVos, 1998).

In such a way, biological as well as socioeconomic nature, and religious prescription, are integrated into the family in Confucianism. Family is the manifestation of the Heavenly principle that reflects nature and the moral imperative (Hahm C., 2004). As a result, family in Confucian society acts as a strategic unit in accessing religious citizenship, political power, social reputation, and economic resources. Individuals who are alienated from their families not only deviate from a deep social norm but also face substantial difficulties. The interests of individuals and those of their families cannot be separated in Confucian societies (Harris, 1979).

Scarcity of resources heightened the emphasis on family in late *Chosŭn* Korea. The system of opportunity declined dramatically during the late *Chosŭn* dynasty, when class boundaries weakened and population pressure increased (Lee H.-J., 1991; Jeong J.-Y., 1991), leading to intense social and economic competition. From the perspective of the individual families, the crisis for survival threatened remembrance and representation of ancestors, and their strategic response was therefore urgent and acute.

The families' response to this crisis was "organizational integration." Primogeniture, solidification of rights to ancestral rites, establishment of consanguineous villages, publication of genealogy books and collected writings of ancestors, and erection of memorial halls and shrines are only some examples (Deuchler, 1992). Consolidation of the right of primogeniture boosted the eldest son as the center of the family, after which the hierarchical unity of family was reorganized to increase the family's competitiveness. Likewise, the establishment of consanguineous villages reflected a strategic plan to reduce decision-making time and transaction costs by concentrating resources at a physical locality (Coase, 1988[1937]; Williamson, 1973; Jacobs, 1985). Families could share, confirm, and intensify remembrance and representation of that locality's ancestors through the publication of genealogy books and collected works of ancestors, construction of memorial halls and shrines, and so forth.

Through these strategic practices, individuals' immersion and devotion to the family were dramatically heightened as a means for survival under competitive conditions. The imperative endowed upon family by Confucianism in the normative domain was intensified by the politico-economic reality. The dismantling of the Confucian state by the Japanese, liberation of Korea by US Forces, and the devastating Korean War that divided the country only reinforced the trend. Through experience and learning about competition to survive, family became the supreme value as well as a practical reference point for every Korean. This is the historical origin of familism in Korea. However, subsequent developmental processes in modern Korean history only served to strengthen, rather than weaken, these trends.

Modern Pressures for Better Representation

Individuals are never independent or absolute in Korean society due to the domination of the culture of familism. Individuals exist as parts constituting the whole in the form of family, that is, as unity,[8] not as independent units (Bell and Hahm C., 2003; Lew S. C. and Kim T. E., 2001). Likewise, individuals are a "totality of roles" in relation to the family and cannot have absolute independent meaning by themselves (Rosemont, 1988). If this is the case, then what is the obligation of the parts to the unity of the family? Or what are the roles of totality in relation to family?

These questions require further examination of the meaning of remembrance and representation of one's ancestors. First of all, remembrance involves the offspring's conscious understanding of the physical appearance or lives of the parents during their lifetimes, and representation involves practicing to reveal the parents' characteristics during their lives through a specific form. These two are complementary and cyclical: the parents are represented through remembrance and remembered through representation. From an analytical perspective, however, representation encounters more threats than remembrance in modern contexts.

The traditional form of representation (or ritual) has become obsolete in modern times. Still, representation is not abandoned, only expanded (Lee K. K., 1998: 259–261): representation is now manifested as revealing and extending the life of the parents by transferring that life to the child. Inevitably, representation is the offspring's practice by proxy on behalf of the dead parents, and if this meaning is extended, representation is the process through which the offspring lives the parents' lives on their behalf. This "proxy life" used to be objectified by institutionalized rituals of filial piety in traditional society, but the conditions for proxy life have mostly been destroyed in modern society. Today, representation needs to be practiced and confirmed throughout the offspring's entire life. Modern familism had to renew its operating mechanism while still preserving its essence of remembrance and representation. The modern religious drive for a better proxy life took new forms.

Korean modernization in the late twentieth century is widely acknowledged as a model of remarkable economic growth. No comparable experience can be found in world history, except in other Confucian countries. This has naturally generated much interest in its background, and unique Korean characteristics in particular have garnered much attention (Hamilton and Biggart, 1988; Kuk M.-H., 1999). Reinvigorated interest in Confucian familism is significant in this regard. Confucian discipline, collective devotion, familial mobilization of resources, and strong attachment to education have been pointed out as major forces behind Korea's economic growth (Pye, 1985, 2000; Maison et al., 1980; Berger, 1988; Hofheinz and Calder, 1982; Kahn, 1979; MacFarquhar, 1980; Tai, 1989; Tu, 1996; Vogel, 1991).

However, there is dissonance with respect to the broader socioeconomic causes of Korea's economic growth (Amsden, 1989; Wade, 1990; Fukuyama, 1995b; Bell and Hahm C., 2003; Shin J. S. and Chang H. J., 2003; Kim H. A., 2004; Davis, 2004) as well as the functional role that Confucianism might play. Few efforts have been made to explain how Confucianism drives economic development, and many arguments for its role do little more than point out how Confucianism and rapid growth managed to coexist. The missing link of *how* Confucianism might contribute to economic growth is not spelled out. Here, we link religiously prescribed remembrance and representation of ancestors to strengthened motives for children's education and labor ethics. In doing so, we articulate the internal psychological mechanism through which filial piety instills responsibilities of representation into family members.

It is well known that familism played a major role in mobilization of resources in the course of modernization and economic growth in Korea (Park H., 1992). Mobilization, induced from outside, especially from the top (the state), was an important factor, but this does not explain work ethic or other mechanisms at the individual level. One source of this internal mobilization "from the bottom" was the desire not to lose the competition of remembering and representing ancestors. Efforts to represent ancestors based on remembrance imbue familial mobilization of resources with powerful religious motives. This phenomenon may be labeled "the economic effect of representation." Three mechanisms or pressures have significant consequences in the modern representing process.

The first is the pressure of "developmental representation." As the traditional means of representation have been abolished, representation needs to be proved during the entire lifetime of the offspring according to the logic of proxy life. Does my life as the continuation of my parents' lives remember my ancestors well? Do I represent my ancestors well? These questions generate considerable anxiety.[9] Moreover, in contrast to traditional society, the objective criterion to resolve this anxiety becomes vague. The only practical criterion in this regard is the achievement of a better life, an improvement in life over that led by the ancestors. If not, the life of the offspring cannot be recognized as proper and appropriate representation. Anxiety can only be escaped by improving one's life or at least maintaining the standard of living of one's ancestors. From the perspective of proxy life, a declining living standard is dereliction of obligation, a failure in representation, and therefore a failure in filial piety.

Development can be assessed using various standards. However, the first and foremost is economic. Although the goal of "rising in the world and achieving fame" (立身揚名) encompasses political power, sociocultural authority, and other dimensions, the most obvious measure lies in economic success, because it is the foundation for familial gains in other areas. Economic improvement was not only the ultimate goal but also the most objective criterion of developmental representation, especially in the early stages of industrialization. To achieve economic improvement, economic motives were highly stimulated by those who were engaged in proxy life. These motives were manifest in the first instance through labor effort. It is generally known that self-sacrificing labor was a somewhat unique characteristic of Korean industrialization, but there was an additional component that went beyond the general economic motives found in capitalist development; the component was religious pressure in the form of developmental representation.

The second modern pressure is that of "successive representation." Developmental representation is not limited to one's lifetime. Remembrance and representation are imperative practices that should be continued by individuals of successive generations, thereby continually confirming the ancestors' existence. Individuals as part of the family lineage should remember and represent their ancestors and are also responsible for passing on remembrance and representation to the descendents. Each individual is a mediating link. Therefore, descendants, or children, have great importance. Children exist to remember and represent not only their immediate ancestors but also the ancestors before them. Reproducing and rearing a child is not a choice but an imperative in Confucianism; an offspring is not only my child but is also a child of my ancestors.

A child serves two functions in this sense: the means of representing me and my ancestors, and the new "subject" of representation that succeeds me. In the case of the former, a good way to practice the obligation of representation entrusted into my care is making it possible for my offspring to "rise in the world and achieving fame." In the case of the latter, my offspring is the new subject who will continue my obligation of representation in my stead. My offspring is endowed with the imperative obligation of representing the ancestors developmentally, as was I.

The important point is that satisfaction of these two meanings of representation depends on an economic foundation. First, economic means are necessary to provide an opportunity for children to rise in the world and become successful, and to allow children to faithfully represent ancestors after one's death. The latter in particular demands extensive economic means. Although the primary responsibility lies with the children, the parents are charged with the no less momentous responsibility to provide the conditions in which the children can accede to the family lineage without discontinuity. On this point, the obligation reveals itself as pressure for successive representation (Sorensen and Kim S. C., 2004: 174).

Education is the best response to this successive pressure. Empowering children through education is the most apparent method to fulfill the obligation of representation. This explains the enthusiasm for investment in children's education that has been a constant for the past century in Korea (Chang Y. S., 1989a). Especially, the process of preparation for entrance to prestigious universities is a modern objectified ritual to reveal the religious preparation of "better representation" to others: that one's children are on the way to continue the succession. Investing in children can be nothing more than ensuring the continuance of representation, which reaffirms the importance of an economic foundation. This pressure of successive representation, along with the pressure of development, is the source of a powerful economic drive to succeed.

The last modern pressure exerted by the religious effect of representation is that of "collective representation." Subjects who represent ancestors exist as a collective whole. Descendants of ancestors encompass not only me but also those who share memories of those ancestors—that is, my siblings. Here we notice that the obligation of representation covers not only the hierarchical dimension of generations but also the horizontal dimension of brothers and sisters. Although individual brothers and sisters should represent their parents developmentally and successively, each representation contains the collectivity as a whole that cannot be separated from one another. Collective representation means that representation of ancestors should not be mine alone but ours as well.

Collectivity of representation contains a significant implication: sharing of the obligation of representation. Representation of ancestors not only does end up in improving my own life but should also be proved through the lives of my brothers and sisters, thereby sharing the obligation by us all. In fact, levels of representation cannot but differ among brothers and sisters. A brother's or sister's lack of economic capability can cause a crisis in collective representation. This pressure is no less considerable in that the possible failure of representation by individual family members could damage collective representation. Therefore, a sense of responsibility—collective responsibility among siblings—to guarantee successful representation arises.

Pressure for collective representations has a number of significant effects. Internally, tacit pressure acts among brothers and sisters to spur competition among them for economic advancement. They should stimulate and supervise each other's secular performance so that every family member can fulfill their totality of roles and contribute to collective representation. Externally, pressure for collective representation also spurs competition with other families and enhances the mutual aid for same family members in need. It is precisely in this context that the mutual aid given and received among brothers and sisters is appreciated and rewarded (Janelli and Janelli, 1982: 104). Such a norm of mutual aid originated from the obligation of collective representation and consequently played the role of assurance on the familial level of representation.

These pressures help us explain a number of real-world circumstances. Self-sacrificing female factory workers supported their entire families, including brothers studying at college, out of their meager salaries in the 1960s and 1970s. Even low-income families would spend large amounts of money on exam preparation of their children so that they could climb up the educational ladder. Modernization in Korea would have been impossible if not for the high emphasis placed on economic success, with self-sacrificing, or sometimes self-exploiting (Ringmar, 2005), input of labor, and dedicated concerns on children's education as pivotal mechanisms for economic growth.

Continuities and Changes in Confucian Familism

The religious characteristic implied in familism reveals its most patent and typical features in the context of traditional society, due to the prevalence of Confucianism in *Chosŭn* Korea. Does this mean that the religious foundation of familism no longer exists in modern Korea? Does familism have nothing to do with religious aspects in contemporary Korean society where secular principles dominate? Does the principle of filial piety as a religious imperative no longer operate through familism? Are the economic effects of familism therefore now muted?

The religious desire to remember and represent ancestors in the form of filial piety is the original foundation of familism in Korea. However, modern conditions that differ from traditional society drastically secularized the religious orientation of Confucianism itself. Today few Koreans seem to accept Confucianism as a religion (Koh B. I., 1996: 281). Confucianism as an institutionalized religion has disappeared in everyday life, and the deep religious meaning attached to filial piety cannot easily be perceived. Then how can Confucianism and filial piety still be seen as sources of economic growth?

At this point, attention should be paid to a telling article in a prominent foreign journal. According to Shim J. H. (1984), "Korean Christians are Confucians in Christian cloaks." In the eyes of foreigners, Koreans are situated within the framework of foreign religion, particularly Protestant Christianity (Lee J.-Y., 1988), but in reality they are living under the influence of Confucianism.[10] Although Confucianism as a historically institutionalized religion has largely disappeared, Confucianism as an orientation that is internalized in everyday life still dominates modern Korean society. Confucianism is still alive not as an objectified religion but as a cultural ethos that has been adapted to modern conditions. In this sense, classification of Confucianism as a system of life and culture remains meaningful (Chan, 1999: 212–213). Although the former has been weakened on the formal and institutional level, the latter has not.

Such Confucian legacy in modern Korea is clearly demonstrated in Table 2.1. It shows a cross-tabulation of "practicing ancestor rites" by "religion" based on a nationwide probability proportional to size (PPS) sample of 1,003 questionnaires surveyed in May 2000 (Shin K.-Y., et al., Korea Social Science Data Archive, data # A1-2000-0003). First of all, the table shows the distribution of religious belief in modern Korea: Protestant (24%), Catholic (9%), Buddhist (28%), and no religion (37%). Distribution of religion in Korea *per se* indeed shows no sign of Confucian tradition at all.[11] However, if you ask a question to the same sample whether they are practicing ancestor rites or not, 73% respond yes. In this important regard, about three-quarters of Koreans are found to be still Confucian. Especially people in the categories of "no religion" and "Buddhism" have the highest yes rate, reaching to almost 90%. Even 78% in the Catholic category respond yes. The lowest yes category is, of course, Protestant, but the rate of Protestants practicing ancestor rites is still 37%.[12] As far as ancestor rites are concerned, Korea is still predominantly Confucian. Indeed, as the journal article suggests, Korean Christians are Confucians under a Christian cloak.

Table 2.2 provides information on the future of religious orientation in Korea. The table is based on a survey asking a sample of 319 young local primary and middle school students in 2008 whether they will practice ancestor rites when they grow up (Lee S.-Y., 2008: 221 and 229). Surprisingly, the rates belonging to "won't do" are only 14.2% and 7.0% for male and female students, respectively. The rest of them, including "don't know" and "no response," consist of 85.8% male and 93.0% female students, and they are found not to reject Confucian tradition of practicing ancestor rites when they grow up. Besides, there exists a Confucian proactive portion of 63.6% male and 60.1% female students who manifest clearly that they will do the rituals in the future. This trend shows no difference between male and female students.

Further survey evidence that modern Korea is still predominantly Confucian, as far as filial piety and ancestor rites are concerned, comes from a survey of housewives. An absolute majority of housewives, who

Table 2.1 Practice of ancestor rites by religion, 2000

Religion	Practicing ancestor rites, N (row %) (column %)[a]					
	Yes		No		Total	
Protestant	90	(37.2) (12.2)	152	(62.8) (56.7)	242	(100) (24.1)
Catholic	71	(78.0) (9.7)	20	(22.0) (7.5)	91	(100) (9.1)
Buddhism	250	(88.7) (34.0)	32	(11.3) (11.9)	282	(100) (28.1)
Others	16	(94.1) (2.2)	1	(5.9) (0.4)	17	(100) (1.7)
No religion	308	(83.3) (41.9)	63	(17.0) (23.5)	371	(100) (37.0)
Total	735	(73.3) (100)	268	(26.7) (100)	1,003	(100) (100)

Source: Shin, K.-Y. et al., Korea Social Science Data Archive (KOSSDA, data # A1-2000-0003). Recited from Lew, Choi, and Wang (2011: 186).

Note: a. For each answer, the number of responses is followed by the row percentage (in parentheses) and then the column percentage (in parentheses).

Table 2.2 Youth's opinion on future practice of ancestor rites, 2008 (Unit: %)

Do you think you will practice ancestor rite when you grow up?								
"Will do"		"Won't do"		"Don't know"		"No response"		Total (N = 319)
M	F	M	F	M	F	M	F	M (194) F (125)
63.6	60.1	14.2	7.0	19.9	28.7	2.3	4.2	100 100

Source: Lee S.-Y. (2008: 221 and 229). Recited from Lew, Choi, and Wang (2011: 187).

Note: The sample is made of local (southeast region of Korea) students and is composed equally of 10th, 13th, and 15th graders: M = male and F = female students.

make the most substantial "sacrifice" for ancestor rites in the form of cooking and serving, responds that the ritual is "necessary." Out of a sample of 249 housewives, living in two Southern coastal cities of *Pusan* and *Yeosu*, interviewed in September 2003 (Jung B.-M. et al., 2004: 137 and 148), only 17% of the responses claimed that the ritual is unnecessary. On the other hand, those who think that the ritual is necessary make up 83.1% of the whole sample, including a strong 55% who responded absolutely (see Table 2.3).

The reality still witnessed today is nationwide migration of millions of Koreans heading for their hometowns on traditional holidays (*Chusŏk* or Thanksgiving and *Sŏl* or the Lunar New Year Day) to pay respect to their ancestors, and many rigidly adhering to interment burial despite a serious lack of available land.[13] Korea has a unique market where commodities of "filial piety tourism" or "filial piety insurance" for elderly parents are widespread. The habitual visits presidential candidates pay to their ancestors' tombs ahead of presidential elections show exactly the same context. Attendance at ancestors' memorial ceremonies is a fundamental appointment most Korean cannot defy, and a sense of guilt accompanies nonattendance even without condemnation by others. Alternatively, Christian memorial services replace Confucian remembrance ceremonies. Although we may not take notice of the internalized religious nature of remembrance and representation of ancestors, it has become a habit of the heart for every Korean (Sorensen and Kim S. C., 2004: 171–174).

In sum, in the course of modernization, traditional means for remembering and representing have disappeared. Except for the memorial ceremony, all other objective means or rituals have disappeared and their absolute religious meaning abridged to a certain extent. Modernity in Korea deconstructed traditional forms of remembrance and representation. The need to renew these means of remembering

Table 2.3   Housewives' opinion on ancestor rites, 2003 (Unit: N (%))

Do you think ancestor rites are necessary?						
"Absolutely"	"So and so"	"Not at all"	"Don't know"	"No response"		Total
137 (55.0)	70 (28.1)	17 (6.8)	15 (6.0)	10 (4.0)		249 (99.9)

Source: Jung B.-M. et al. (2004: 137 and 148). Recited from Lew, Choi, and Wang (2011: 188).

Note: The sample is drawn from local housewives in *Pusan* (150) and *Yŏsu* (100). Number of responses comes first (percentage in parentheses).

and representing or replace them with another form nonetheless persists; the abolition of traditional means is not an indication of an absence of desire or obligation to remember and represent.[14]

In the modernization process, the mode of remembrance and representation has been renewed or transformed from its constrained form—such as memorial ceremonies—to a generalized form of "exaltation of the life of one's children." The great importance attached to education, which is a specific phenomenon in Confucian society, is an expression of a strong desire to realize this exaltation of life. A vignette by Janelli and Yim D. H. (2004: 135) summarizes this transformation well:

> In *Naeari*, the creation of an ancestral hall for collective rites was viewed as a simplification of ritual practices and, by implication, a curtailment of filial piety.... Arguing against the creation of the hall, one elder proclaimed that ancestor rites were a form of filial piety. Those favoring the hall did not challenge this moral norm but chose instead to define it more broadly. They pointed out that by creating the hall, the lineage would no longer need the extensive land holdings that were used to finance all the separate rites at gravesites. Some of these ritual estates could then be sold to provide funds for the education of promising descendants, which would also be a form of filial piety, they maintained.

Conclusion

Many studies have highlighted Confucian culture and familism as positive reasons for Korea's success. A central weakness of these studies is the failure to identify the mechanisms through which aspects of Confucianism and familism enabled success. We emphasize the significance of filial piety. As a religious ethos, filial piety internalizes responsibility for remembering and representing ancestors among Koreans in general, which transforms itself through familial practice into motives for economic success. The religious imperative of filial piety is the hidden source of self-sacrificing labor and adherence to education in Korea, and thereby we may label it as a Korea-specific or Confucian-specific "spirit" of capitalism.[15] It would not be an exaggeration to call the Korean economy of the last 50 years an economy of filial piety.

The main effects of the religious impetus to remember and represent ancestors are found in three sociocultural pressures: developmental, successive, and collective.[16]

With the strategy of the developmental state from the top, the economy of filial piety from the bottom has constituted the other side of the coin of economic development in Korea since the 1960s. Korean development in the 1960s and 1970s heavily depended on mobilization of human resources. Familial representation was decisive in channeling dedicated labor and education-obsessed parental concerns to the process of industrialization. Representation under conditions of abject poverty became "economic representation." From a macro-perspective, it was effective in establishing a dedicated, disciplined, and educated workforce. Self-sacrificing labor coupled with educational enthusiasm was the central mode of the practice of economic representation.

The developmental state of Korea derived familial mobilization from the economy of filial piety, and successful economic growth was achieved through efficient distribution and management of that economy. "Developmental, collective, and successive representations" hold remarkable significance in this process. The state minimized the cost of social welfare by relying on familial mutual aid generated by these pressures of representation. Instead, the state appropriated the curtailed cost for construction of economic infrastructure, which consequently paved the way for maximizing macroeconomic growth. Family-like affective ties or associations, mediated by school or local networks, internalized responsibility for one another as an ethos and were functionally connected with the mobilization mechanism of the developmental state.

Notes

* Chapter 2 is from an article, "Confucian Ethics and the Spirit of Capitalism in Korea: The Significance of Filial Piety," *Journal of East Asian Studies*, Volume 11 Number 2 (2011), pp. 171–196.

1. These virtuosi are exemplary figures who are considered the ideal model in Confucianism (Hahm C.-B., 1998; Hahm C., 2004). They are the ones who have mastered the religious solution of Confucianism by gaining knowledge through investigation of objects

and cultivation of the mind (Taylor, 1990: 39–52; de Bary, 1998: 100–102). Realistically, however, these are limited to only a few.
2. Filial piety is considered the first virtue in Chinese culture. While China has always had a diversity of religious beliefs, most of these beliefs embraced filial piety. This relationship was extended by analogy to a series of five relationships or five cardinal relationships (五倫 *Wulun* in Chinese): father and son (父子), ruler and subject (君臣), husband and wife (夫婦), elder and younger brother (兄弟), and friend and friend (朋友).
3. *Fung Yu-lan* (馮友蘭, 1952) estimates that the Confucian world is where the sacred and the profane are unified as one, and in this sense, Confucianism is the synthesized principle that encompasses religion and reality.
4. This is similar to Weber's thesis on Protestantism, in that Protestants are attached to the objectified evidence of wealth in order to subjugate tension and unrest as well as strengthen the subjective conviction of salvation (Weber, 1951[1920]).
5. The process of competitive diffusion of intensified clan rules on ancestor memorial services, the publication of genealogy books and collected works of ancestors, and the erection of ancestral memorial halls and shrines in late *Chosŭn* dynasty, can be viewed in this context (Deuchler, 1992).
6. According to Putnam (1993a), the sociocultural orientation of southern Italy can be explained from the perspective of familism as well.
7. Weber found a clue to kinship "relativization" in an incident recorded in Galatians about the symbolic significance of the "conference at Antioch." According to this record, St. Paul overcame the kinship exclusivity of St. Peter and tolerated uncircumcised Gentiles by agreeing to hold rituals and communion with the Gentiles. For Weber, this incident is a sign of progress made in modern Western history in which the familial (kin) boundary is crossed to advance into universalism (Weber, 1961[1923]: 335).
8. Family is the unity when compared to individuals. However, each family can be a part of a greater and more fundamental principle, the Heavenly Principle (天理). As such, the worldview of Confucianism made up of links between unity and parts. In any case, those alienated from this links, that is, separate entities, cannot exist (Choi B.-Y., 1999).
9. "A lineage woman told us that her first son died in childhood, shortly after her husband's family had failed to perform a death-day rite for one of their ancestors. Someone later told her that omitting the rite had caused her child's death" (Janelli and Janelli, 1982: 157).
10. An example of this can be "the Christian memorial service" in Korea (Sorensen and Kim S. C., 2004: 173). In fact, memorial services that mourn the dead are a phenomenon specific to Korean Christians and cannot be found in the Christian Bible or its doctrines. Korean

Christians in general show a negative response to Confucian memorial rituals, but paradoxically, Christian memorial services practiced now have many implications as they are Christian adaptations of traditional Confucian values.
11. 2005 Census that includes "Confucianism" as a response category reports: "Protestant" 18.3%, "Catholic" 10.9%, "Buddhist" 23.1%, "Confucian" 0.2%, "other religion" 0.5%, and "no religion" 46.5% (Korea National Statistical Office, 2008: 583).
12. In Korea, it is generally admitted that Protestant orders have strictly banned Confucian memorial rites requiring bows and sacrifices to the dead while Catholic orders have maintained a moderate view on these rites (Lee J. Y., 1988). This difference in missionary strategies creates a significant attitudinal gap between Protestants and Catholics toward the issue of Confucian ancestor rites. Catholics are more tolerant than Protestant. For example, one Protestant online news reports that, out of 100 lay believers, 56 think that practicing "traditional ancestor rite" is a serious problem since it is an "idol worship" (http://www.unionpress.co.kr/news/print_paper.php?number=4676, searched on Sep 20, 2010). The same report describes 26, out of 100, believe it is no problem because it is just a traditional custom. However, Catholics show an opposing tendency: "the proportion of Korean Catholics who practice ancestor rite increased from 69.4% in 1987 to 88.0% in 1998" (*Hankyoreh* Daily, April 11, 1998).
13. Cremation has been considered to be a serious violation of filial piety in Confucianism.
14. Recently a large academic conference was cohosted to review and search new forms and methods of Confucian ancestor rituals fitting to modern context by the Korean Studies Advancement Center and the World Confucianism Festival Community to commemorate the 600 years of Confucianism in Korea on September 16–17, 2010 at the Seoul Museum of History (*Chosun* Daily, Sep 15, 2010). The conference attracted so much public attention that seats were entirely filled, and the general public was forced to stand and listen.
15. Redding (1990) and Yao (2002) applied similar logic to overseas Chinese capitalism.
16. This unexpectedly reminds one of the economization processes of religious ethics that transformed the Protestant desire for salvation into abstinent labor. In this sense, serious comparative studies of these two aspects are urgently required.

Part II

The Social Dimension: Affective Networks

Chapter 3

Affective Networks, Social Capital, and Modernity in Korea*

with Mi-Hye Chang and Tae-Eun Kim

Introduction

In the previous chapter, the focus was placed on the psychological effect of Confucianism in Korea. This chapter and the following chapters pay greater attention to distinctive features of Korean society. One of the seeming anomalies of this otherwise rapid and apparently thorough transition to modernity in Korea is the continued presence of strong "affective networks" (緣故關係, *yuangu guanxi* in Chinese, *yŏn'go kwankye* in Korean). Indeed, one of the most striking characteristics of modern Korean society is the intricately webbed nexus among state/nonstate and official/nonofficial sectors. As was clearly revealed during the Asian financial crisis of 1997, many hitherto successful Asian economies, including that of South Korea, were characterized by strong state–business ties and business-to-business ties, which went beyond the kind usually found in modern capitalist economies.

After the crisis these were thoroughly criticized as the stuff of "crony capitalism," responsible for continued lackluster performance of most Asian economies in recent years. The policy recommendations that were forthcoming and the reforms undertaken since 1997 in South Korea have, for the most part, focused on dismantling the now discredited economic model, with a special emphasis placed on eradicating "cronyism" and the affective networks that permeate the society. The assumption, explicit or otherwise, is that cronyism is not only inefficient but also characteristic of a premodern agrarian society and as such should disappear as modernization and rationalization proceed.

However, despite the best efforts of many, the affective networks of South Korea hardly seem to be in decline. Even though some business practices that overtly reflect cronyism have been done away with, South Korean society and politics are still beholden to affective networks. This chapter argues that the network society has served Koreans very well in achieving their prized goal of economic development. Despite the recent economic crisis, the efficiency and efficacy of the network society for both economic and political purposes have yet to run their course. Moreover, the Korean tendency to form and treasure affective networks is derived from a worldview deeply rooted in Korean history, tradition, and philosophy, namely, Confucianism.

If we continue on the assumption that the affective network is simply a remnant of a bygone era and, as such, something to be gotten rid of as quickly as possible, the fight will be a long one. If we argue that the only way to upgrade the economy and consolidate democracy is to do away with affective networks, nothing short of a complete transformation of the Korean worldview and way of life will do. However, it is perhaps time to reevaluate some of the assumptions behind such recommendations. It is also timely to retrace and rethink the role of the affective network in South Korea's process of modernization and for its future. Could it be that the affective network society is efficacious not only in the short run but also for a fully industrialized democracy? Could it be that the affective network is more than just a crude "functional equivalent" of more "rational" and "advanced" means of organizing and ordering society, economy, and politics?

Answers to such questions require us to consider some of the most basic and cherished assumptions of modern economics and politics. Time and again we are faced with the "anomaly" of East Asian countries seemingly defying the "laws" of modernity. Then again, such events as the East Asian financial crisis of 1997 and the continuing decline of some of East Asia's formerly mighty economies seem to "confirm" suspicions that something was indeed "rotten" in East Asia. However, in this chapter and the one that follows, we would like to challenge such assumptions by arguing that the affective networks so characteristic of South Korea will remain and that there are reasons, not only historical, cultural, and philosophical, but also economic, social, and political, to support our view.

Affective Networks and Social Capital

It is now time to discuss the question of whether "social capital" does indeed exist in Korean society and, if so, in what form. Social capital designates a specific network of human relations that "mediates" profit-seeking market behavior. Accordingly, business groups such as corporate organizations that are dominant in the profit-seeking market are not our concern here. For the same reason, bureaucratic organizations such as governments that control behavior using power relations do not need to be covered either. Hence, in this section we intend to target the nongovernment and nonprofit sectors of Korea and consider the diverse social groups that exist as subjects of this discussion.

To start the process of examination, it is necessary to establish categories for defining the diverse social groups that exist in the nonprofit and nongovernmental sectors. Generally speaking, there are two different types of networks that create social capital. The first type is network formation due to voluntary association.[1] In this network, admission and withdrawal are made according to the choice of the person concerned and, for that reason, the members affiliated with this group share a specific ideology, interest, or concern. Representative examples of this type of network are the various clubs or citizens' associations. The second type is network formation due to affective relationships. In this network, because membership is determined by common experiences rather than the choice of the person concerned, there is a greater possibility that communitarian concerns between members are higher than in the case of the voluntary association. Clan organizations, regional (locality-based) associations, and alumni associations, which are formed in accordance with affective networks such as kinship, hometown, and school ties, are representative examples.

On the other hand, in addition to the criteria of group membership rules, nonprofit/nongovernment organizations can also be classified by whether the aim of their activities is to pursue public good or private good.[2] However, in this case, because the criteria for classifying public and private goods are not clear, it is not easy to establish any single, distinct criterion. For example, when a local organization operating as a unit in a specific region claims that it undertakes activities speaking for the general interests of the local people, we are not sure whether this organization should be viewed as a group for public good or private good. Although this group can be viewed as having a public nature when assessing the aim of the activity by the standards of those within the region, however, when assessed according to the standards of people outside of the region, it is also possible to see it as merely a product of "group egoism" (集團利己主義). Recently, the debate surrounding the role of citizens' groups in Korea has gained much public interest due to their ambiguous position that cannot clarify such problem.[3]

Although incomplete, however, we will take the discussion up to the present point as a basis for determining a framework of analysis for classifying the groups in Korea's nonprofit/nongovernment sector in the following way. First, we intend to adopt two criteria. One criterion is the membership rule of the group, whether it is "voluntary" or based on "affective network." The other criterion concerns whether the aim of the activities of the group is in the interests of a "public good" or a "private good." In principle, there may be 2 × 2 = 4 spaces into which it is analytically possible to divide groups. However, in reality, as discussed, it is impossible to classify clearly whether the activities that are manifested along with affective network are ultimately in the interests of public or private good. Consequently, two spaces were combined into one and the groups have been divided into three types. Table 3.1 arranges the results of this classification.

The most fundamental problem when using this diagram to classify groups is to determine at what frequency and how these three types of groups are distributed in the Korean nonprofit/nongovernmental sector. Without empirical investigation, however, it is impossible to answer this question.[4] However, based on objective knowledge and subjective experience, it can be conjectured that in comparison to any other country, Korea has many C-type groups that are formed along with affective networks such as kinship, regionalism, and school ties and that the activities of these groups are vigorous. On the other hand, this situation can be diagnosed in reverse by arguing that the formation and activities of the B-type group, which is based on "civility" as described by Tocqueville (1969) or Putnam (1993a), have

Table 3.1 Classification of groups

Membership rule	Aim of activities	
	Private good	Public good
Voluntary	Type A (clubs)	Type B (citizens' groups)
Nonvoluntary (affective network)	Type C (kinship, regional, alumni networks)	

still not reached satisfactory levels. Meanwhile, it is difficult to find any basis for making distinctly special predictions about the A-type, namely, the voluntary as well as private interest group.

Inevitably, the question now centers on how to evaluate the Korean society based on the active presence of C-type groups formed along with affective networks from the perspective of social capital. In retrospect, the works of Coleman (1988), Putnam (1993a), and Bourdieu (1986) concluded that social capital does not necessarily have to take the form of voluntary associations. This is because social capital can, through "the closed network," produce "generalized reciprocity" by supplying a public good—trust—"among members." In this sense, the affective network groups in Korean society, on the contrary, furnish a source of extremely strong social capital.

Paradoxically, as a consequence of the existence of affective network groups, it does not seem inappropriate to hear Korea appraised as a "Heaven of social capital." Further, as Putnam (1993a: 169) emphasizes, social capital, including the affective network in Korea, is a "moral resource whose supply increases rather than decreases through use and which become depleted if not used." Far from being a zero-sum game, accumulation of social capital in an affective network never diminishes the chance to accumulate social capital in another affective network.

Of course, affective networks are not exclusive to Korea. As summarized in Table 3.2, business organizations in East Asia are based on various forms of affective network (Hamilton, Zeil, and Kim W. J., 1990), even though the system of corporate governance varies from country to country. In Taiwan, family-oriented small and medium-sized enterprises comprise the majority, whereas most Japanese enterprises are organized under *keiretsu* (系列) and subcontract relationships characterized by simultaneous horizontal and vertical relations. Korean enterprises, for their part, are organized in a patriarchal and strictly vertical manner (Hamilton and Biggart, 1988; Lew S. C., 1999). In China, *xiangzhen* (鄉鎭) enterprise is an example of business organization formed by extended regional connections based on a conception of the traditional Chinese family (家 *jia* in Chinese) (Lew S. C. and Kim T. E., 2001).

These business organizations and systems of enterprises have been responsible for the explosive economic growth that the region has experienced over the past four decades. It is argued that the institutional isomorphism and embeddedness between business organization and cultural context found in East Asia have been advantageous to rapid growth by reducing transaction costs involved in economic

Table 3.2 Institutionalization of affective networks in East Asian business organizations

	Cultural sphere		Economic sphere
Korea	Familism, affective network, groupism, paternalism	Regionalism, academic cliquism, familism	*chaebols* conglomerate (財閥)	Hierarchically arranged large-scale network of enterprises
Japan		Academic cliquism, paternalism	*keiretsu* subcontract relation (系列)	Horizontal connection among big enterprises and vertical connection between big enterprise and small and medium-sized enterprises
China		Familism, *guanxi* (relation, 關係)	*xiangzhen* enterprise (鄉鎮企業)	Various forms of nonstate-owned corporate organization, existing in both rural and urban areas, owned and managed by farmers' groups
Taiwan			*jiazu* enterprise family enterprise (家族企業)	Corporate organization based on noncontractual relations among family members

Source: Lew S. C., Chang M. H., and Kim T. E. (2003: 207).

activities (Williamson, 1989; Chang H. J., 1993: 147–148). East Asia has successfully responded to the pressure from the capitalist world economy by building up social capital needed for the development of capitalism and democracy (Coleman, 1988; Putnam, 1995).

Modern Manifestations of Affective Networks

Affective networks in Korea are mainly based upon three factors: blood ties (血緣), school ties (學緣), and regional or locality ties (地緣). Korean businesses are famous for the family-based organizational characteristics (Janelli and Yim D. H., 1993). Most of the largest *chaebol* (conglomerates), including the most internationally competitive ones such as Samsung, Hyundai, and LG, are still controlled by the founder's family members, usually brothers, sons, nephews, and grandsons. The importance of blood ties is even greater for smaller companies. Whereas the largest conglomerates make some effort, albeit usually halfheartedly, to adopt global standards by being less obvious about favoring members of the founding family, the smaller companies feel no such compunction. In fact, for most Korean businessmen, the most important motivation for building their businesses is to pass it on to their children as part of their "patrimony."

Affective networks based on school ties are especially important in government and politics. The graduates of elite schools and universities dominate the political and economic sectors to a degree rarely witnessed in other societies. The highest echelons of the Korean bureaucracy have traditionally been occupied by members of the "KS," graduates of the elite *Kyung-gi* High School and Seoul National University. Since the abolition of the high school entrance examination in 1974, the importance of elite high schools has diminished somewhat, but the dominance of Seoul National University within the government bureaucracy continues unabated to this day. Little wonder, then, that every schoolchild in Korea and their parents dream of being accepted at Seoul National University.

Indeed, Korean zeal for education is inextricably linked with the Korean penchant for forming affective network, as school tie has always been one of the most important ways to form such networks. As such, there is a fierce competition to get into better schools, one of the surest ways of climbing up the social ladder. Elite colleges and universities are preferred as much, if not more, for their alumni network as for the quality of education they offer. This results in an infamously competitive college entrance examination system in preparation for which many Korean families invest exorbitant amounts of resources, financial and otherwise. The importance of school ties as a basis upon which to build affective networks explains the ubiquitous alumni organizations and meetings.

Most Koreans attend the meetings of the alumni organizations of their elementary, middle, or high schools as well as those of their colleges, graduate, or postgraduate programs on a regular basis. In recent years, the Internet has become a new medium for building and strengthening school ties in Korea. One of the most successful Internet businesses in Korea was "iloveschool" that specializes in locating long-lost school friends and building up alumni networks in cyberspace far before the coming of "facebook" service. This is an indication that the affective network is not necessarily incompatible with modern technology and society. In fact, if anything, at least in this case, the most modern technology and the most traditional aspects of Korea are mutually reinforcing.

In many cases, school ties are combined with regional ties, the third factor most often used by Koreans to form affective networks. For example, former presidents Chun Doo Hwan and Roh Tae Woo were classmates at the military academy, and it was during their administrations that many of their classmates occupied important posts in the government. It was also during this period that the clique popularly known as the "TK" group came to dominate Korean politics and the economy. The "T" stood for *Taegu*, the name of the city from which most of them hailed. The "K" stood for *Kyung-book* High School, the elite high school in *Taegu*. During President Kim Young Sam's administration, the highest echelons of Korea's power elite were populated by the "PK" group where the "P" stood for *Pusan*, the home city of its members including the president himself, and the "K" for *Kyŏngnam* High School, the elite high school in *Pusan*. With the accession of President Kim Dae Jung, graduates of *Mokpo* High School and people from his province, *Chŏllanamdo*, were clearly in the ascendancy.

Since the transition to democracy, regional networks have played an increasingly important role in Korean politics. In fact, it could be argued that regionalist sentiments enabled the first "turnover" of government to the opposition in the presidential election of 1997, when Kim Dae Jung was elected. Kim Dae Jung was able to win the presidency only because, in addition to the overwhelming support that he received from his home region of *Honam* (Southwest of Korea), he was also able to rally to his side the sentiments of another region, namely the *Choongchung* (central part of Korea) region with its political leader Kim Jong Pil, who also had grievances against the *Yŏngnam* (Southeast of Korea) region that had dominated Korean politics till then. If such a regime change was the driving force of democratic consolidation, as it clearly was, then regionalism was a major force behind democratization in Korea. Although regionalism was indeed used as a means to maintain power by authoritarian regimes in the past, it also made possible for Korea to take another important step toward consolidating democracy.

Most analysts of the Korean politics would agree that regional sentiments have been exacerbated during Kim Dae Jung's presidency and that such sentiments were one of the decisive factors in the 2002 presidential election for Rho Moo Hyun. Some rather cynical observers have noted that the "progressive" outlook for which the people from the *Honam* region have celebrated is in reality nothing but a reaction to politics dominated by the people from *Yeongnam*. Given that behavior pattern of the *Honam* government follows the identical regionalist route for which the previous governments were severely criticized, their erstwhile "progressivism" seems to have been just another form of regionalism in disguise (Lee K.-Y., 1998; Lew S.-C. and Shim J.-B., 1990).

Given the importance of affective networks, it is little wonder that Koreans invest significant amounts of time and energy attending innumerable social gatherings such as weddings, funerals, and alumni meetings, as well as more traditional social groups such as *kye* (契, a traditional way of saving among close friends or micro-credit rotating), *hyangwuhoi* (鄉友會, social gatherings of people from the same hometown), or *chongchinhoi* (宗親會, an extended family reunion). This is in sharp contrast to the conspicuous lack of commitment to and involvement in the voluntary citizens' groups or "civic organizations" deemed essential for a thriving democracy (Lew S.-C. and Kim Y.-M., 2000).

Although many Koreans would gladly pay US$10 for a round of drinks for "old buddies," few are willing to pay even half that amount in fees and dues to citizens' groups. Even in the smallest localities, town elite gatherings—such as *palgakhoe* in the city of *Jinju*, the American Armed Forces Air Base Golf Club in the city of *Kunsan*, and other social clubs, such as the Lions Club, the Junior Chamber of Commerce, and the Rotary Club—function as the focal points of affective networks linked by blood, school, and regional ties. A broadcasting company once conducted a survey of over 40 citizens' groups in the country and every single one of them acknowledged that a local power group based on family, school, and regional ties exists in their regions (Yang S.-W. and Cho S.-K., 1999).

Confucianism and Affective Networks

The persistence of affective networks in Korean society cannot, however, be explained solely in terms of its rationality or efficiency in the context of rapid industrialization. Affective networks continue to exert their influence on Korea because they receive powerful ideational support and reinforcement from neo-Confucianism, which provided the normative foundations for Korean politics and society during the past five centuries. In order to understand the theoretical as well as normative bases of affective networks in Korea, we must look into the theory and history of neo-Confucianism in Korea, however briefly.

Neo-Confucianism refers to various new interpretations of Confucianism that arose during the *Song* (宋) dynasty in China, which saw a great revival of ancient schools of thought and government. The most dominant of these neo-Confucian schools was the one articulated by *Zhu Xi* (朱熹) and it was his take on Confucianism, called *xing-li-xue* (性理學), which was imported by the founders of the *Chosŭn* dynasty in late fourteenth-century Korea. One of the most striking features of neo-Confucianism was the emphasis that it placed on the importance of the family or the clan. *Zhu Xi* had made clear and elaborate provisions, both theoretical as well as institutional, for the reconstruction and strengthening of the institution of the family. The clan, or the family writ large, was the institution of choice for *Zhu Xi* just as it had been for Confucius because it was where filial piety, loyalty, trust, and other values essential for the affective society could flourish. As a sociopolitical institution, it provided the sense of continuity, permanence, and identity that the highly bureaucratized, impersonal, and commercialized society of imperial *Song* could not.

For neo-Confucians who followed in *Zhu Xi*'s footsteps, the family was as important as the dynasty. The dynasty, or the state, was where one's sense of loyalty and public service laid. Neo-Confucian scholars thought the purpose of their education and self-cultivation was public service, which mostly meant serving in the imperial bureaucracy. The state thus provided them with a sense of achievement as well as prestige, wealth, power, and honor. However, the family, or the clan, was the other pillar of a Confucian scholar-bureaucrat's self-identity and the object of his loyalty, expressed in terms of filial piety. It was in the family that one learned the most basic and fundamental values of Confucianism, including a sense of justice, trust, affection, order, and propriety, the Five Cardinal Principles. It is only after one has mastered these values and rules of propriety that one can then go out into the world as a truly "public" person.

In modern Western political discourses, home provides the space where emotional connection and ties are cultivated and strengthened among close companions (Ringmar, 2005). It also functions as a shelter from the impersonal public sphere (Duncan, 1998: 13). In Confucianism, however, home is where moral discipline and the training of a public person are carried out, and accordingly, ties that bind the family, relatives, and other affective networks are considered public in nature rather than private (Duncan, 1998: 19). Home is the public sphere where one is taught one's rights and duties, responsibility, and power (Lew S. C. and Kim T. E., 2001). Confucians viewed public and private spheres to be in harmony rather than in conflict.

The Confucian "citizen," thus produced, is able to make the clear distinction between the public and the private, just as Western counterpart does. In fact, like the ancient Greeks, the Confucian citizen clearly privileged the public over the private. The difference is that the distinction is not based upon a family–state dichotomy. It is possible to act in a "public" (公) and just manner in the household just as it is possible to do so in public: "Master *Zeng* said: 'Be circumspect in funerary services and continue sacrifices to the distant ancestors, and the virtue (德) of the common people will thrive.'"[5] Or, "Where exemplary persons (君子) are earnestly committed to their parents, the people will aspire to authoritative conduct (仁); where they do not neglect their old friends, the people will not be indifferent to each other."[6] Conversely, it is possible to act in a "private" (私) and hence self-interested manner in the family as well as in the public realm. Again, the family is the realm in which one is taught the values of the public (公). In fact, the training for the public starts with self-cultivation (修身) and the sense of the public thus acquired is then expected to be applied and practiced in the realm of the state and the world. This is the philosophy expressed in the famous opening lines of *The Great Learning* (大學), one of the *Four Books* of neo-Confucianism:

> The ancients who wished to illustrate illustrious virtue throughout the kingdom, first ordered well their own States. Wishing to order well their States, they first regulated their families. Wishing to regulate their families, they first cultivated their persons. Wishing to cultivate their persons, they first rectified their hearts. Wishing to rectify their hearts, they first sought to be sincere in their thoughts, they first extended to the utmost their knowledge. Such extension of knowledge lay in the investigation of things.[7]

What we have then, in Confucianism, is a philosophy of the public that does not follow or respect those dichotomies essential for the concept in the Western tradition, namely, "individual versus group," "state versus civil society," and "public versus private sectors." As we have seen, this does not mean that it lacks a sense of the public as opposed to the private. Confucians are able to make the distinction between "cronyism" and a "just" order. It is simply that they are not nearly distinguished along the dichotomous lines so dear to Western political discourse.

In fact, it is the particularly strong sense of the "public" over the "private" among the Korean public that has brought about the repeated prosecution and jailing of high-ranking government officials, army generals, politicians (including former presidents), and businessmen (including founders of major conglomerates). It is the

Confucian sense of the public that has been the force behind the resistance against authoritarian rule and the yearning for democracy. It is also this sense of the public that undergirds the seemingly endless series of "reforms" we have seen in Korean politics, including market-oriented ones. "Civil society" in Korea also gains its theoretical impetus as much from the Confucian sense of the public as from the theories of civil society imported from the West in recent years.

To be sure, this is in no way to say that the *Chosŭn* Confucians or their descendants were able to maintain and practice such fine distinctions all the time. *Chosŭn* Confucians and modern-day Koreans have had more than their share of bouts with corruption arising from the neglect or conscious manipulation of the fine distinctions between the public and the private. However, it is to say that Koreans continue to be influenced by the neo-Confucian terms of discourse, which provide the opportunities for abuse and corruption of the values that they prescribe as well as the normative standards from which to criticize such abuses. Moreover, it is to say that the importance Koreans place on the family and other affective networks is not the result of their inability to make the distinction between the public and the private, as some have argued, but the result of a worldview that operates on values and assumptions different from those of Western political discourse.

Previous Studies on Affective Networks

In recent years, an increasing number of scholars have been looking into affective networks by applying the theories of social capital or organizational analysis of social institutions. Studies that analyze regionalism utilizing these new approaches, for the most part, define regionalism as a version of factionalism, particularism, or even "mob mentality." As such, it is regarded as the manifestation of an underdeveloped political process (Kim M.-J., 1993; Son H.-C., 1993). Some understand regionalism to have been produced as part of a political strategy, especially since the 1960s when authoritarian governments were seeking ways to maintain their grip on power. It is argued that President Park Chung Hee's regime fermented regionalism as a way to garner support from his home region for his repressive regime. Others argue that the authoritarian government accused the people of *Honam* of inciting regionalism when in reality they were simply trying to express their grievances against the government's economic policies that overtly favored the *Yŏngnam* region. Even the pro-democracy movement led by Kim Dae Jung and many of his followers, who happened to be from the *Honam* region, was portrayed as nothing more than an expression of regionalist sentiment (Choi J.-J., 1991; Jung K.-S., 1997; Choi S.-M., 1999).[8]

According to studies that adopt rational choice theories (Kim Y.-H., 1996; Kim S.-U., 1993), trust in private networks rather than in the law and institutions made positive contributions to rapid industrialization. Individuals' decisions to rely on affective networks is rational in the sense that they help reduce uncertainty and transaction costs in a sociopolitical environment characterized by instability and uncertainty: "when uncertainty of the system is high, affective networks provide trustworthy membership and predictable conduct; therefore, people employ networks as a means to reduce uncertainty" (Kim Y.-H., 1996: 106). The preference for affective networks, then, was the result of strategic choices made by rational individuals under particular constraints. Affective networks based on "primary" ties can provide the sense of trust essential for the exchange of various kinds of political and economic resources when other institutions are underdeveloped. During social upheavals, the social cost of establishing trust can rise to such levels that the cost of official contracts is higher than that incurred by transactions based on personal trust. Accordingly, people are able to gain access to scarce resources most effectively and efficiently by conducting their transactions through affective networks.

Yet another approach regards affective networks as the result of changes and distortions brought about by the "developmental state" through its active intervention in the market. Traditional familism of the past, affective and communitarian, arose from the labor-intensive agrarian environment. However, during the industrialization process, it was transformed into an instrument for the maximization of narrowly perceived and exclusively defined family interest to survive and win in the newly emerging fierce capitalistic competition. The developmental state intervened in the market by allocating scarce resources according to its own design, thus creating and maintaining massive inequality in the distribution of social wealth. In this process, individuals had to engage in a battle for survival, a battle to become the beneficiaries rather than the victims of the policies of the developmental state. In an environment that lacked procedural or institutional competition mechanisms that ensured fairness and equal opportunity, everyone attempted to gain access to the powers through the affective networks at their disposal (Kim D.-N., 1997).

In a similar vein, others have argued that rapid industrialization dissolved traditional communitarian ties without substituting a new principle of social integration to replace the old one. As a result, only a "lawless jungle" emerged in which individuals were forced to depend on primary groups or affective networks (Kim S.-U., 1993). Still others have argued that the reason affective networks became so important was because people relied on them as a counterweight to the sense of dislocation and alienation they experienced in the newly rising urban and industrialized centers that offered only temporary and anonymous relationships (Song B., 1997).

The assumption common to these analyses of affective networks in Korea is that they are nothing more than expressions of parochial interests, nepotism, and other forms of premodern "irrationalism" (無理), obstructing modern, rational, and hence universal institutions and standards. As such, what is called for is unceasing effort to replace the "narrowly defined and closed connections" with "general and open networks" (Kim Y.-H., 1996). Another assumption common to these analyses is that "premodern" agrarian societies have affective and communitarian social relations while "modern" industrialized ones are competitive and guided by rational regulations and principles: "a demand for structural clearness and fairness of competition will gradually put pressure for change on the existing balance of a connection-oriented society. Therefore, market competition will replace existing connections in social and political sectors as well" (Lee J.-H., 1999a: 49). Affective networks function effectively during the transitional phase when rational organizations that can generate true public trust and effective and efficient means of resource mobilization and allocation are lacking.

Alternative Views on Affective Networks

As we have seen, affective networks seem to be firmly rooted in Korean society. As such, they are also one of the keys to understanding the logic of contemporary Korean society. However, their existence directly contradicts some of the basic assumptions of modernization theory, which claims that the traditional community is necessarily weakened as industrialization increases social mobility among different social classes. This is why most analysts seem to agree that the affective networks will soon disappear as the market economy and democracy take further root in Korea. If they fail to disappear as expected and hoped for, then it is imperative that every effort be made to eradicate them as quickly and thoroughly as possible.

However, as of yet there is no clear-cut reason why affective networks should be viewed in such an unrelentingly negative light in the context of a modern society. It is unclear whether the influence of affective networks will necessarily decrease as society develops, or they will continue to exist and perhaps even be strengthened under certain circumstances. For example, affective networks lower the cost of supervision and provide economic efficiency. They are highly effective means for monitoring and controlling behavior. When a person is recruited by a company through recommendation or connection, he/she tends to work harder not to disappoint those who recommended him/her and to secure his/her position within the network of personal relations provided by that connection. Again, "connections by blood (family), region, and/or school working in reality are all means to reduce transactional cost. If horizontal and vertical connections are correlated with already existing affective networks, they create a strong trust" (Kim Y.-H., 1996: 111).

The claim that competition among network groups leads to conflict and is always counterproductive, while the existence of many civic organizations and interest groups will ensure more rational and reasonable resolutions for conflicts of interests, does not seem to hold water either, at least in the case of Korea. Korean labor unions and other more recently formed interest groups modeled after modern Western ones do not necessarily lend themselves to peaceful resolution of disputes. If anything, they seem to have exacerbated the vehemence and violence, which accompany many disputes that have arisen in Korea in recent years. The claim that modern Western-style organizations reduce transactions costs cannot be taken as a given.

Another common assumption is that affective networks are essentially private organizations and hence are in fundamental conflict with public civil society. Lee J.-H. (1999a: 50) argues: "a well-balanced connection-oriented society will diminish civil society while the collapse of the connection-oriented society will strengthen civil society." However, where can citizens who wish to participate in institutionalized voluntary activities learn to make rational decisions and acquire a strong sense of political identity? In many cases, the family, the quintessential affective network, functions as the realm in which we receive socialization and acquire our basic dispositions and beliefs as citizens. Cohen and Arato (1992) acknowledge the importance of the family and argue that the followings belong to the spheres of civil society: family or nonofficial groups and voluntary organizations that provide diversity and autonomy of lifestyle; cultural and communication systems; spheres for private self-development and ethical choice; and general law and fundamental rights that are needed to divide private life from the public sector. In this regard, there is no intrinsic reason why families and other affective networks cannot function as the training ground for a sense of public life and citizenship.

The most problematic aspect of affective networks most often referred to is that they block outsiders from accessing their resources, and unfairly so. Again, Lee J.-H. (1999b: 236) argues: "if a group of actors forms an exclusive clique...it would become more effective in the short run. However, in the long run, it is bound to have an ill effect on all, that is to say, it will ultimately lead to inefficient distribution of resources in the society and cause institutional mistrust." That is, "as reciprocity in the groups and personal trust created by cliquish connection accumulate on an exclusive basis, trust in general others outside the in-group or 'the rules of the game' which should generally be applied are inevitably damaged. Such groups damage fairness of competition and diminish possibility of productive transactions, eventually bringing about inefficiency in the distribution of resources" (Lee J.-H., 1999a: 49).

Affective networks create social relations not through impersonal contracts based on overt calculations of self-interest but through voluntary agreements among participants, thus strengthening interpersonal ties and furthering efficiency in certain transactions. The downside of them is that the trust among the in-group members cannot easily be extended to those outside the group or to the level of general trust. Thus, the biggest problem of affective networks is seen as the existence of an "exclusive inner group" (Lee J.-H., 1999a: 47).

However, one of the issues often overlooked in discussing positive as well as negative effects of affective networks is the fact that, in many cases, affective networks lack clear boundaries between outer and inner groups. Individuals can and do belong to not just one but several affective networks simultaneously in reality. A typical Korean belongs to numerous alumni associations. He or she typically belongs to numerous *hyangwuhoi* (鄉友會, social gatherings of people from the same hometown) simultaneously, ones based on people from the same *Myŏn* (village), *Kun* (county), or *Do* (province), among others. Ultimately, they all belong to the community of the Korean people. Even the family has porous boundaries as it extends beyond the nuclear family composed of parents and their children to include not only members of an extended family such as aunts, uncles, and cousins but also everyone with the same "choronyms" (Hahm C., 2000, 2003). Also, any family members on both father's and mother's sides, as well as in-laws, could typically be included in one's "family" (Lee K.-Y., 1998).

In this respect, the boundary that divides inner and outer groups is highly flexible. By contrast, many of the networks or groups characteristic of modern societies tend to be much more exclusive with clear-cut boundaries. For instance, if an individual is a member of a certain class, he or she cannot be a member of another class simultaneously. Also, if he or she belongs to a particular political party, he or she cannot belong to another political party at the same time. A similar case can be made in regard to civic groups. In the West, if one participates in the activities of a particular voluntary association, he or she is likely to stay and devote most of his or her life to that group. On the other hand, a typical Korean belongs to many different groups and organizations because he or she regards the organizations as another means to participate in a new affective network or extend preexisting ones. Hence, the more prominent one is, the more likely that he or she has multiple memberships in several organizations yet not necessarily dedicated to the activities for which these organizations were formed.

The importance of affective networks and their tendency to compete for political power through myriad interlocking channels lead Koreans to place a great deal of importance on politics and the central government as the only means to address their grievances, political or otherwise. "Because other differences are not present, each group tends to be distinguishable from the others only by the personalities of its members and by their relationship to power at the time. Hence groupings are factional; for the issues and interests that forge true parties from factions are absent from the homogeneous, power-bent society" (Henderson, 1968: 5).

According to a survey (Um T.-S., 1997), among 1,000 respondents, 26% chose political reform as the foremost task for the state, and many believed that politicians were the most responsible for the economic crisis of 1997. The flip side of this is that the state is expected to intervene in such problems as corporate restructuring and business–labor relations usually deemed the purview of economic actors or the market. Korean society as a whole and each regional/local society in particular are "narrow societies" in the sense that they are center-oriented societies in which each individual strives to reach the center through various "human channels" (Lim H.-J., 1999). For example, it is often noted that presidents of the student bodies at colleges and universities simply view their position as a means to enter mainstream politics. The same criticism is often leveled at leaders of various nongovernmental organizations and civic groups, as many end up in political parties (Kim S.-K., 1999). As a result, a genuine civil society outside and independent of the state does not exist in Korean society.

As such, politics is identified with the state and government of a particular regime or institution (Lim H.-J., 1999); this explains the Korean tendency to solve problems through abrupt changes in the persons in charge rather than through institutions and procedures. The oft-quoted phrase "human relations are everything" is a reflection of such a view. When a problem emerges, the person in charge is blamed for his/her lack of qualification and bad personality, and an extraordinary person, a leader, with the ability to solve all the problems is sought. Rather than developing and debating policies and institutional measures to remedy governmental and political shortcomings, Korean politicians would rather involve themselves in building new networks. This explains the weakness of political parties in Korea, which have short life spans and are almost wholly dependent on a particular political leader who is the focal point of a giant affective network. Even former president Kim Dae Jung, the champion of Western-style democracy, has single handedly founded and dissolved almost a dozen political parties in his lifetime.[9]

Market and Social Capital

From the perspective of social science, the "market" may be the concept most symbolic of the beginning of the modern era. Ever since Adam Smith vindicated the resource distribution function of the competitive market with the concept of "the invisible hand," the market has been recognized as a firm reality in the neoclassical economics of the Marginal Utility school, in Keynesian macro-economics, which was established in response to the former, and even in Marxist political economy. To those who support the function of resource distribution through competition, the market is an absolute social device and an infallible tool. To those who are concerned about the negative consequences, that is, monopoly, the market must be supplemented by state intervention; nevertheless, the market is considered an important concept and its existence undeniable.

The importance of the market remains unchallenged not only in economics but also in political science and sociology. Competition, rooted in self-interest, has extended into all spheres of society and has endlessly destroyed and replaced existing social and human relations. This process is described as "marketization" or "commodification" of today's modern society. This explanation is the most fundamentally accepted starting point for debates in sociology and political science. Modernization theory, dependency theory, or world-system theory, even mode of production theory, all takes the existence of the market as a premise. Concepts ranging from "status to contract," "primary group to secondary group," and "unequal exchange between the center and the periphery" eloquently express the importance of market.

However, on the other hand, one can indirectly confirm through the experiences of overseas visitors that Korea has a very different type of market compared to that of the West. Some examples include episodes indicating that in Korea, the maintenance of harmonious human relations is a far more important criterion for corporate activities than the quality of products. Of course, such stories are not only applicable in Korea; little needs to be said of China and Japan, both in the sphere of Confucian culture. Going farther afield, similar stories are often heard regarding business in Thailand, in the Buddhist cultural sphere, or in the Muslim cultures of the Middle East. In that case, it is necessary to shift our focus away from the existence of "the market as an abstract concept" to "the market as a concrete mode of function." That is to say, we are interested in whether every market really functions with a unified mode across space and time.

The concrete mode of function of the market experienced by people clearly exhibits significant variation in each country or in each culture. Then, what causes such variation? Recently in the field of economic sociology, theoretical and conceptual work examining this question has progressed to a significant level. The debate regarding social capital merits close attention in particular,[10] because the concept of social capital, first originated with Coleman (1988), offers a strong explanation as to why actors pursuing profit in the market exhibit different behavior in cases where they possess social capital and in cases where they do not.

First, it is important to examine Coleman's definition of social capital. He defines social capital by its function:

> It is not a single entity but a variety of different entities, with two elements in common: they all consist of some aspect of social structures, and they facilitate certain actions of actors—whether persons or corporate actors—within the structure. Like other forms of capital, social capital is productive, making possible the achievement of certain ends that in its absence would not be possible....Unlike other forms of capital, social capital inheres in the structure of relations between actors and among actors (Coleman, 1988: S98).

Coleman's argument is directly linked to new institutional economics, which places importance on "transaction costs" that arises within the market (Williamson, 1973).[11] They explain that because those who do not share social capital always face problems of trust, that is, the problem of opportunistic behavior by the transaction partner, it is necessary to introduce reliable safeguards (e.g., insurance or official endorsements). However, if the formation of social capital creates trust between the two participants in a transaction, then safeguards such as insurance merely become cumbersome formalities that increase transaction costs in accordance with the contract. Consequently, social capital is an important mechanism for reducing transaction costs.

According to Coleman (1988: S116–S118), unlike private goods such as physical capital or human capital, social capital has a character strongly similar to that of public goods in the market. Proceeding a step further, he argues for the extreme importance of the existence of social structures such as the "closure of networks" and "appropriable social organizations" that promote the formation of social capital (Coleman, 1988: S105–S109). This is because social capital can be formed when "obligations, expectations, and trustworthiness of structure" exist and thereby provide "information channels" so that "norms and effective sanctions" are available (Coleman, 1988: S101–S105).

Putnam (1993a: 167) refers to social capital as those "features of social organization, such as trust, norms, and networks that can improve the efficiency of society by facilitating coordinated actions." Likewise, he argues that "voluntary cooperation is easier in a community that has inherited a substantial stock of social capital, in the form of norms of reciprocity and networks of civic engagement." He adds that "as with conventional capital, those who have social capital tend to accumulate more" and most forms of social capital, such as trust, have an attribute of "what Albert Hirschman has called 'moral resources'—that is, resources whose supply increases rather than decreases through use and which become depleted if not used" (Putnam, 1993a: 169).

Putnam also points out that "one special feature of social capital, like trust, norms, and networks, is that it is ordinarily a public good, unlike conventional capital" and subsequently explains that "like all public goods, social capital tends to be undervalued and undersupplied by private agents" (Putnam, 1993a: 170). In addition, he contends:

> Norms such as those that under-gird social trust evolve because they lower transaction costs and facilitate cooperation. The most important of these norms is reciprocity. Reciprocity is of two sorts, sometimes called 'balanced (or specific)' and 'generalized (or diffuse)'.... The

norm of generalized reciprocity is a highly productive component of social capital. Communities in which this norm is followed can more efficiently restrain opportunism and resolve problems of collective action.... The norm of generalized reciprocity serves to reconcile self-interest and solidarity.... An effective norm of generalized reciprocity is likely to be associated with dense network of social exchange (Putnam, 1993a: 172).

French sociologist Pierre Bourdieu (1986: 248) defines social capital as "the aggregate of the actual or potential resources which are linked to possession of a durable network of more or less institutionalized relationships of mutual acquaintance and recognition—or in other words, to membership in a group–which provides each of its members with the backing of the collectivity-owned capital, a 'credential' which entitles them to credit, in the various senses of the word." Moreover, he argues that "the volume of the social capital possessed by a given agent thus depends on the size of the network of connections he can effectively mobilize and on the volume of the capital (economic, cultural, or symbolic) possessed in his own right by each of those to whom he is connected" (Bourdieu, 1986: 249). Furthermore, he points out that activities in the market selected by a particular group or individual take on different appearances according to the extent of institutionalization of this social capital.

Coleman, Putnam, and Bourdieu, by emphasizing the function and role of social capital, are ultimately arguing that the modes of function of the market take on a different appearance according to the form and conditions in which institutionalized social capital is accumulated. That is, they are arguing that the appearance of the concrete market can differ according to the "embeddedness" of economic action (Granovetter, 1985). Moreover, all three make clear that the existence of a "community" based on "closure of network" and "generalized reciprocity" are indispensable conditions to establish the concept of social capital. They succinctly point out that through the closed network, that is, the community, social capital supplies a public good that the market cannot offer, which is trust.

Ultimately, this is a view in complete opposition to the "previous studies on affective networks." Moreover, in contrast to Lee J.-Y. (1998) and many others with similar positions, formation and accumulation of social capital cannot be possible in open networks. The moment that a network is opened, the specific, concrete, and embedded context of the economic action disappears, and in its place, an abstract and de-personalized market characterized by unlimited competition takes over. However, this kind of market is merely one that is separate from the market that we experience in the flesh on a daily basis. This is because embedded social capital is always extant in a market in which concrete economic activities occur.

Conclusion: An Alternate Modernity?

Most scholars until now have regarded affective networks as transitional features of the Korean society, the side effects of a temporary social malaise brought about by rapid economic growth, or the lingering features of the premodern era soon to disappear. However, affective networks do not simply appear to be premodern practices or anomalous remnants of a bygone era soon to disappear (Hahm C. and Bell, 2004). Studies that regard affective networks only as "functional alternative" to better institutional means fail to give due recognition to the effectiveness and even the compatibility of affective networks with modern society and underestimate their durability.

Moreover, as we have seen, families and clans were of central importance in the organization of society in traditional Korea. In particular, the neo-Confucianism that was adopted as the "state religion" during the *Chosŭn* dynasty put family and clans on equal footing with the state (Hahm C., 2003). Confucianism also continues to provide normative justifications for practices that in modern Western terms can easily be regarded as cronyism and nepotism. Given that Korean society is still highly influenced by Confucian values, it is little wonder that the importance of families, clans, and networks based on blood ties continues to this day.

Perhaps the question that needs to be asked is not how and how soon these networks can be replaced with more rational ones, but how it is that they not only have produced astonishing growth in the past but also continue to do so in the present. What is behind such practices that seem to defy the logic of increasing industrialization and democratization? How is it that South Korea is able to record remarkable economic growth and political progress while social practices often described as "transitory" continue to coexist and sometimes even to grow? How should we interpret the existence and persistence of diverse and strong affective networks during and after unprecedented economic growth and radical social change? Could it be that Koreans have found in their tradition resources that can also be put to good use in a modern society? If the remarkable progress of capitalism and democracy in South Korea is inseparably linked to and made possible by such networks, perhaps it is indeed the case that the relationship between affective networks and modernity is more than one of a passing variety.

According to many studies, the traditional principle of "mutual help" has survived in the form of "personalism" in the urban community of contemporary Korea (Chang Y. S., 1980, 1989a, 1989b, 1991, 2003). In the process of industrialization and democratization, personalism simultaneously played both positive and negative roles, which later on laid the foundation for the distinct dynamics of Korean modernization (Chang Y. S., 1991). If one accepts this analysis, it can be understood that modernization in Western society is, on the contrary, a process in which industrialization and democratization were achieved while the norms and morals of traditional society are thoroughly dismantled on the basis of the establishment of individualism. On the other hand, modernization in Korea began when traditional Confucian personalism met the market system and constitutional government was imported from the outside. However, at the same time, rather than saying that tradition was dismantled, it can be argued that as a consequence of this union, tradition has remained and has altered itself (or been altered) to take on the role of a stepping stone in the development of one of the most dynamic forms of capitalism and democracy in the world.

Accordingly, the following equation can be suggested: the personalism of Chang Y. S. (2003) is in fact the same concept as social capital as explained in this chapter. Further, we can argue that it exists in Korean society in the concrete form of the affective network. On the other hand, if one understands Western democracy and capitalism as a system based on individualism, then it can also be argued that democracy in the West is merely a system that institutionalizes mistrust among people (Lee J.-Y., 1998). To solve this problem of mistrust, as seen previously, the West repeatedly emphasizes the importance of social capital as a means of securing trust in the market. However, social capital in the West is increasingly weakening, as the famous phrase "Bowling Alone" suggests (Putnam, 1995).

If one considers that the completion of modern society is to guarantee maximum choice to free individuals, then paradoxically, the appearance of postmodernism starts from the question of how these free individuals will be able to form meaningful relationships with each other (Hahm C.-B., 1998; Hahm C., 2000). When examining the issue in this manner, as opposed to Western society in which mistrust has become institutionalized, Korean society already has the social capital to solve the problem of "inter-subjectivity" that is necessary in the development of postmodernism. That is, the process of modernization has not destroyed personalism or the human relations based thereon, and affective networks remain in their entirety.

If we suppose that the individualism of the modern West terms this situation in Korea "Asian Values," then paradoxically, the situation suggests Asian Values have ample social capital required for the present transition of Western modernity into postmodernity. This is because while contracts in the market may be effective in the pursuit of interests, they merely connote commodified values that are of no assistance in the formation and expansion of meaningful human relations. The Confucian traditions that have survived in spite of modernization, and the affective human relations that are the basis of such traditions, should be reevaluated as resources in the postmodern era that will guarantee our future.

Notes

* About half of chapter 3 is from a book chapter, "Affective Networks and Modernity: The Case of Korea," pp. 201–217, in Daniel A. Bell and Hahm Chaibong (eds.), 2003, *Confucianism for the Modern World*. Cambridge: Cambridge University Press.

1. In his book, *Democracy in America*, Tocqueville (1969) asserts that the formation of civic community through voluntary association played an extremely important role in the development of American democracy. Through the concept of "civic engagement," Putnam (1993a) also shows that voluntary associations took charge in the decisive role of social capital in Italy's democratic development. Meanwhile, in the same context, as phenomena such as "Bowling Alone" increase, Putnam (1995) cautions that the United States is facing a crisis of depletion of social capital.
2. In addition to membership rules and aim of activities, there are numerous criteria for classifying the groups in the nonprofit and nongovernmental sectors. For example, they can be divided by sectors such as religious group or welfare group, and so on.
3. The role of citizens' groups regarding each of the reform policies of the Kim Dae Jung and Rho Moo Hyun administration has been criticized because it appeared similar to the nature and power of the Red Guards (*Choson Daily*, July 13, 2001). In particular, the Rejection and Defeat Campaign (落薦落選運動), unfolded by citizens groups at the time of the parliamentary election in the first half of 2000, serves as a good example (*Donga Daily*, February 8, 2000), and the Korean Constitutional Court's final verdict on August 30, 2000 decreed that the campaign was "illegal." The court explained that "an election campaign to 'defeat' a certain candidate signifies 'support' for the other candidate."

4. For an empirical analysis on social capital in a variety of groups in Korea, see Lew S.-C. et al. (2008).
5. *Analects* 1: 9.
6. *Analects* 8: 3.
7. *The Great Learning* 1: 4.
8. Regionalism is evident in Korean politics, and scholars take different academic approaches and stances on regionalism depending on where they come from. They could be grouped into adhering to either the "hegemonic regionalism" of *Yŏngnam* or the "progressive or resistant regionalism" of *Honam* (Hwang T.-Y., 1997; Nam Y.-S., 1992).
9. Kim Dae Jung started political career as a member of old Democratic Party in the 1950s, and subsequently, depending on political situation, changed party membership or created new parties (Kim J. H. and Lew S. C., 1995). Until he stepped down from the president in 2003, only a few examples of the parties he created or belonged are as follows: New Democratic Party (新民黨) in 1967, Democratic Reunification Party (統一民主黨) in 1979, New Korea Democratic Party (新韓民主黨) in 1983, Peace and Democratic Party (平和民主黨) in 1987, New Democratic Union (新民主聯合) in 1991, Democratic Party (民主黨) in 1991, New Political National Congress (新政治國民會議) in 1995, and New Millennium Democratic Party (新千年民主黨) in 2000.
10. In addition to Coleman (1988), Putnam (1993a; 1995), and Bourdieu (1986), who are the focus of examination in this writing, the issue of social capital has also been debated by Fukuyama (1995a, 1995c), Pye (1999), Edwards and Foley (1998), and so on.
11. Oliver Williamson (1973), the most representative scholar in new institutional economics, says in his book *Market and Hierarchies* that corporations make hierarchies that internalize transactions in order to suppress opportunism in the market.

Chapter 4

Historical Development of Affective Networks in Korea: The Nongovernmental Sector and Confucian Tradition

with Mi-Hye Chang

The Nongovernmental Sector

Society can be divided into three sectors: the "state," which presupposes coercive power; the "market," in which individuals seek profit; and "voluntary activities," which rest on neither coercion nor profit. In this threefold model, the "nongovernmental" sector represents the third sector where voluntary activities go on (Hall, 1992). Studies on the nongovernmental sector emphasize its autonomy as a distinctive characteristic in comparison to the other two sectors (Wuthnow, 1991). The functions and roles of the nongovernmental sector and its historical development can be better understood when compared with two other sectors, the state and the market (Habermas, 1989).

The development of the nongovernmental sector has been generally explained within the context of the development of the modern nation-state and the expansion of a capitalist economy. The emergence of the absolutist state in the West, which established a universal bureaucratic system, destroyed the inherited privileges of feudalism and regionalism (Keane, 1988). This process provided Western societies with a modern legal system that guaranteed equal rights and freedom to all citizens regardless of their heritage, class, or occupation; at the same time, it transformed conditional property rights to absolute property rights so that profit seeking in the market did not face as much uncertainty (Anderson, 1974).[1] Rule of law in the modern Western state weakened the influence of kinship, privilege, tradition, convention, and authority. Thus, the process of modernization can be equated with the disintegration of the premodern feudalistic legacy.

In most Western countries, the importance of the nongovernmental sector has increased in response to the financial crisis of the state caused by worldwide economic volatility and the expansion of welfare policies since the 1970s (Kramer, 1984). In non-Western societies, although the nongovernmental sector has been passive under authoritarian rule, recent trends toward democratization have drawn close attention to the role of this sector's potential to check the power of the state (Oxburn, 1995). This sector has been poorly developed in former socialist societies, where the state assumed complete control over power and resources. However, these societies are experiencing rapid development in this sector since the collapse of communist regimes in 1989 (Wank, 1991).

Modernization or industrialization in non-Western societies is generally understood as a process in which free-market institutions, through the logic of profit maximization, overwhelm society, while the nation-state effectively monopolizes control over society through the means of violence. The question is, how can we explain the survival of the nongovernmental sector under such expansion of the first and second sectors? It seems to be that the scale and scope of the nongovernmental sector largely depend on how it builds up relations with the other two sectors in a different historical and cultural context.

Any analysis of the development of non-Western societies that conceptualizes the process as a linear transformation toward a Western-style democracy and market economy, without considering historical context, will be unable to answer important questions. How is it that many East Asian countries can enjoy relatively high standards of living and still take for granted social monitoring and control by the state? Why is the state's subsidized welfare relatively weaker in this region than in the West? Why are tradition and authority still revered more than in the West? Why is the institution of family still strong, and why do East Asians appear to be obsessed with education? Why does the devotion toward work appear at the family level rather than at the individual level in these countries? Why do we not see a strong culture of mutual criticism or a strong trend toward the formation of consensus through discussion? To answer these questions, close attention must be given to each society's cultural, institutional, and historical distinctiveness (Schwartz, 1996).

As modernization has been mostly focused on the state and business realms, that is, the first and second sectors, the characteristics of traditional social bonds have been relatively well preserved in the nongovernmental sector. However, it has been generally assumed that the process of modernization, be it industrialization of the economy in the second sector or democratization of politics in the first sector, would shrink traditional communities in the third sector. Nevertheless, Korean reality shows that strong family ties and a sense of belonging to the community still persist. At the same time, the cultural norms that underscore veneration of authority and hierarchy, as well as vertical social order, are still very influential. As seen in various examples—the authoritarian and coercive control of the state, the organizational convention that emphasizes hierarchical order and submission rather than individual autonomy, the powerful influence of affective networks in employment and promotion, and regionalism (or localism) particularly noticeable in electoral politics—it is true that the characteristics of the nongovernmental sector have rather deeply penetrated into the state and market in Korean society.

In a study of the development of Korean society, it would be a mistake to disregard the unique characteristics of the nongovernmental sector and its strong influence on society in general. However, almost all theoretical as well as empirical studies on the nongovernmental sector in Korea attempted to find common traits between Korean society and Western societies, rather than address differences. For this reason, little serious research has been performed in this area.

Existing Studies on the Nongovernmental Sector in Korea

First, it may be in order to delineate the existing discussions on Korea's nongovernmental sector. Studies in this area have employed various concepts, such as "civil society," "nongovernmental organizations" (NGOs), the "third sector," "public foundations," and "interest groups" without explicitly using the concept of the nongovernmental sector. However, at a more general level, we can identify three major categories of discussion.

The first approach uses the concept of civil society as its central idea. These scholars analyze civil society in Korea after democratization from a Marxist perspective (Choi J.-J., 1996; Son H.-C., 1995; Yu P.-M. and Kim H.-K., 1995). Nevertheless, such an analysis is rooted in the scholar's normative opinion on the preferred direction in which Korean society (or government) should advance and how civil movements should be activated, without due consideration of the reality of Korean society. Those who belong to this category conceptualize civil society as an autonomous sphere that arose during the transition from authoritarian rule to democracy. They assume the dichotomy of the state and civil society, and argue that the state should be checked, criticized, and eventually become democratic through a strengthened civil society (Kang M.-K., 1995).

The most serious weakness of this approach stems from its uncritical acceptance of a Western ideal type of civil society and its application to Korean reality. Rather than noticing various forms of the nongovernmental sector that exist between the market and state, they underline only the role of dissident groups that mobilize the democratization movement or environmentalist groups that lead "new" social movements. They are obsessed with the normative justification of active civil movements as a check on the market and state, and lack any concrete definition or empirical study of civil groups' legal and institutional forms, the details of their activities, the size of their members or budget, and status of financial independence.

The second approach focuses on the voluntary public services of NGOs. These studies pay attention to ways in which the state and private businesses cooperate with each other to support voluntary activities. Research on the management and regulation of public foundations is a specific example of this kind of study (Park T.-G., 1995). Nevertheless, such attempts are also limited, in terms of giving full consideration to the particular context of Korean culture and institutions. Rather than objectively viewing the differences between Korean and Western NGOs, they focus on the conditions of economic development and the growth of the middle class that accompanied the development of NGOs in the West. Consequently, although they admit that the size and activities of Korean NGOs are far behind those of Western ones at this moment, they expect that as the private sector continues to grow these organizations will develop in a fashion similar to NGOs in the West (Park T.-G., 1995: 3). This approach is unable to answer why the development of the nongovernmental sector does not coincide with economic development in Korea. Furthermore, this approach cannot offer any answer to the question of how differences in sociohistorical contexts can be accommodated.

The third approach encompasses the literature on interest groups. By viewing the nongovernmental sector as a social sphere within the context of Western-style interest groups, these studies analyze Korean society from a liberal and pluralistic perspective (Kim Y.-R., 1996). They argue that as society becomes structurally divided, each group pursues its own interests and each individual organizes or participates in interest groups to pursue his or her own interests. In this sense, they conceptualize interest groups as an organized body of individuals who share goals and try to influence public policy (Berry, 1989:

4). Naturally, they assume that interest groups do not advocate the interests of nonmembers, thus creating competition between different interest groups and making consensus difficult to attain. Hence, from this perspective, NGOs cannot necessarily be considered agents of the common good.

In this pluralistic approach, civil society is not a unitary realm but consists of a variety of groups with conflicting interests. Additionally, this perspective argues that the activities of the nongovernmental sector cannot replace the role of the state. Those who advocate this approach are sensitive to the potential problems of receiving financial support from the state or businesses. At the same time, however, they tend to neglect the other potential of the nongovernmental sector, where the everyday life of people outside of the state and market sector can contribute to the development of new cultural as well as institutional trends. Most importantly, they completely ignore the difference between Western political culture, in which individuals organize themselves to protect and advocate their interests and rights, and Korean political culture, which emphasizes individual sacrifice for the sake of the community or society in general.

As evident in the above discussion, existing studies of the nongovernmental sector have applied their own concepts to their respective areas of interest, overlooking the potential benefits that could be gained by incorporating ideas from other approaches. In addition, since their approaches are based on Western experiences, in which individuals freely associate through a fair, free, and competitive political process, they disregard the cultural context that creates distinctive characteristics in the nongovernmental sector in Korea. In particular, there have been no efforts to incorporate the roles affective networks have played in the evolution of this sector.

The Nongovernmental Sector and Affective Networks

Up until now, classifications of the nongovernmental sector have been offered using criteria such as goals and functions, legal status, or financial sources (Weiss and Gordenker, 1996). The most frequently employed typology is the definition by Salamon and Anheier (1996), which classifies NGOs depending on their structures and forms of management. It defines the nongovernmental sector as having four characteristics: "redistribution," "autonomy from government control," "financial independence," and "voluntary participation."

Let us take a closer look at affective networks in relation to these criteria. The memberships of an affective network are determined by birthplace, alumni relations, and kinship (chapter 3). Therefore, they are not necessarily voluntary associations since memberships are ascribed mainly by birth (kinship). However, alumni ties are a mixture of educational attainment and birth ascription because schooling becomes competitive rather than compulsory,[2] as one goes up the ladder toward higher education. In addition, regional ties are also not determined solely by birthplace, as one can change residence from one location to another. Therefore, affective networks are a mixture of voluntary as well as nonvoluntary association. Regardless of the nature of membership, they all provide a sense of belonging, like primary groups, since intimacy among members is high. At the same time, affective networks exclusively pursue their own interests, which distinguish them from public foundations (Shin Y.-K., 1993), social welfare foundations (Yi H.-K., 1995), and NGOs (Yu P.-M. and Kim H.-K., 1995). In this context, affective networks may be regarded as "primary interest groups."

Nevertheless, since affective networks are financially independent from the government or business sector, they are free from the influence of the state or market. But important contributors to affective networks include incumbent or former high-ranking government officials or business managers. For this reason, affective networks are vulnerable in restricting or monitoring the activities of the state or businesses. Despite such "internal relationships," because affective networks formally exist outside the sphere of the state authority and the profit-seeking activities of the market, they cannot be directly controlled by the state's administration nor by the market's logic of profit maximization.

In short, since affective networks do not seek profit or distribute profits to their members, and because they are independent of state financial support and restrictions, their characteristics are similar to those of the nongovernmental sector as defined by Salamon and Anheier (1996). However, because membership in the affective network is not necessarily based on voluntary participation but on ascribed characteristics such as birth, there are also some aspects that contradict with the frequently adopted definition of the nongovernmental sector elsewhere. Therefore, the concept of the nongovernmental sector should be revised to include affective networks as well as to reflect the presence of Confucian traditions in the sector.

What are the specific organizational characteristics of affective networks? First, an affective network usually has a two-tiered membership of financial sponsors and regular members. Regular members are greater in number, but they do not actively participate in organizational activities in general and keep only nominal memberships. Whereas higher-ranking members of an affective network are usually older, assume more active roles, and have a strongly bonded commitment, lower-ranking members are younger, less intense in their solidarity, and weaker in their commitment. In this regard, there is a large gap in the roles between active and nominal members. However, in special events, such as political elections, they become the target of mass mobilization.

Second, an affective network is nonprofessional in character and interested in general rather than specific goals. Of course, the most important goal of any affective network is "promoting friendship" (親睦圖謀) and "mutual help" (相互扶助) among members. In addition, since membership is determined primarily by ascription, there are only limited numbers of professionals in any specified field, be it politics, economy, society, or culture. Therefore, affective network tends to have the nature of a totality, or generality, rather than of specialization. As such, activities of an affective network routinely consist of commonplace human events such as births, weddings, or deaths. Major activities include publishing newsletters so that every member is aware of how others are doing, and this naturally leads to the activity of collecting small gift or money from members and donating them to the member in concern to pay congratulations or condolences.

For these reasons, an affective network has entirely different properties from that of an NGO, which tends to be more professional. Although other parts of the nongovernmental sector, especially NGOs, have often been oppressed and controlled by authoritarian regimes, affective networks have been left intact. In addition, most members of affective networks devote time and effort to their organization without any monetary reward. This is why affective networks are able to maintain spontaneous reciprocity, "generalized reciprocity" (Sahlins, 1972) in particular, which mutually benefits members and their families in times of need. As such, affective network offers precisely the function that Ringmar (2005) calls "surviving capitalism" in which "we learned to live with the market and remained almost human."

Confucian Tradition in the Nongovernmental Sector

To explain the unique characteristics of the nongovernmental sector in Korea, we return again to Confucian cultural tradition and its institutional practice. Of course, the influence of Confucianism, be it state ideology, cultural orientation, or institutional practice, varies in accordance with historical contexts. A difference does exist between the *Chosŏn* dynasty in which economy was based on social status and coercive labor, and contemporary Korea where economy is based on free labor and equal opportunity for everyone.

Nevertheless, it is an undeniable fact that modern Korean society is deeply rooted in Confucianism (Koh B. I., 1996; Koh B.-I., 1996). Confucianism acts to refract values, institutions, and practices that have been imported from the West to Korea. For a better understanding of the refraction process, an illustration of the differences between Confucian and Western Enlightenment thought is useful. This comparison can be made with respect to four different issues of basic social order: ideas on human rights, perspectives on the individual and society, roles of the state, and ways to deal with conflicts between individuals.

The origin and development of the nongovernmental sector in the West is closely related to the tradition of liberal democracy. The Enlightenment tradition gave birth to the ideal of the autonomous individual, free from any hierarchy or authority. An autonomous individual is not coerced by the will of others and is free from any social restraints. A free individual has the right to determine his or her own life and actions, and citizenship is the concept adopted to legally express the independent rights of the individual. In the West, the development of citizenship was the process by which individuals found protection by liberating themselves from the illegitimate power or abuse of the privileged. Therefore, the Western notion of human rights has nothing to do with the social roles of individuals; it is a "fundamental concept of human rights," which insists upon the equal rights of all people regardless of their ascribed characteristics such as gender, race, or class (Hahm C.-B., 1998).

By contrast, due to the influence of Confucianism in Korean society, an individual is not identified separately from his or her particular social role. The Western notion of an isolated, abstract individual or free autonomous individual does not exist in Korean tradition; rather, individuals are always identified by their social roles and in relation to others (Rosemont, 1988: 177). The concept of duties and rights of an autonomous individual is absent in Confucian principles (Lee S.-H., 1998: 214). In this regard, the Confucian notion of human rights may vary according to social context. Indeed, this Confucian concept conflicts with the Western fundamentalist notion of human rights and can be labeled as a "variable concept of human rights" (Chan, 1999).

From the perspective of Western individualism, a society consists of selfish individuals who are apathetic toward each other. The ideal form of the Confucian community, however, is one in which *ye* (禮), the highest moral value, is fully realized throughout society and where individual selfishness has been overcome (Ames, 1988). From the Confucian perspective, advocating one's rights without consideration of others is regarded as egocentric; individual rights should be restrained rather than protected. Confucian principles emphasize caring and communitarian reciprocity rather than expressing one's rights, and these principles should be practiced more strictly in intimate relationships. This kind of relationship based on social roles is, of course, not the same as the Western relationship based on equality. It is rather natural to limit and order the roles in a hierarchical manner according to social status and position (Lee S. H., 1992: 251).

In Korean society, because an individual is identified in relation to his or her social roles, there is no autonomous individual who exists as a subject of contract or agent of legal rights. In addition, because Confucianism lacks the Western sense of the autonomous individual, profit-seeking activity in the free market also focuses more on collective interests rather than on individual interests. For instance, even legally protected rights such as taking a vacation or observing standard work hours are often not exercised by workers in Korea, because they are conscious of their manager's *nunch'i* (*nunch'i* refers to a situation in which one is expected to be conscious of the other's thought or mood). Social practice in Korea has not allowed the development of a culture in which one can demand one's rights before others.

Even in the perception of the state's role, there is a difference between East and West. In the classical Western theory of the liberal state, respect for individual rights is a basic duty of the state, thereby limiting its role considerably. However, the principle of "paternal intervention," which prevails in Confucianism, places the people/monarch relationship in parallel with the child/parent relationship. Such a view of the state is characteristic of Confucian East Asia and has become the basis for justifying political intervention from the center.

The difference between East and West is also prominent in resolving conflict among individuals. As Hobbes remarked, in the West's "war of all against all," it is inevitable that the interests of individuals will, at times, come into conflict. However, Korean society denies the inevitability of conflict itself and idealizes the society in which every member participates in constructing a family-like community in order to achieve social harmony. When a conflict inevitably occurs, instead of taking legal action, compromise and arbitration are used to resolve the conflict. This is particularly true if conflict arises among family members or acquaintances. As such, moral instruction and arbitration are emphasized as a means of negotiations rather than legal action (Chen, 2003). In a culture underscoring social harmony instead of conflict, if a person stubbornly promotes his or her rights, he or she is viewed as disrupting the harmony of the community. Thus, humility and deference toward others are valued over raising one's voice, and collective interests are valued over individual interests.

In order to explain how the nongovernmental sector in Korea differs from its Western counterparts, competing views of individual rights, of relationships between individual and society, of the state role, and the ways in which a conflict is resolved must be considered. Without such consideration, one cannot explain why there is such a strong attachment and devotion to affective networks on the basis of kinship, regional identity, and alumni relationships in Korea. In fact, it is the presence of these affective networks that gives the nongovernmental sector a distinctive flavor, and this phenomenon is deeply rooted in Korea's enduring Confucian tradition (Hahm P. C., 1986: 282–317).

Furthermore, the affective network functions as a primary provider of welfare, because such assistance from the state or market is highly insufficient in Korea. In East Asia, there has been a strong tradition that communities or affective networks offer help when an individual or individual family faces difficulties which cannot be overcome by themselves (Chang Y. S., 2003). It is true that those traditions of communitarian culture have been weakened as modernization advances. However, even today, the influences of families, or clan, or blood ties, remain as strong as ever, and affective networks based on school or regional ties play no less significant role than before in the everyday lives of Korean people.

Historical Origin and Development of Affective Networks

Most existing studies of civil society or NGOs in Korea assume that civil society in Korea only come to exist in recent years, particularly after the democratization of 1987. They presuppose that the development of the nongovernmental sector in Korea is not different from that of the West in which the development of the modern state or market is critical (Chung C. H., 1997). They argue that various interest groups and voluntary associations, especially the mass media, played the role of arbitrator between individuals and the state, and between private and public sectors in the process of democratization (Han S. J., 1997). The backdrop for the advent of a new political culture was the emergence of professionals and the middle class as a result of a developing economy that fostered a fledgling pluralistic social structure.

When focusing solely on the emergence of the Western type of nongovernmental sector, one tends to overlook organizational as well as constructional differences due to tradition and cultural norms. According to Cho H. I. (1997), the concept of civil society in Korea is not new. Rather, it is fulfilling a traditional role of checking the abuse of state power, albeit in a revitalized form. Cho H. I. argues that the *sarim* (士林, literati out of state office) intellectual group in the *Chosŏn* dynasty played the same role as that of the Western civil society, because it existed outside of the state and restricted the king's power so as to protect the people. As the moral leaders of local communities, they influenced local politics through *hyang'yak* (鄉約, village pact) and served as a check on state power by sending appeals directly to the king (上疏, presenting a memorial to the King).

If that is the case, then how do we distinguish civil society in Confucian and Western traditions? While the Western civil society has grown as an opposing power to the state, Confucian civil society does not view itself as being necessarily antigovernment (Steinberg, 1997). In the Confucian order, the state may infringe upon citizen's rights but can protect them as well. Thus, Confucianism itself does not presuppose an a priori role of the state but presumes the state to be neutral. The primary task of the government according to the Confucian principle is to understand the people's will in a moral sense, rather than guaranteeing free and equal citizenship in a legal sense. This Confucian perspective provided moral justification for the *sarim* to restrain state power. Thus, the antigovernment element found in the Western model of civil society cannot be assumed to exist in the Korean tradition.

Because the *sarim* groups started to form from family origin and school (private Confucian academy) ties, and they placed high value on holding office by virtue of passing the state examination, they can be interpreted as a traditional form of affective network that played a middle role in checking state power. By defining the *sarim* as a traditional form of affective network, we can reconcile the two opposing arguments of Cho H. I. and Steinberg. On the one hand, Cho H. I. (1997) argued that *sarim* was an equivalent of Western civil society because it existed outside the government and balanced state power. On the other hand, Steinberg (1997) insisted that *sarim* was a part of the state because it does not show any sign of heterodoxy. However, if we acknowledge that the *sarim* were affective networks based on

Confucian values, we can explain that they existed outside of the government in the formal sense but functioned informally as if they were government agents. As argued in chapter 6, as well as in other parts of this chapter, the boundary of affective networks was vague and blurred from the beginning, and this characteristic allowed affective networks to have an "internal relation" to the state and market sector.

The *sarim* affective networks, the functional equivalent of civil society in Korea, have undergone many changes in the course of modernization, and in some ways they have influenced government (Choi J.-S., 1975, 1983 [1965]). After the state changed from dynasty to republic, direct appeals to the king lost their meaning. In so much as political processes such as elections or mass communication have become important forums for public opinion, affective networks have sought to expand into new social organizations such as political parties or mass media so as to maintain their influence in sociopolitical issues.

Regionalism, which becomes a major factor in every election, is a good representation of affective networks' new role in contemporary Korea. The influence of alumni is equally important, as some Koreans opt to use an analogy of Korea as the Republic of Seoul National University. Such examples are not confined to the state sector. Their influence in the market can also be found in the organizational characteristics of *chaebol* (Orru, Biggart, and Hamilton, 1991), which played a leading role in globalizing Korean business. Affective networks exist officially only in the third sector of the nongovernmental realm, but their roles and functions extend deeply into the state and market sector.

The Functions and Roles of Affective Networks

The role of the nongovernmental sector, which is situated between the state and the market, is closely related to the roles of the other two sectors. The nongovernmental sector supplements various aspects of the other two sectors, such as the financial crisis of the state and capitalist market failure. Nongovernmental sector services are relatively more flexible and resilient than those of the state and market sector, which are often hierarchical and rigid, or competitive. The nongovernmental sector, especially the affective network, has the advantage of satisfying diverse demands simultaneously as a result of its comprehensive and general characteristics of organization.

The role of the affective network can be divided into several types. Economically, an affective network provides welfare services offered by neither the state nor market. By influencing policy formation and execution, an affective network can protect or reflect its member's interests. Also, an affective network facilitates a sense of belonging to isolated individuals who want to be part of a community. An affective network offers a shelter for vulnerable individuals who have to confront the powerful state or market forces. Affective networks naturally protect individuals from the unlimited expansion of the state and the limitless competition of the market (Ringmar, 2005).

The reason why an affective network is effective is that, unlike the Western nongovernmental sector, their members can belong to both an affective network and an institution in one of the other two sectors through employment. Due to this dual characteristic, members may be government bureaucrats or business managers. It seems more plausible from this perspective to argue that the affective network in Korea exists within both the state and market sectors rather than independently, as is the opposite case of the nongovernmental sector in the West. Given these conditions, politicians, bureaucrats, or business managers may construct their own affective network and take advantage of it as a means to further their own interests.

Due to this overlap in membership, the affective network's influence on the decision-making procedure of the state or businesses can be strong. However, at the same time, it is not necessarily true that such an influence can be beneficial for the common good, because an affective network itself may take advantage of the overlapping membership. Accordingly, it is unlikely that affective networks speak for the underprivileged to enhance democratic rights. Furthermore, one should acknowledge that there are numerous cases where affective networks provide scholarships or fraternity facilities for their members or member's children. However, at the same time, it is true that those opportunities are limited to network members.

In terms of psychological functions, however, affective networks may provide a sense of belonging and solidarity as well as protection for members from brutal competition. Individuals may gain what they want from the network without having to compete with the anonymous mass simply by virtue of being a member of the affective network. It is true that voluntary associations in Korea are not as active as in the West. Under such circumstances, by grouping along affective networks, individuals who lacked a sense of belonging can experience psychological relief. Nostalgia for the gradual disappearance of communities in contemporary society also leads to (or causes) the formation of these affective networks.

Although human relations in business and government organizations are rank–order hierarchies, human relations in affective networks are not so hierarchical. Instead, they show a more humanistic character depending on age: senior/junior or older/younger. Thus, relationships in this group are not based on command submission, but generosity and communitarian reciprocity. Relations in the market sector are based on exact give-and-take and competitive exchange. But in an affective network, it is conventional for those who have more or are older to become benefactors, thus making it nonacquisitive and noncompetitive. Although affective networks do not explicitly assume the role of providing public service and assistance to the underprivileged, they serve to protect individuals from market competition and hierarchical bureaucracy.

Affective Networks and Social Development

Korea's democratization in 1987 was a historic moment in the sense that political democracy in the past had always been sacrificed for the sake of economic growth. In the process, individual freedoms were promoted, including freedom of expression, which created an autonomous space where voluntary associations could be freely organized. Although Korea consciously modeled itself after a Western-style liberal democracy, emphasizing individual freedom and rights, there has not been much discussion over whether such a model is applicable to a society in which historical and cultural background differs so dramatically (Callahan, 1998).

It has been implicitly conceded that Western values such as political pluralism, respect for diverse values, and individual autonomy are universally applicable to all societies. In a similar context, Korea has recognized the expansion of the rule of law, and the peaceful change of power through free and fair elections as necessary political goals. Nevertheless, Korea has been learning that a peaceful transition of power through free and fair elections is only a preliminary condition for democratic development. There is a limit to the extent of change that can be brought about within such a short time by means of explosive social action such as the June Uprising of 1987; it takes much longer to change cultural orientations and the consciousness of the people (Kim S. H., 1998). Institutional changes and administrative reforms thus far have had little effect on regionalism, the self-centeredness of groups, and the preference given to one's school ties over and above ability. In witnessing the patron–client relationship corrupting politicians or administrators, we are skeptical about the existence of universal and rational criteria in Korean society. This has been considered by many to be the ultimate cause of the 1997 economic crisis.

These facts show that Korea is still under the influence of affective networks. Contrary to common assumptions, this influence has not declined but grown. This fact may suggest that Western universalism is not sufficient—whether be it in industrial economy, in democratic politics, or in rational culture. We have to search for a model that can take into account Korea's distinctive cultural and institutional characteristics, especially the powerful influence of affective networks.

It may be "politically correct" to view the strong influence of affective networks and Korea's communitarian tradition as obstacles to democracy. However, depending on the definition of democracy (Bell, 1996), those are not necessarily politically incorrect things. If democracy is defined as the practical and empirical selection process of political leaders and form of government rather than a concept dealing with morality or rationalization, then the question as to whether the change of government can be achieved through electoral or violent means, such as *coup d'état*, becomes very important. If we define democracy in a narrow sense of the word, having the right to choose a leader from and among candidates is indeed an important criterion.

Nevertheless, since the process of democratization cannot sidestep bureaucratization, the level of participation by citizens is limited when making decisions on issues that require professional and practical knowledge. Indeed, substantial participation of the masses is even restricted in Western democracies, which we usually picture as being the prototype of democracy. Western democracy presupposes highly qualified political elites who can put diverse public opinions together and then select correct policies (Cohen and Arato, 1992).

If we accept the fact that political participation is not equally open to all members of even Western societies, we can argue that Confucian political ideology—which admits social inequality due to social status and role, or alternatively, to the level of self-cultivation, such as exemplary person (君子) or commoner (小人), and expects the people to abide by the virtue of their leader—also has no less value than Western democracy (Chan, 1997). The ideology of "ruling by virtue" (德治) is based on the thought that when a ruler is virtuous, the subject will naturally follow. This not only works as a ruling ideology but also applies to all human relations, such as in the filial relationship between parent and child, the reverence shown toward family elders, and the deference shown toward one's seniors.

Because relationships between members of affective networks are based on rule by virtue, they lack the Western notion of equality between individuals; the relationships are hierarchical in that they emphasize seniority and one's social role. In this context, questions such as whether an individual can make decisions by himself/herself, whether individuals can decide to participate autonomously, or whether a consensus can be reached through equal participation in public forums cannot be answered merely by legal and formal procedures such as holding a free election. These questions can be solved only by considering a wider historical context in which cultural orientations and institutional norms have been laid down and shared by the public.

If we pursue the institutionalization of formal democracy while ignoring its cultural and normative context, the strong influence of affective networks can only be perceived as an obstacle to either modernization or democratization. But the influence of affective networks, whether positive or negative, is so strong that it cannot be eliminated by legal or institutional reforms; we have to accept this reality while charting Korea's own distinctive course.

The Western tradition of liberalism is based on individual freedom. However, Korean culture has prioritized society over the individual. The Western tradition of liberalism idealizes a society in which each individual can make decisions and act upon them autonomously without interference from state authorities or others. Confucian tradition has pursued more active forms, or contents, of freedom, that is, self-discipline or self-cultivation, which enables individuals to internalize norms of the community as his/her own will. If we disregard such an extensive definition of freedom and merely follow the narrow notions of liberal democracy, which is based on atomic as well as absolute individual, we can easily fall prey to the fallacy of universalism.

Korea's communitarian tradition has emphasized individuals as members of social networks and thus has allowed individual freedoms to be restricted in order to benefit the whole of society. Consequently, a blind pursuit of the expansion of Western-style citizenship in Korea may not help us in preparing future development. We have to acknowledge that the development of democracy is not linear, but rather can vary according to differences in value orientations. Undoubtedly, it is a difficult task to maintain a balance between individuals and community, rights and duties, and freedom and social harmony. Nonetheless, this is an endeavor we must accomplish in order to achieve democracy in a proactive way.

This effort will enable us to continue to utilize the resources provided by our culture, which brings individuals together, while pursuing modernization. Success in carrying out these tasks will allow us to rediscover the merits of Confucian tradition, which prioritizes the well-being of the whole community while restricting excessive individualism. The functions and roles of our nongovernmental sector, especially of affective networks, can provide an avenue in searching for a new direction in social development.

Notes

1. Anderson (1974) analyzes this process as a rediscovering process of the Roman legal tradition. He argues that Roman law consisted of civil laws, which regulated economic transactions between citizens, and public laws, which determined political relations between the state and society. While civil laws advocated the interests of commerce and the industrial bourgeoisie, public laws expressed and stabilized the authority of the absolute monarchy. The modern state was thus able to overturn the feudal order with these two legal systems.
2. Compulsory education is up to middle school in Korea as of 2012.

Part III

The Political Dimension: State–Society Relations

Chapter 5

Confucian Capitalism of Park Chung Hee: Possibilities and Limits

The Rise of "Confucian Capitalism"

Until very recently, debate has been ongoing as to whether integration between capitalism and Confucianism can be achieved. We now have a clear answer to this question. Numerous examples—the economic prosperity of Japan, followed by the remarkable economic development in Korea, Taiwan, Singapore, and Hong Kong, and the more recent economic booms in China and Vietnam—show that Confucianism can be incorporated into capitalism. The two philosophies have found a fruitful common ground even as scholars continued to wrestle with this matter.

By the mid-twentieth century, when Japan was the only example of a working Confucian capitalist society, skepticism was predominant regarding the ultimate success of such societies. The prevailing interpretation has been that Confucianism's value system, which categorizes vocations into high and low classes and ranks social order in a hierarchical manner (士農工商: literati, farmers, artisans, and traders in descending order), would suppress free market activities. Such arguments only had to make an exception of Japan (Morishima, 1981).

As the four East Asian "Tigers" became new exceptions (Barette and Whyte, 1982), the debate on Confucian capitalism fueled another controversy. New interpretations of the role of Confucianism emerged (Kahn, 1979). Some observers attributed the competitiveness of East Asian exports to "education fever" in the public and a strict work ethic (Clegg, Higgins, and Spybey, 1990), whereas others argued that the strong administrative capabilities of state bureaucrats with Confucian backgrounds contributed significantly to the development of these new economies (Johnson, 1985; Haggard, 1990).

As even socialist nations such as China and Vietnam adopted market economies in the late 1980s, theories suggesting that Confucianism would be an obstacle to capitalist development were muted. Instead, theories that assert the indispensability of Confucianism for the development of capitalism in East Asia are now widely advanced. The coining of the term "Confucian capitalism" is indicative of this trend (Tai, 1989; Tu, 1991; Rozman, 1992; Berger and Borer, 1997).[1]

If the integration of Confucianism and capitalism has become a historical fact, then we should not ask whether integration is possible but how it became possible. What specific elements of Confucianism proved conducive to capitalism? Was Confucianism the Asian functional equivalent of the Western Protestant ethic that led capitalist development in Europe and North America?

Debates on Asian Values

There have been ongoing debates on "Asian values" (Kim D. J., 1994; Zakaria, 1994; Bell, 1996, 2008; Christie, 1997; Chan, 1997). Favorable assessments were at the forefront before Korea had to ask help from the International Monetary Fund (IMF) in 1997, but after the IMF there have been more negative assessments. It should be noted, however, that the focus of such debate is not on the content of value systems as compared to that of Western countries. Rather, debates deal with monetary measures such as economic success or failure. Therefore, when Asian economies were booming, the validity of Asian values was spotlighted. As Asian economies experience downturn, problems of the Asian values become targets of criticism.

What are Western values that correspond to Asian values? Needless to say, it is the European value system which brought economic development to modern Europe. Protestant values, which denied the very basis of Catholicism, played a vital role in transforming Europe from the Middle Ages to the Modern Era. Two notable events paved the way for Protestant values to be settled as the value system of modern Europe. The first event was separation of religion from politics. If a state, which dealt with worldly matters, did not separate itself from church whose concern was sacred issues, the values of the Middle Ages could have not been altered. The rise of the absolutist state in Europe, which was established during the Renaissance era and formed throughout the Reformation, signaled the birth of a state separated from religion (Anderson, 1974).

The second event was separation of the economy from the newly formed state. If the economy did not separate itself from the control of a state, which decided reallocation process based on political motives, a rapid rise in productivity—as witnessed during the industrial revolution—would not have been achieved in Europe. Protestant values voiced an ideology called "laissez-faire" and successfully separated the European market from states. European history shows that the bourgeoisie, the main player in market, broke down the absolute state run by aristocracy and placed the pursuit of self-interest, or profit, as the main value in Europe (Polanyi, 2001[1944]).

After Europe experienced these two separation processes, Protestant values took their place as the leading value system in Europe. The teachings of Protestantism emphasize frugality and one's own effort to be near the absolute being in order to obtain salvation. It became a cultural basis, along with changes in social structure, that eventually gave birth to capitalism in modern Europe (Weber, 1930[1920]).

If so, then what social and historical backgrounds underlay the development of Asian values? Asian values, of course, incorporate many ideas, and it may be correct to say that all non-European values are Asian values. Islam in the Middle East, Hinduism in India, and Buddhism in the Southeast Asia can all, in a broader sense, be included in Asian values. Recently, however, the subject of interest is the Confucian value system in East Asia.

The history of East Asia differs a great deal from that of Europe (Schwartz, 1996). First of all, as a worldly religion from the beginning, Confucianism admitted no room for separation of the state from religion. The teachings of Confucianism, dating back to several hundred years before the birth of Christ, are not concerned so much with sacred matters such as the salvation of individuals. From the beginning, Confucianism has been a value system that mainly concerns with governing the state. Accordingly, the second separation in Europe identified earlier—separation of politics and economy—did not show the slightest hint of appearing in East Asia. Under the Confucian value system, separation of production from political redistribution is to renounce the designated role of the state (Hall and Ames, 1987; Tu, 1996).

Therefore, recent debates on Asian values, which do not take such historical and social contexts into account, cannot be valid. The importance of family and community as well as functions/dysfunctions of affective networks, based on blood (family), region, and/or school, become significant only when they are considered within the historic-structural characteristics of the society. Debates on Asian values, which ignore social context and only consider immediate outcomes, such as economic success or failure, should be discouraged.

Weber and Modernization Theory

Max Weber argued that the Protestant ethic, which advocated diligence and frugality, overturned the feudal order and became a determinant factor in Western Europe's capitalist development. Because Protestantism provided a unique set of ethics that was particularly suited to profit-seeking activities, Western Europe was able to nurture "rational" capitalism for the first time in world history (Weber, 1930[1920]). Although Weber (1951[1920]) described various complex conditions that prevented China from developing into a capitalist society, he claimed that the most important factor was that the Confucian precept, "adaptation to this world," was antithetical to capitalist development. It was precisely the opposite of the "transcendence over this world" prescribed by Protestantism that induced hard work.[2]

Weber's negative interpretation of Confucianism became the classic explanation as to why capitalism was underdeveloped in China. Of course, many theorists do not think Weber's explanation is all that simple. They contend that Weber did not limit his explanation of the development of capitalism solely to the religious value system (Collins, 1980). He did not ignore the importance of social structural contexts of particular religious beliefs. Nevertheless, his analysis was subsequently boiled down into dogma and gained wide currency. If the Protestant ethic played a progressive role in destroying the medieval feudal order in Western Europe, Confucian ethics functioned conservatively to maintain a medieval order in China.

This perspective, however, cannot answer a number of questions. First, is it therefore impossible for the non-Western world, without the influence of the Protestant ethic, to develop capitalist economies? Consideration of this question generated so-called "modernization theory," according to which the non-Western world should follow supposedly rational Western norms and methods in order to transform their premodern value systems into modern ones. This perspective, along with the prevailing economic and military hegemony of the West, provided a prescription for non-Western societies to "modernize" themselves.

The second question centers on the effort to explain the economic development achieved by non-Western societies without the benefit of the Protestant ethic. This question is crucial to understanding the early industrialization of Japan. There was indeed a plausible explanation: Japan developed capitalism because its society was operating under a "functional equivalent" of Protestant ethics during the Tokugawa period (Bellah, 1957). This explanation inspired a new intellectual movement in many nations that wanted to develop capitalism to review their histories and search for their own functional equivalents. The philosophy of "practical learning" (實學, shilhak) in eighteenth-century Korea and neo-Confucianism in China were some examples of Eastern systems that were reinterpreted and reassessed as functional equivalents of Protestant ethics (Metzger, 1977). Nevertheless, despite such reassessments, it is clear that these nations did not indigenously develop capitalism, unlike the cases of Western Europe and Japan, so these theories were suspected.

Given these two problems, the simplified Weberian analysis does not convincingly explain capitalist development in the non-Western world. Explaining such development through the presence or absence of a particular value system is a logical leap. Development must be determined by the social structural conditions faced by groups, not their values alone. A comparison of East and West should consider the structural conditions in which various groups or agents, carrying particular values, were positioned.

The "agent" of Protestant ethics in the West was, of course, the bourgeoisie. In medieval feudal society, they were in a marginal position. The value system of Protestant ethics that developed after the Reformation supported their struggle against conservative landlords who were supported by the established Roman Catholic Church. In comparison, the agents of Confucian ethics were the literati, who had never lost their dominant position throughout the medieval period in China. Even when dynasties changed and when foreigners invaded, their privilege and status remained stable and dominant through the institution of civil service examinations (科擧制度). The Protestants of medieval Europe challenged the status quo, whereas Confucianism was already the philosophy of the privileged in medieval East Asia. Therefore, contrasting social conditions existed for agents with different goals.

Modernization theory, which simplified Weber's analysis and dogmatically attempted to explain the emergence of capitalism in the non-Western world by the presence or absence of particular value systems, has been confronted with a dilemma. The role of the value system cannot be adequately analyzed unless the properties of the surrounding social structure are also taken into consideration, because the outcomes of values vary depending on the structural conditions in which their agents are placed. Due to such structural differences, Protestant ethics played a "progressive" role in the West, whereas Confucianism played a "conservative" role in the East.

History of Confucian and Capitalist Integration: State–Business Collusion

Capitalism did not develop indigenously in East Asia. Confucian society, ruled by the literati, had to overcome many obstacles over an extended period of time until capitalism emerged. The first obstacle was Western imperialism. In the face of an imperialist invasion, East Asia was forced to choose between two options: socialism or capitalism. The Confucian states that chose socialism were China, Vietnam, and North Korea. The leaders and people of these nations purged the literati landlords and constructed socialist institutions. Ironically, the new communist leaders of these states inherited the structural role of the former literati. When the party elites planned their economies, they monopolized the duty, or right, to "integrate society and maintain order."

Socialism in Confucian East Asia, as in Christian Eastern Europe, could not overcome its inherent limits. The recent transition to market economies in both regions plainly indicates these limitations. In the end, for China and Vietnam, socialism was only a stage on the long road to capitalism. As party leaders were reluctantly forced to make this transition, the two countries experienced rapid growth. During this process, the party elites enjoyed the privilege of monopolizing national decision-making, just as had the literati bureaucrats of an earlier stage.

On the other hand, Confucian nations that had embraced capitalism early on readily accepted the market economy as a basic principle. Nevertheless, even in these nations the state was deeply involved in the market and in planning the economy, which proved a success. The success of state intervention brought about the new concept of the "developmental state" (Johnson, 1982; Amsden, 1989), which was capable of "governing the market" (Wade, 1990).

Thus, the role of state bureaucrats in nations that inaugurated market economies after liberation from colonial rule was not much different from that of literati bureaucrats in the past. The bureaucrats of Confucian capitalism had to create markets from scratch, accumulate scarce capital, and mobilize abundant labor. The only difference from the past was that the bureaucrats' role of "integrating society and maintaining order" assumed a new form under capitalism. But the agents remained the same state bureaucrats as before.

Two different historic developments in East Asia resulted in the acceptance of capitalism through decision-making by state bureaucrats, regardless of whether or not their countries had experienced socialism. The Meiji Restoration of Japan followed a similar pattern, although at an earlier time (Ornatowski, 1996). All of these developments in East Asia involved reactivation of the dominant role of the literati under capitalism, with this process again being administered by state bureaucrats. After this long and oblique process, the modern state bureaucrats who had assumed the same structural role played earlier by the literati decided to implement a capitalist order in East Asia. Once they had made this decision, they already possessed effective methods of implementation.

Capitalism in Confucian societies was established through top-down implementation by state bureaucrats. Therefore, this brand of capitalism differs dramatically from its Western counterpart. Western capitalism had to break down the medieval feudal order before it was able to take off. To ensure the success of this struggle, the bourgeoisie needed new social apparatuses: universal citizenship to resist aristocratic power, autonomous cities to transform peasants into free workers, and guilds for vocational groups to protect their interests. In short, the bourgeoisie needed to construct a "civil society" that would enable them to stand up to established aristocratic power.

On the other hand, capitalism in East Asia did not require such a fundamental makeover. The civil society and voluntary associations so crucial to the development of Western capitalism did not play an important role in the East. Instead, state bureaucrats organized capitalism in their own fashion. Decision-making by bureaucrats created markets, accumulated capital, and made wage earners available for these markets. The private sector was mobilized according to the needs and plans of the state. Traditional Confucian affective networks (緣故), mainly based on blood (血緣), locality (地緣), and school (學緣), were utilized to this end.[3]

Confucian capitalism, which exemplified state-led industrialization, thus emerged from a context entirely different from that of the West. The state controlled entry into and exit from markets, dictated who could accumulate capital, and managed and disciplined labor. Civil society and free markets in the Western mode were unnecessary for the development of Confucian capitalism. The Eastern variety of capitalism did not result from a struggle against a dominant class. Instead, it was chosen by the dominant group. Obstacles may have cropped up in the course of the state bureaucrats' decision to implement a capitalist order but the bureaucracy was powerful enough to overcome such limitations.

Park Chung Hee (朴正熙) of South Korea, Chiang Kai-Shek (蔣介石) of Taiwan, Lee Kuan Yew (李光耀) of Singapore, and Deng

Xiaoping (鄧小平) of China were political leaders who demonstrated the dynamics of Confucian capitalism to the world—perhaps too vividly. In these countries, economic goals were achieved with precision and speed according to the well-calculated plans of capable bureaucrats. In this process, entrepreneurs who actively followed state policies could accumulate enormous wealth, whereas those who disobeyed were brutally excluded.

The dynamics of Confucian capitalism presume effective state intervention in the market. Such intervention inherited two traditional Confucian orders (Jacobs, 1958, 1985). First, the policy decisions of state bureaucrats superseded decision-making by businesses. The state granted favors to firms that conformed to its policies and applied sanctions against those who were in opposition. Preferential financing and tax audits were double edges of the state's ever-present sword.

The second Confucian tenet borrowed for the development of Asian capitalism relates to the organization of business and civil society. As civil society and free markets developed, the affective ties of family, hometown, or school, which had all waned in the West, were reinforced in the East. The strength of "Confucian familism" is particularly evident in the cases of Korea's *chaebol* and Japan's *zaibatsu* business organization (Hattori, 1989, 1997). Chinese enterprises, which are the dominant business groups in Southeast Asian economies, also reflect the importance of kin and regional networks in their organizational characteristics (Wong, 1985; Redding, 1990; Hamilton, Zeile, and Kim W. J., 1990; Gold, Guthrie, and Wank 2002; Yao, 2002).

Market intervention characterized by state favoritism and affective networks—two mechanisms that define the dynamics of Confucian capitalism—diminished in the course of development of Western capitalism, because both mechanisms were directly opposed to free market principles. In Western capitalism, the problem of "trust," which is indispensable for stable economic activities, was solved by the growth of autonomous markets and the reduction of the state's role. On the other hand, in East Asia, government intervention and affective networks provided the "trust" that was needed to stabilize economic activities. Confucian capitalism in East Asia needed government guarantees so that business could reduce "transaction costs" (Williamson, 1973, 1985).[4]

To obtain guarantees, businessmen depended on their affective ties for access to favors from state bureaucrats. In other words, "rent seeking" has become the most effective method of accumulating capital under a "rent-granting" government (Lew S. C., 2000: 6). Businessmen have used their affective networks to receive and maintain state favors. "State–business collusion" (政經癒着) is a term that describes this structural characteristic, which became an essential mechanism necessary to incorporate Confucian traditions into capitalism.

Legitimacy in Confucian Capitalism

Do state–business collusion and rent-seeking activities eventually result in social waste? Proponents of mainstream neoclassical economics and rational choice theory, developed from the Western experience, would clearly answer "yes." They argue that if the state intervenes in competitive markets for political reasons, businesses will have to engage in nonproductive lobbying to obtain favors, resulting in social waste and corruption instead of increased productivity (Buchanan, Tollison, and Tullock, 1980).

If these claims are true, then how can they explain the remarkable economic development achieved in East Asia? Some may insist that state–business collusion was largely absent from East Asian capitalism. They may contend that known cases of corrupt favor seeking are negligible relative to the size of economy. Nevertheless, the majority of observers still believe that state–business collusion was a pervasive, intrinsic, and even common phenomenon in Confucian East Asia.

In particular, Korea experienced a series of significant political scandals implicating every single former president. Two former presidents, Chun Doo Hwan and Rho Tae Woo, were sent behind bars for collecting slush funds from businesses. The son of President Kim Young Sam was summoned by the National Assembly for alleged corruption and eventually arrested by prosecutors (the *Hanbo* Steel scandal).[5] President Kim Dae Jung had to go through the same process twice and had his two sons jailed for precisely the same reason as President Kim Young Sam. Finally, the last former president, Rho Moo Hyun, who stepped down in 2008, committed suicide as a lawful investigation on alleged bribery approached his family. It seems that no administration in Korea is immune to negative stories of state–business collusion. State–business collusion has been a structural part of Confucian capitalism in Korea ever since it first developed.

If that is the case, how does the development of the failed *Hanbo* Group differ from that of other *chaebols* in Korea? All the *chaebol* conglomerates developed with the benefit of enormous state support and favors. It is a well-known fact that the Korean government has long granted favors to *chaebol*—including market entry barriers, financial supports, and tax breaks—which enabled them to capture markets and monopolize their share of the pie. In this process, it is very possible that state–business collusion was a routine practice, however secret.

Can neoclassical economists explain how it has been possible to simultaneously pursue rent-seeking and sustain double-digit economic growth? Why didn't state–business collusion result in social waste and economic bankruptcy? The answer to these questions can be found in the conjoining of Confucianism and capitalism. As mentioned earlier, the mechanism that integrated Confucianism and capitalism was different from the mechanism that bound Protestantism and capitalism. Therefore, it is impossible to compare East Asia, where the dominant group confronted no challenges from the bottom and decided to accept capitalism by itself, and Western Europe, where capitalism was achieved only after a long bourgeoisie struggle against the feudal dominant class.

The Western bourgeoisie demanded civil society and free markets from the feudal elites, and they succeeded. Western economic historians explain that the bourgeoisie gained autonomy from the state through expansion of property rights (North and Thomas, 1973). Through this process, the bourgeoisie could better guarantee their economic activities and gain stability, thereby reducing transaction costs of economic activity and ensuring the basis of steady economic growth.

Then, why do we not see pervasive corruption causing the economy to collapse? How can Confucian capitalism allow state–business collusion and at the same time prevent corruption and maintain a high growth rate? The *Hanbo* Steel scandal may serve to explain this phenomenon. Public opinion polls on corruption in Korea show general disapproval of *Hanbo* Steel and more favorable opinion toward *Pohang* Steel (POSCO). Both firms developed by benefiting from state subsidies and favors. Then why is POSCO acceptable and *Hanbo* not? The answer to this question may shed some light on the secrets of Confucian capitalism's continuous success.

In the Korean case, the dynamics of Confucian capitalism began when General Park Chung Hee assumed power through a military *coup* in 1961. Ever since, the state has provided myriad favors to *chaebols*, leading to their phenomenal growth. However, the state maintained an important criterion in distributing favors. For example, the *chaebol* must succeed in international competition. This reflects the government's so-called export-oriented industrialization policy. If export performance was low, or if a *chaebol* failed to produce domestic substitutes for imports, favors were immediately withdrawn. The fact that financial support was based on letters of credit from banks, particularly foreign banks, is evidence for this criterion. Performance in the foreign market, where political connections could not play a role, was employed as the ultimate criterion in state rent granting.

Although the state was deeply involved in market affairs through favors, it never abandoned the performance principle. The state periodically screened rent recipients, mostly *chaebols*, on the basis of individual performance to maintain a minimum, if not maximum, level of efficiency and competitiveness in the market (Chang H. J., 1994: 147–148). In other words, to a certain extent the state chose to maintain a competitive mechanism in the market. The state was cautious lest favors become concentrated on a few businesses that in the end were not sufficiently competitive or efficient to survive in the global market. Thus, the state constantly monitored the performance of firms benefiting from its favors.

The fact that the order of Korea's top ten *chaebols* has fluctuated greatly over time clearly shows this concern on the part of the state. No *chaebol* could escape government oversight and ensure favors forever. As shown in Table 5.1, the survival rate of Korean firms was extremely low at the earlier stage of economic development. Among the top 100 firms of 1965, only 22 firms were able to remain at the top in 1975. Among the top 100 firms of 1975, only 30 firms were able to keep the same status in 1985. The extreme diversity of individual firms constituting the top 100 list over a ten-year interval displays the volatility of Korean firms in the course of economic development. Although the numbers in Table 5.1 are not limited to *chaebol* firms, there is no doubt that *chaebol* firms comprise the majority among the 100 largest firms at each time point.

If Table 5.1 is implicit, Table 5.2 is explicit in demonstrating the extreme volatility in individual mobility patterns of *chaebols*. Among

Table 5.1 Survival of 100 largest firms in Korea, ten-year intervals, 1965–1985

	1965	1975	1985
1965	100	22	19
1975		100	30
1985			100

Source: Gong B.-H. (1993: 16).

Table 5.2 List of top ten *chaebols*, three time points

Rank	Late 1950s	Mid-1960s	Mid-1970s
1	Samsung	Samsung*	Samsung*
2	Samho	Samho*	Lucky-Goldstar*
3	Gaipoong	Lucky-Goldstar*	Hyundai
4	Tai Han	Tai Han*	Hanjin
5	Lucky-Goldstar	Gaipoong*	Ssangyong*
6	Dongyang	Samyang	Sunkyung
7	Keukdong	Ssangyong	Korea Explosives
8	Hankook Glass	Hwashin	Dainong
9	Donglip	Panbon	Dong Ah
10	Tai Chang	Dongyang*	Hanil Syn

Source: Kim E. M. (1997: 124).
Note: *Chaebols* that retain positions on the list over time.

the top ten *chaebols* in the late 1950s, only six were able to maintain the same status by the mid-1960s. Among the top ten *chaebols* in mid-1960s, only three were able to keep the same status by the mid-1970s. For the entire period of 20 years, only two *chaebols*, Samsung and Lucky-Goldstar, were able to sustain their top ten *chaebol* status. The rest of the list is filled with new *chaebols* at each time point, which indicates extreme individual competition, resulting in a volatile pattern of mobility.

Two characteristics emerge from the examination of the growth and mobility pattern of *chaebols* in Korea. First, *chaebols*, taken together, show a tremendous growth in economic power, reflecting the overwhelming state favors extended to them during the Park era. Second, the volatility in rankings of *chaebols* during the same period indicates that most *chaebols* were not able to transform state favors into once-and-for-all privileges. *Chaebols* suffered constantly from the continuous pressure of individual competition to gain state favors. "Support combined with discipline" was the key to understanding the phenomenal growth of the Korean economy (Chibber, 1999, 2002; Davis, 2004, Chang H. J., 2006).

The international competitiveness required by export-oriented industrialization and the maintenance of competitive mechanisms in the domestic market were the two principles that the Korean state adapted as benchmarks to discipline the economy. At the same time, the Korean public agreed with these principles. As long as these principles were applied, the public was not concerned about state favors to businesses. In fact, the public pressured the state to do so; while public opinion opposed businesses monopolizing state favors through corrupt collusion, most regarded competitive businesses as deserving of favors. Most Koreans were even proud of such successful firms.

Now, the difference between *Hanbo* and POSCO becomes clearer. The state's favors for POSCO were "legitimate," while favors for *Hanbo* were "illegitimate." Both firms might have tried a variety of strategies to secure state favors. In these attempts, they might have bribed government officials or mobilized networks of families, compatriots, and schoolmates. However, *Hanbo* has never proven its capability to compete in international or even domestic markets, and this renders *Hanbo's* corruption unforgivable.

The question of legitimacy raises a very controversial issue in Confucian capitalism. What criteria can be used to explain the dynamics of Confucian capitalism, which prevented the development of Western rationality, that is, rationality based on market autonomy? From what perspective can we examine "institutionalized" state–business collusion? Some insist that free market values should be promoted in East Asia. They argue that civil society, which checks the state, should become more active and that free competition in the market should be expanded, so that Western rationality could be rapidly disseminated. However, Confucian capitalism does not support the growth of social groups who can order and promote such values. In Confucian capitalism, governmental organizations are preferred over private associations, state–business collusion is more prevalent than free market, and affective networks are more important than class solidarity. Of course, this situation is the product of a long historical process in which literati-bureaucrat dominance integrated with capitalist economics.

If Confucian capitalism had failed, then we would likely agree that such structural and historical conditions unique to East Asia should be immediately scrapped. However, whether we like it or not, during the past 50 years Confucian capitalism has been appraised as one of the most dynamic and successful forms of capitalism in the world. Should Korea abandon it? Should Korean society heighten class consciousness and grant "cultural hegemony" to the capitalist class in order to build rational Western capitalism?

Implementing Western rationality, that is, separation of the market from the state,[6] in Korea, or in East Asia, where the historical context is entirely different from the West, might be akin to searching for fish in trees (緣木求魚). Besides, there is no concrete evidence that the order and legitimacy of Confucian capitalism are necessarily inferior to those of Western Protestant capitalism. If the order and legitimacy produced by Confucian literati were so inferior, the *Chosŭn* dynasty—based on Confucianism—could hardly have lasted for 500 years.

The Korean economy has been successful because the state granted favors based on clear criteria that have proven to be productive for the national economy. This principle of modern Korean capitalism is similar to the *Chosŭn* dynasty system in which the state recruited its bureaucrats based on the results of competitive civil service examinations. The more qualified candidates who passed the exam were proven to govern the people more efficiently. We can also explain why the economy was stagnant during the Rhee Syngman regime (1948–1960) for the same reason. The Rhee administration lacked clear and productive principles, which were supported by the public. He arbitrarily selected his cronies for government favors. Rhee was never a disciplinary leader as far as the economy was concerned.

To conclude the discussion on legitimacy in Confucian capitalism, the state may well grant favors to business; however, its criteria and targets should be clear and productive enough to gain the people's consent. Otherwise, favors will be viewed as lacking in legitimacy, thus creating suspicions of corruption. Such suspicions are not unusual in Confucian traditions; under the literati's domination in the *Chosŭn* dynasty, Confucian scholars and inspectors played such a role. In modern Confucian capitalism, the media and intellectuals, including university students, have inherited the "watchdog" role.

If the state does not adequately respond to such suspicions, Confucian capitalism cannot earn legitimacy, which can eventually result in popular resistance to the state. Student resistance to Rhee Syngman's corruption and dictatorship is a good example. These protests gained popular support and curtailed "illegitimate collusion." Conversely, a similar logic can be found in the nearly two decades of Park Chung Hee's Confucian capitalist regime. Although the press and university students continued to suspect government dealings with business, Confucian capitalism during the Park regime was disciplinary, systematic, and efficient (Kim H. A., 2004; Davis, 2004, Chang H. J., 2006). Thus, the state earned considerable popular support and the regime was sustained. In fact, without the economic development of the Park period, Korea would not be able to enjoy today's "dynamic" capitalism.

"Checks and Balances" in Confucian Capitalism

In East Asia's state-led economies, neither civil society nor labor unions can be the moderator of Confucian capitalism. Journalists and intellectuals have observed the holders of power under the Confucian context. They cannot be categorized as an interest group, occupational association, or social class. During the *Chosŭn* dynasty, it was the literati, cultivated and learned in the classics, who became state bureaucrats by the examination recruitment system. At the same time, they appealed to the state when it abused its power; they also civilized the populace and maintained order at the village level (Deuchler, 1992). They were indeed the pillars of *Chosŭn* society. The heirs of the literati are today's journalists and intellectuals, who question the state's discretionary use of power and aim to enlighten the people.

Individual journalists and intellectuals do not hesitate to become state officials whenever they have the opportunity, as the *Chosŭn* literati did. Indeed, they often have the chance to make such a career change. In the meantime, they play the role of power monitor. This pattern of "checks and balances" still remains in place and surprisingly minimizes the negative consequences of Confucian capitalism. Today, universities as well as the media monitor state power, and at the same time they provide a talented pool of candidates for state offices. The "religious fever" for higher education,[7] the obsession with becoming a state official, and the continuous recruitment of officials from academia and journalism all demonstrate the functionality of these groups. The "dual" role of literati officials has now been inherited by modern intellectuals, and it has become a mechanism for "checks and balances" in Confucian capitalism.

Therefore, searching for models of arbitrators for the Confucian order in the Western notion of civil society that resisted feudal aristocrats, or in labor unions that struggled against the capitalist class, is futile. The mediators of Confucian capitalism are intellectuals, not workers. Their structural conditions and ideological orientations are not based on Western Protestantism, which starts from below, but rather on East Asian Confucianism from above. It is improbable that Western civil society or the free market, where the political goals of nonsectarian as well as voluntary associations and the profit seeking of interest groups are fundamental criteria, can be independent and universal in the Confucian context.

For example, one of the most influential and supposedly nongovernmental organizations (NGOs) in Korea, the People's Solidarity for Participatory Democracy (PSPD), has been under severe criticism of being a governmental or near-governmental organization (*DongA* Daily, 2006). It was reported that in the 12 years since the organization's creation in 1995, among 416 members who held rank as organizational officers, one-third or 150, were advanced to 313 high-ranking government positions (Lew S.-C. and Wang H.-S., 2006). The transformation of civic organizations to pro-government groups and their gain in political power have been significantly concentrated in the administrations of Kim Dae Jung and Rho Moo Hyun. Prior to democratization, civic organizations were primarily antigovernment or nongovernment, but NGOs in the post-democratization period have been pro-government or acting as an extension of government.[8]

This issue is already reviewed in chapter 4 of this volume in depth to argue that the antigovernment element found in the Western model of civil society cannot be assumed to exist in the Korean Confucian tradition. The following editorial in a major newspaper entitled "Are Civic Groups Fulfilling Their Role?" clearly demonstrates this point (English *JoongAng* Daily, 2006).

> One-third or 150 senior members of the nation's leading civic organization [People's Solidarity for Participatory Democracy: PSPD] have been seated in high-ranking government posts or participated in committees set up by the government. They have advanced into pivotal positions, such as prime minister, deputy prime minister, and minister, wielding strong influence over state affairs....
>
> How can those civic group members monitor state power when they have already gained authority? Once forging ties with the government, they will inevitably have to move their focus to understanding and cooperation. In President Roh Moo-hyun's administration, which garnered the nickname "committee republic" for creating numerous state committees, many critics have already pointed out that government policies almost always coincide with those proposed by the PSPD. And the government may find it difficult to deny the accusation because it has actually brought that criticism upon itself by inviting so many members from civic groups....
>
> The PSPD has indeed voiced objection to a range of corruption cases and violations of human rights. Its contributions so far are undeniable. However, its degeneration into sort of a subordinate government organization will bring misfortune to everyone.

Korea's labor movements now also face similar criticism. For instance, organized labor in *chaebol* firms, such as the *Hyundai* Motor Labor Union, enjoy salaries over three times higher than gross domestic product (GDP) per capita. However, their policy platforms exclude any concerns on the issue of marginalized laborers, that is, irregular and temporary workers who are suffering at the minimum wage level (Kim D.-H., 2009). Still, *Hyundai* Motor Union repeats its "militant struggle" every year for the sake of collective bargaining. Universal class solidarity is hardly found in today's labor movement in Korea. The current self-serving aristocratic nature of the labor movement is far from being an arbitrator for the general public or Confucian capitalism.

Possibilities and Limits of Confucian Capitalism

The total population of potential Confucian capitalist countries (including overseas Chinese and Koreans) comprises over one-fourth of the world's population.[9] Their recent economic growth rate is also significantly higher than the world standard. In particular, the growth rate of the world's most populated country, China, is amazing. At the same time, Vietnam follows China by a narrow margin. Although other Confucian countries, that is, Korea, Singapore, Taiwan, and Hong Kong, no longer show double digit growth rates, they are still performing relatively well in comparison to the rest of the world. Japan is the only country that has recently lagged behind in terms of growth. However, Japan's economy continues to be ranked second largest in the world for several decades.

Of course, several lines of negative evaluations on Confucian capitalism and its future exist. The first pessimism comes from mainstream economists who view the East Asian economy as identical to former communist bloc economies (Krugman, 1994). More specifically, this stance argues that, due to the same reasons behind the socialist economy's growth and sudden collapse, the Confucian economy will also experience a plunge. This view argues that Confucian capitalism does not base itself on technological innovation, efficiency, or productivity, but relies heavily on state mobilization and monitoring to produce quantitative results in a short period of time. Nevertheless, this perspective considers only the "production cost" side of economic activities. The persistent growth of Confucian capitalism requires us to ask more fundamental question about the sociocultural context, which engenders growth by reducing transaction costs. We have to face the reality of state–business collusion and affective networks that lie behind this remarkable success.

On the contrary, the view of Fukuyama (1995a), who pays attention to "trust" as social capital, is more progressive because it furthers the consideration of sociocultural contexts.[10] Fukuyama argues that the industrial structure is determined by the predominant organizational pattern, which in turn is determined by level of trust. That is, low-trust family-oriented economic activities engender an industrial structure based on small- or medium-size firms, whereas a high-trust voluntary association-oriented economy produces an industrial structure that relies on big firms such as corporations. Nevertheless, his analysis does not adequately fit the empirical realities of Confucian capitalism. His argument cannot explain how a low-trust society such as Taiwan can have a high-tech computer industry, or how a low-trust society such as Korea has developed advanced heavy and chemical industries.

Huntington (1993) is perhaps the author who may most enthusiastically accept the concept of Confucian capitalism, as he argues that the future world will form a new global order through conflict among civilizations. Nevertheless, it should be noted that his discussion of "Confucian civilization" starts from the West-centric interest in preservation of hegemony in the international politics. The economic success of Confucian capitalism is not the only goal that should be achieved. However, it is more important to alleviate doubts and cautions by making Confucian capitalism more understandable. It should begin by turning attention to the sociocultural as well as historical characteristics of Confucian societies.

Korean society is strongly influenced by a traditionally centralized social structure. Over 500 years of Confucian dynasty rule and Japanese colonial and American military governments contributed to Korean society's tendency toward centralized power rather than decentralization. It was centralized bureaucratic authority that led nation building after liberation, economic progress after military *coup d'etat* in 1961, and democratization after the June 29, 1987 Declaration of President Roh Tae Woo. The degree and scope of Korean state bureaucrats' rule and control over other areas of society are greater than those of any other country (Henderson, 1968).

The centralized ruling structure of Korean society played a vital role during the process of rapid economic development in recent years. With planning and executing, as well as supervising and mobilizing from above, the Korean economy boasted the world's highest growth rate for over 30 years. Although different periods show differences in degree and scope of state intervention in the market, it is basically assumed that the government and private sector took the role of superior and inferior, respectively. Due to such hierarchical relation between the government and enterprises, Korea earned a notorious fame as an interventionist state where, in some cases, fundamental order of the market economy was not obeyed. However, it is also true that the Korean economy grew remarkably in such a short period of time as a result of this developmental state ideology.

Confucian capitalism, which has been gaining interests recently, attracts much attention because East Asian countries belonging to the Confucian sphere of influence show a model of economic development different from that of "Christian Protestant capitalism" (MacFarquhar, 1980; Rozman, 1991). The history of integration between Confucianism and capitalism in East Asia differs from the history of integration between Protestantism and capitalism in Europe. Protestantism and capitalism were combined in Europe during the process of overcoming a decentralized ruling order, namely feudalism. On the other hand, in East Asia, Confucianism and capitalism were combined while maintaining centralized rule. Hence, European capitalism started "from below," whereas East Asian capitalism started "from above."

These two different kinds of capitalism contrast not only in terms of their origin but also in their course of development. The "bourgeoisie," which stood against the aristocracy, nurtured themselves to become not only an economic but also political and cultural ruling class. They built a "capitalist state" and drew the working class to their side (Gramsci, 1971). In East Asia, state bureaucrats not only fostered a "bourgeoisie" with no economic autonomy but also guided them politically and culturally to establish a "capitalist state." Moreover, the state directly controls, regulates, and protects the working class (Deyo, 1989). While the most important means to accumulate capital in Europe was the independent "economic competitive power" of the bourgeoisie, in East Asia it was "political collaboration" with a ruling power under Confucian capitalism.

"Protestant" capitalism emphasizes the establishment of "exclusive property rights" in all economic transactions as a precondition to ensure potential forecasting of economic activity (North and Thomas, 1973). If there is no private ownership, "transaction" (Williamson, 1985) between two concerned parties in the market faces uncertainty and "social trust" (Fukuyama, 1995a) cannot be maintained. However, instead of exclusive and private ownership, in Confucian capitalism intervention and the guarantee of a political group that officially speaks for the good and interest of the public (i.e., bureaucracy in power) are the most important criteria for all economic transactions (Jacobs, 1985). Even though the modern legal system does protect private property, in a state of emergency such as a national crisis, a demand of a third party, an intellectual group in particular, often assumes priority. A demand, usually addressed to moral standards, assumes priority over a contract between two concerned parties under the law, and the state endorses such demands (Hahm P. C., 1986).

In the process of overcoming economic hardship caused by the 1997 economic crisis in Korea, such characteristics of Confucian capitalism were evident again. For example, demanding *chaebols* to donate private property or to close down decision-making agencies (企劃調整室, business office of planning and coordination), and the so-called Big Deal that asks *chaebols* to exchange large-scale businesses in order to mitigate diversification and promote specialization, were moral demands from an intellectual group backed up by political authority. Meanwhile, the various reform policies of President Kim Dae Jung have been quite effective in meeting such demands, although many of them are without due process of law (i.e., failed to take legislative steps in the National Assembly).[11]

Public opinion questioning or expressing opposition against these reforms has not been found in abundance. An overwhelming majority of the public wholeheartedly supported the reform policy of the new president regardless of legal problems. It should be noted that such conditions are an exact repetition of the early years of the Kim Young Sam administration when it carried out audits and inspections of political circles and that of the early years of the Chun Doo Hwan and Roh Tae Woo administration when the National Security Legislature Council (國保委) or Social Purification Committee (社會淨化委員會) wielded power (Kim J. H. and Lew S. C., 1995: 186). In spite of the IMF intervention, Confucian capitalism is sure to survive.

Conclusion: Confucian Values in Korea

A father and a younger brother's family who lived in a house owned by a sister were asked to move out when they could not pay the monthly rent. When her demand was not realized, she resorted to court action to exercise her property rights; a primary court and Court of Appeal ruled in her favor. However, although it acknowledged her property rights, the Supreme Court decided that exercising her right would transgress moral standards. Thus, the Supreme Court sent the case back to a lower court.

The case mentioned above is an actual Supreme Court decision delivered on June 12, 1998. Nearly all the media in Korea headlined this incident the day after it happened. What could have been the reason? The general public agreed with the Supreme Court decision that placed family morality above right to property. That is, taking care of an old and sick parent is more important than exercising one's property rights. It seems that Korean society is not yet ready to accept individualistic values based on exclusive property rights. Or, alternatively, it could be more correct to say that dominant public sentiment in Korea may "never" accept such values.

It has been over a century since "modernization," which implies "Westernization," began in Korea. Korea continuously pursed modernization since it was forced to open the ports to foreigners in 1876. Political institutions and the economic system as well as value orientation and lifestyles underwent significant changes. Not only particular individuals but also everyone tried their best to make a new society modeled after the European system and values. As a result, Korea achieved substantial success; as of the summer of 1997, Koreans were convinced of successful modernization and proud of attaining industrialization and democratization.

However, when expectations of success turned into conviction, a new crisis emerged. The intervention of the IMF, triggered by a crisis in foreign exchange markets, once threatened Korea's existence, encroaching not only on the financial market but on the real economy as well. There were voices that demand the neoliberal reform requested by the IMF be made to penetrate the economy as well as every nook and corner of society to enhance efficiency. The Korean President at that time, Kim Dae Jung, during his visit to the United States, even delivered a speech stating that Korea believes in American values and that there is no need to worry about investing in Korea (*Hankook* Daily, 2nd page, June 14, 1998).

"Freedom" is the core of American values. Democracy is attainable only when freedom of speech, press, association, and assembly are guaranteed. In this sense, the American value, freedom, is significant in that it functions to ensure universal democracy. Accordingly, Korea pursued a democracy modeled after the United States with all its might and accepted the universality of freedom. However, Korea was engrossed in carrying out modernization and did not pay much attention to historical inheritance and social conditions that existed on the other side of the American value.

"Individualism" is inherent in the concept of freedom. Western history presents the separation process of individuals from state intervention in Europe. Modern individuals are now free from the church of the Middle Ages or the political power of the state in the Age of Absolutism. After obtaining religious and political freedom, individuals appealed for economic freedom and established a free market economy. After economic freedom, individuals in Europe are now demanding freedom from family as a final step. Increasing numbers of single families or single households is a symptom of such a trend.

However, Koreans are not quite certain whether the European modernization process is desirable. A value system that prioritizes family morality and a value system that advocates individualism are never compatible with each other. Koreans only perceived the superficial side of the concept and neglected the historical process of "separation of the individual from family." Koreans were too occupied with blindly imitating American pursuit of freedom. Such a tendency may grow even more after the IMF intervention. Can "warm morality" and "cold-hearted individualism" reside in a mutual existence? Koreans may have to make a difficult decision in choosing only one of the two alternatives.

Notes

1. Some have used the term "Confucian capitalism" to describe the characteristics of overseas Chinese economic activities and their success (Yao, 2002).
2. Chapter 2 of this volume is dedicated to an in-depth discussion of this issue.
3. In China these networks, or relationships, are called *Guanxi* (關係) (Gold, Guthrie, and Wank, 2002).
4. "Transaction costs" contrasts to "production costs." Instead of limiting the notion of economic cost to only production costs, Williamson (1973) proposes to expand the concept to all necessary costs involved in securing social apparatuses that enable transactions (e.g., trust). According to him, a "hierarchical organization" is an alternative to the "horizontal market" in mitigating transaction costs. Similarly, Granovetter (1985) emphasizes the "embeddedness" of economic actions.
5. Banks were pressured by government officials to extend loans to the insolvent *Hanbo* Steel.
6. As long as the discipline of "political economy" exists, "state and business" or "politics and market" can never be truly separated.
7. Chapter 2 of this volume discusses on the issue of "education fever" in relation to the Confucian religious value of filial piety.
8. This situation, however, was reversed again after opposition leader Lee Myung Bak became president in 2008.
9. Estimated populations of Confucianist nations in 2008 are as follows: China (1,330 M), Japan (127 M), Vietnam (86 M), S. Korea (48 M), N. Korea (23 M), Taiwan (23 M), Hong Kong (7 M), Singapore (5 M), Chinese Abroad (39 M), and Korean Abroad (7 M). http://www.nationmaster.com/graph/peo_pop-people-population (accessed on August 26, 2009).
10. Fukuyama (1995a) distinguishes "low-trust societies" (China, Taiwan, Korea, France, and Italy) of which economic activities are based on an organizational form of "family" from "high-trust

societies" (Japan, Germany, and US) where economic activities unfold in "voluntary associations."
11. The Korean National Assembly was not convened to carry out its duties after Kim Dae Jung came to power. As of summer of 1998, reforms were executed by the administrative authority without any legal basis. Chapter 7 of this volume provides a close look at this issue.

Chapter 6

Generalized Reciprocity between Strong State and Strong Society: Park Chung Hee and the Korean Developmental Path

with Hye Suk Wang

Introduction

The economic success of Korea has been attributed mainly to the initiatives of a "strong state." It is commonly assumed that society, in contrast to the state, was weak and passive yet was effectively mobilized by the state's rigorous planning efforts. We challenge this interpretation. The "developmental state" (Johnson, 1982), autonomous as well as embedded (Evans, 1995) during the Park Chung Hee era, cannot be explained by the simple dichotomy of "strong state and weak society" (Migdal, 1988). We rather find that Korea during the Park era was a showcase of synergy between a strong state and a strong society.

At the macro-level, state bureaucrats, seeking a strong state, embedded themselves in the middle class, especially the rural middle class who comprised the majority of Korean society at that time, in order to adopt a "disciplinary ethos" (Davis, 2004: 13). Employing the work ethic of small-holding peasants, Park tried to inculcate the belief among state bureaucrats that incompetence and idleness were betraying the Mother country. This disciplinary ethos was the moral basis of the government in exerting control over society, which includes landlords, capitalists, and labor. The leader's role in setting an example of moderation was the most important condition in achieving this moral imperative.

On the other hand, at the micro-level, individuals belonged to various groups, such as families, villages, and even factories, through traditional networks based on blood (*hyul-yon*: 血緣), locality (*chi-yon*: 地

緣), and school ties (*hak-yon*: 學緣). These network-based groups, discussed in more detail in chapters 2 and 3, engendered strong attachment and devotion. Although secondary group activities, including voluntary associations, were not so prominent at the time, primary group ties allowed people to join a variety of cross-cutting communities. The factors necessary for the development of a strong interwoven society were already in place in Korea.

After disciplining itself, the state employed several redistributive strategies to reward the better-performing groups at the micro-level and induce their competition to create developmental synergy. The New Village Movement (*Saemaeul Undong*) and state favoritism toward business groups (*chaebols*) under the name of the industrial policies of Park were only a few among many examples of these strategies. It turned out that these strategies generated enormous concern and devotion of individuals to their own group, because the out-group competition, induced by the state's redistributive policies, intensified in-group commitment (Portes, 1998). Individuals internalized and reinforced group-integrity norms. Synergy between "strong state and strong society" was generated to produce an outcome that exceeded all expectations.

Group integrity, found at both the macro- and micro-level, played a critical role in preventing the free-riding problem or the tragedy of the commons. At all levels, people came to internalize the norm that the development of the collective group would lead to the development of the individual. The norm of reciprocity, especially "generalized reciprocity" (Polanyi, 1957; Sahlins, 1972), was the ultimate source for developing an autonomous and, at the same time, embedded state.

Korea: Strong State and Weak Society?

The literature has debated the economic rationality and technical expediency of development policies selected and pursued in Park Chung Hee's Korea (Amsden, 1989; Johnson, 1982; Wade, 1990; Woo-Cumings, 1999; World Bank, 1993; Shin J. S. and Chang H. J., 2003). They stress the strategic role of the government industrial policy and the state intervention with financial support and discipline. However, they do not fully address why other developing countries produce different outcomes in spite of implementing industrial policies similar to Korea. Especially in regard to state-capitalist relations, many literature stress the importance of state autonomy in the development process and assume that "the Korean state was sufficiently autonomous from its capitalist class that it could simply impose a new developmental strategy with little regard for how firms would react" (Chibber, 2003: 52). This is true to some extent. As we argued in chapter 5, the state did have adequate autonomy to discipline the private sector.

However, they do not clearly explain how the state could aggressively orchestrate big firms' growth and activities, sometimes even assigning individual firms to specific projects. Conventionally, Korea is categorized as a combination of "weak society and strong state" (Migdal, 1988: 269).[1] The Korean society is depicted as premodern and under-organized, lacking any internal or autonomous mechanism of self-organization. However, as Evans (1995) argues, the combination of strong state and weak society is more likely to result in a "rogue" state, predation, and corruption. Table 6.1 summarizes types of developing countries and their state–society relations suggested by Evans (1995: 12–18). To be a developmental state, a strong society is required to respond to, and check, a strong state.

Based on this typology, this chapter articulates the "synergy" between a strong state and strong society in Park Chung Hee's Korea. Two distinctive features of the Korean developmental path will be highlighted. First, further attention is paid to the normative dimension of the state discussed in chapter 5, such as shared norms among bureaucrats and the leader's orientation. Second, we focus on how a strong and responsive society is required for the creation of a developmental state. In Third World countries, strong societies often resist the state. However, in Korea, society took an alternate track of active and voluntary cooperation with the state. To be sure, in Park Chung Hee's Korea, we observe several occasions of violent demonstrations not to mention political repression. However, it is still true that, in spite of contention, state initiatives achieved fruitful consequences in collaboration with a variety of social actors. What allowed the state's quest for development to be backed up by society in such a way as to create synergy between the two?

Table 6.1 Types of developing countries

		State	
		Strong	Weak
Society	Strong	Developmental state (synergy)	Captive state
	Weak	Predatory state	Collapsed state

In order to define a "strong" or "weak" society, we rely on the social capital literature. Social capital is defined as "features of social organization, such as trust, norms, and networks that can improve the efficiency of society by facilitating coordinated actions" (Putnam, 1993a: 167). According to Putnam (1993a: 169), "voluntary cooperation is easier in a community that has inherited a substantial stock of social capital, in the form of norms of reciprocity and networks of civic engagement." Social capital is crucial for economic and political development. Without social capital, economic and political institutions cannot work properly (Woolcock and Narayan, 2000). A society with a rich social capital is a strong society that can produce a developmental synergy when combined with a strong state.

Woolcock (1998: 172 and 177), as summarized in Table 6.2, suggests a general conceptual framework that incorporates various forms of social capital at the micro- and macro-levels and the in- and out-group dimensions.[2] He employs two key concepts: "embeddedness" and "autonomy."[3] The concept of embeddedness stresses the fact that individual actors are inherently enmeshed in a broader range of socioeconomic and political institutions around them, that is, social contexts. As such, embeddedness at the micro-level refers to the degree of integration of individuals by "in-group networks" in the communities to which they belong (c: **Integration**). At the macro-level, embeddedness indicates the degree the state and the society can respond to each other (a: **Synergy**). At the micro-level, the concept of autonomy is employed to indicate the extent to which community members have access to "out-group networks" beyond their community (d: **Linkage**). At the macro-level, autonomy is the extent to which the state exercises organizational integrity in such a way that institutional cohesion and capacity can be maintained *vis-à-vis* the society (b: **Organizational Integrity**).[4] These concepts were explored in chapter 5 and will return in our discussion of the 1997 financial crisis in chapter 7.

Table 6.2 Forms of social capital

	Embeddedness	Autonomy
Top-down: the state	a. Synergy: state–society relations (out-group)	b. Organizational integrity: institutional cohesion and capacity (in-group)
Bottom-up: social groups	c. Integration: in-group networks	d. Linkage: out-group networks

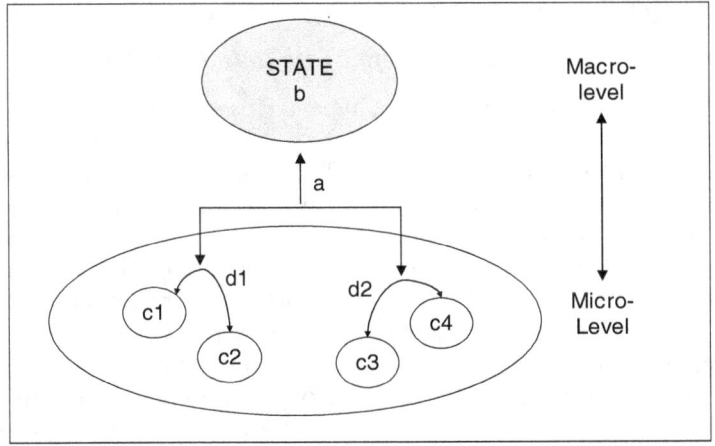

c1 & c2: villages
c3 & c4: business groups

Figure 6.1 Synergy between strong state and strong society

Figure 6.1 visualizes these concepts according to the logic of discussion in this chapter. First, we examine in more detail the organizational integrity of the state at the macro-level (**b** in Figure 6.1). It does not focus on how well designed and skillfully maintained the bureaucracy was during the Park era but focuses on what made for a robust and consistent bureaucracy committed to national goals. Second, we observe the integration of various groups at the micro-level on the basis of social capital theory (**c** in Figure 6.1), focusing on how these various groups internalized self-organizing community norms and thus enhanced in-group integration.

Finally, we turn to the articulation of the developmental synergy between strong state and strong society (**a** and **d** in Figure 6.1). In doing so, we aim to affirm the state's role in redistributing resources among micro-level social groups. We will highlight the explanation on how the state governed competition among such groups and prevented collective action from producing inefficiency and underdevelopment such as amoral familism. We argue that the most important element of the developmental synergy is the norm of generalized reciprocity, by which "leadership," "competition and reward," and "participation" play critical roles. This chapter provides empirical evidence for these arguments by considering the New Village Movement (*Saemaeul Undong*) and industrial policies of the Park government.

Strong State and Strong Society: The Park Chung Hee Era

The Making of Strong State (b in Figure 6.1)

Most literature on Korean development fails to answer the following question: why did state bureaucrats not pursue private interests through rent seeking (Kim H. A., 2004: 74). In fact, many strong states in underdeveloped countries, on the basis of their high level of autonomy and their weak societies, extracted resources for private ends and thereby degenerated into predatory states (Evans, 1995). One example is North Korea. The high level of state autonomy itself can result in either a developmental or predatory state if not combined with other factors. One factor is the intra-state (in-group) factor, a disciplinary ethos that provides organizational integrity in the state. The other factor is the extra-state factor, the presence of strong society endowed with a diverse and affluent stock of social capital that actively responds to the state.

It has been argued that the most distinctive character of the Korean developmental state is "support with discipline" (Shin J. S. and Chang H. J., 2003; Davis, 2004). Park's state was a disciplinary state with respect to not only society but the state itself. Why was the state charged with such a disciplinary ethos? Davis (2004: 13) finds the source of this ethos in the "rural-middle-class embeddedness of the state." The inauguration of Park Chung Hee's regime meant that political leaders from the rural middle class held state power for the first time in Korean history (Davis, 2004: 86). Unlike the former president Rhee, Park was supported by the military forces—most of them, including Park himself, were sons of the rural middle class. Park considered the "natural diligence and disciplined life of small peasants" as an ideal and demonized the "lavishness, excessive consumption, and corruption of the landlords and capitalists" (Davis, 2004: 104). He believed that the rural middle class was "industrious, self-disciplined, and capable of restraining consumption" (Davis, 2004: 105)—core elements of an ethic for developing the economy through savings. Park shared the perception of the rural middle class that most rural problems were caused by the usurious and import-addicted leisure class.

To amend the behavior of amoral capitalists, Park firmly believed that the state should have more direct control over resources and redistribute these resources to the rural middle class (Davis, 2004: 99). "Imposing a rural-based, disciplinary orientation onto a capitalist class" was the most important way to establish sound state ethics and to achieve the economic development (Davis, 2004: 108).

Furthermore, Park extended this disciplinary ethos to the entire society, including the capitalist class and the emerging working class. However, this ethos was most strictly imposed on state bureaucrats (Davis, 2004: 103). It turned out that this political motivation received wide-ranging support from the rural as well as the urban middle class.[5]

State discipline on bureaucrats was practiced in various ways. In particular, Park stressed capacity and efficiency in public administration and service. Inefficiency reflected the absence of discipline and commitment to the state, which was morally reproved and harshly punished (Kim H. A., 2004: 72–76). At the same time, he employed diverse disciplinary tools to enhance bureaucrats' administrative efficiency and develop a reward system based on their performance (Davis, 2004: 106). His endless commitment to discipline bureaucrats eventually succeeded; thus, the bureaucrats internalized the ethos as a viable norm.[6] The bureaucrats were convinced that their commitment to self-discipline would contribute to the development of the nation, and it would bring about, in turn, improvement of private as well as public life. Underlying this conviction was the belief that an increase in public goods as a whole would enhance the private good and their families' good as well. It seems they all shared the statist view that the prosperity of the state would extend to individuals (Kim H. A., 2004).

Based on this internal norm, the state was able to maintain a high level of organizational integrity, cohesiveness, and capacity, to discipline society, including the capitalist class (Chibber, 1999, 2003). Therefore, Park's regime was able to enhance its autonomy and to employ the mechanisms of control outlined in chapter 5. Their orientation toward the rural middle class and the consequent support from the majority of people offered leverage to control and govern the rent-seeking activities of commercial and financial capitalists. This paved the way for economic development under the guidance and governance of the state.

Potential of Strong Society (c in Figure 6.1)

Much work on the Korean Miracle highlights the role of institutions and the formal sector. However, without the complementary role of the civil society, a top-down developmental strategy would have failed (Leys, 1996).[7] Recent research on "social capital" reflects the importance of the social sector in economic and political development (Putnam, 1993a; Platteau, 1994a, 1994b; Portes, 1998; Woolcock, 1998).[8]

One of the notable characteristics of Korean society is the intricately webbed nexus among state/nonstate and official/nonofficial sectors. These networks, discussed in more detail in chapters 2 and 3, are mainly based on blood, school, or locality and may be called "affective networks." Affective networks are firmly rooted in Korean society and are key in "enabling collective actions which return goods in excess of those the individual might achieve by acting alone" (Warren, 2008: 125).[9]

As we saw in chapter 2, family ties, the most representative type of affective networks in Korea, significantly contribute to economic development. Every family network in Korea shares the Confucian ethic of filial piety. The religiosity of filial piety requires material institutionalization, chiefly through the ritual of ancestor worship. Every family in Korea is forced to engage in this competition of ritual display. The norm of filial piety has the unintended consequence of generating a moral drive for economic improvement in order to perform a better ritual.

This mechanism can be extended to other forms of affective networks woven through school ties, regional ties, or acquaintanceship. It turns out that affective network facilitates cooperation, not competition, among individuals belonging to the same community. The norms shared by affective networks prevent the selfish and maleficent behavior of group members and allow them to contribute to the creation of collective goods and thus maintain in-group integrity (chapter 3). The trust among group members enhances collective action for economic improvement of the group. In-group networks help mobilize the resources and channel effective communication. For this reason, we regard traditional affective networks as "social capital."[10]

However, a strong society endowed with rich social capital comprises only half of the picture. Rather, a strong society must be seen in the context of the diffused (weak) or developmental state. The most problematic aspect of affective networks, as many previous studies have pointed out, is that they block outsiders from accessing resources on a fair basis. Positive returns to individuals within given social networks can be negative externalities to those outside those networks (Warren, 2008: 126). Such a condition may negatively affect fairness of competition, diminish the possibility of productive transactions, and eventually bring about inefficiency in distribution of resources (Lee J.-H., 1999a). A strong state encourages the norm of generalized reciprocity in order to make society productive and responsive.

Developmental Synergy through Generalized Reciprocity

The most fundamental element in bringing about synergy between a strong state and a strong society is the norm of generalized reciprocity. The term "generalized" is adopted here to emphasize the unconditional aspect of reciprocity, following anthropological usage. In economics, the term reciprocity carries a specific condition of exchange, that is, equal and simultaneous exchange between two parties.[11] However, there are many occasions when exchange does not take this particular form. For example, an exchange may occur in an asymmetrical way as well as produce lagged returns (Mauss, 1990[1925]). This is especially true when the exchange occurs in a well-integrated community. There have been many studies that offered examples of this kind of reciprocity (Sahlins, 1972). This literature suggests that the norm of generalized reciprocity extends the reciprocal transactions to "others in general" in a given network or community, so that the group maintains a high level of integrity.[12]

We employ this term to explain the developmental synergy in Park Chung Hee's era. We do not intend to devalue the achievements of the Park era by treating it as a primitive or anthropological object of the study. Rather, the goal is to highlight the moral features observed in the developmental dynamic of the Park era which cannot be explained by market rationality. As suggested in chapter 5, the state was motivated to discipline society not for its private rent seeking but for the development of the country. In addition, the state took advantage of a redistributive strategy to enforce competition and reward better-performing groups. Various groups at the micro-level were integrated to respond actively to state initiatives by mobilizing their resources. Two concrete examples demonstrate the generalized reciprocity exercised to bring about synergy between the strong state and strong society: the New Village Movement (*Saemaeul Undong*) and the well-known state policies of export-oriented industrialization.

Village Competitions and State Redistribution: The New Village Movement (a & d1 in Figure 6.1)

The New Village Movement, known as *Saemaeul Undong* in Korean, was instituted with great commitment by Park Chung Hee in the 1970s. The program or movement was envisioned as a highly organized, intensively administered campaign to improve the environmental quality of rural life through projects undertaken by the villagers themselves with government assistance. The bureaucracy, particularly at the regional and local levels, was mobilized on a massive scale to ensure that the program would be carried throughout every village of the whole country. The initial emphasis was on improving village roads and bridges and replacing thatch with tile or composition roofs. Later, government introduced three social values to guide the movement: diligence (勤勉), self-help (自助), and corporation (協同).

There are two contrasting views on the New Village Movement: that of mobilization by a coercive state (Hahn S. J., 1981) and that of voluntary participation by rational peasants (Brandt, 1971; Ho Y. I. and Kim B. H., 1981). Both perspectives are misleading: we must look at the moral aspect of the village competitions. It is true that the state initiated the movement. However, it was neither economic incentives nor rewards but in-group networks and their shared norms that mobilized peasants and villages to empower the movement. Park Geun Hye,[13] the elder daughter of Park Chung Hee who turned into the president of Korea since February 2013, indicates three elements of success in the New Village Movement: leadership, competition and incentives, and people's participation (Park G.-H., 2006). Her insight suggests how the state and society were joined to create a developmental synergy.

First, on leadership, Park's initiatives and bureaucrats' orientation were embedded in rural-middle-class norms. It goes without saying that Park's initiatives were never free from political interest in attracting a wider range of support. However, these shared norms explain why Park and his bureaucrats, as sons of the rural middle class, prioritized rural development (Davis, 2004: 86–87). At the same time, the importance of self-discipline in order to overcome poverty in rural areas was always emphasized. To Park Chung Hee, extending help to those without self-discipline was regarded as a waste of national resources (Park G.-H., 2006). Though the state initiated the movement, Park believed that a movement based on state coercion and predominance alone was doomed to fail sooner or later. He admitted that voluntary participation from the people's side would be keys to making the movement a success. This is why Park Chung Hee adopted a distinctive incentive structure (Kim H. A., 2004).

Initiating the movement, the state introduced competition among rural villages. The government distributed the same amount of resources, for example, cement or steel, to all villages and then allowed them to use such resources as they saw fit. The outcomes varied across villages. The villages that were able to mobilize and organize voluntary participation showed better outcomes. At the next stage, these villages were rewarded with more material resources as well as with a higher moral status. In this way, the state played a pivotal role in mediating and governing competition among villages. Such institutionalization of the redistributive system encouraged competition, and each village was driven to cooperate to produce maximum output.

Voluntary participation was another key element of the success. Participation and mobilization were based on the norms of generalized reciprocity, rather than economic or coercive measures. The fact that the state introduced competition among rural villages, not among individual farmers, created a critical need for cooperation among village members. Considering the situation of those times, individuals in a given village had few linkages connecting themselves to out-groups beyond village boundaries. This situation also enhanced in-group integrity and promoted competition among villages.[14] In the process, the norm of generalized reciprocity relieved conflict among farmers over collective action. This feature of in-group integrity played a critical role as the "forum in and through which there is an attempt to harmonize, when necessary, conflicting demands of individual interests and social good" (Woolcock, 1998: 190). In these forums the norm of generalized reciprocity promoted cooperation toward collective action for producing public goods.

How, then, were problems of opportunistic behavior solved? The norm of generalized reciprocity blurred boundaries between private interests and public interests (Woolcock, 1998: 161). Consequently, village residents came to act without regard to private interest. Balanced "give and take" reciprocity, such as market exchanges, was avoided because it could secularize, or jeopardize, moral relationships. Economic behavior such as dividing yours and mine, or calculating cost and benefits, only hindered in-group cohesion by highlighting boundaries among members.

Finally, this norm of generalized reciprocity, through firmly established affective networks, mobilized resources from the community with few conflicts and enabled state-supported resources to trickle down to the very bottom of the community. The fact that some farmers even donated their land for the sake of the village is firm evidence of this feature (Ministry of Home Affairs, 1980).[15] Moreover, as seen in Table 6.3, a considerable amount of financial resources in the movement was provided by villagers themselves rather than the state. Voluntary cooperation and engagement by villagers based on generalized reciprocity were critical in the movement. Paradoxically, the moral norms and values of "irrational peasants,"[16] once blamed as the root of backwardness by President Park Chung Hee, were keys to the success of the movement. The norm of generalized reciprocity led irrational farmers to become rational peasants.

Table 6.3 Financial resources of the *Saemaeul Undong* (New Village Movement)

(Unit: Hundred Million Korean *won*)

Year	Self-support	(%)	Govt. support					Total	(%)
			National budget	Local budget	Others	Total	(%)		
1971	81	(66.4)	27	14		41	(33.6)	122	(100)
1972	280	(89.5)	20	13		33	(10.5)	313	(100)
1973	769	(78.2)	125	90		215	(21.8)	984	(100)
1974	1,020	(76.8)	121	173	14	308	(23.2)	1,328	(100)
1975	1,306	(44.1)	666	579	408	1,653	(55.9)	2,959	(100)
1976	1,575	(48.8)	484	396	771	1,651	(51.2)	3,226	(100)
1977	2,205	(47.3)	599	723	1,138	2,460	(52.7)	4,665	(100)
1978	2,958	(46.6)	654	773	1,957	3,384	(53.4)	6,342	(100)
1979	3,330	(43.9)	1,258	1,010	1,984	4,252	(56.1)	7,582	(100)

Source: Ministry of Home Affairs (*Naemubu*) (1980: 18).
Unit: Hundred million Korean *won*.

Business Group Competition and State Redistribution: Industrial Policies (a and d2 in Figure 6.1)

Those who are skeptical about state intervention argue that the industrial policies do not work because they often "distort" market signals, are technically difficult to manage, and are liable to capture and corruption by interest groups (World Bank, 1991). This phenomenon is widely observed in the underdeveloped world under the name of "patron–client relations," favoritism, or cronyism. Why do similar relations between politics and business bring different outcomes in Korea? Arguments for the widespread existence of corruption in Korea during the Park era have yet to explain the coexistence of cronyism and development. We can solve this puzzle by applying the same logic of success in the New Village Movement to industrial policies: leadership, competition and incentives, and business groups' (*chaebols*') participation.

First, regarding leadership in industrial policies, we have already shown how Park and his military allies, as sons of the rural middle class, challenged the urban and commercial biases of the Rhee administration (Davis, 2004: 87). Park Chung Hee believed that "many of the problems of rural underdevelopment owed to lavish, improvident, and uncontrolled consumption of greedy capitalists, not just the import substituting industrialists of the Rhee period, but also big bankers and numerous rural-based moneylenders whose pockets grew fat while their countrymen starved and the country suffered" (Davis, 2004: 97). This explains why Park exerted a hard hand to discipline usurious capitalist class from the beginning of his regime, as illustrated in the creation of the Illicit Wealth Accumulation Charge in 1963. The Park regime "imprisoned many prominent businessmen on the charge of having accumulated wealth through 'illicit' means (e.g., using political connection) and later released them in return for their promises to 'serve the nation through enterprise' (企業報國)" (Chang H. J., 2006: 97).

To discipline the market, the state used a strategy of incentives and competition, which were similar to the ones used in the New Village Movement. In the beginning the state provided export subsidies (Amsden, 1989; Chang H. J., 2006). These subsidies were in the form of loans for exporters, tariff rebates on export inputs, or a generous "wastage allowance" to the exporters using domestic resources. The government also provided information on foreign markets through the government trading agency (KOTRA, Korea Trade Agency), and sometimes even the diplomatic service took on such duties.

However, such support was not for every sector or every firm; as indicated in chapter 5, such support was conditional. The government gave such assistance only to targeted industrial sectors, and the recipient sectors had to demonstrate a competitive edge in the international market afterward. The state periodically screened recipients of support, mostly *chaebols*, on the base of market performance to maintain a minimum, if not a maximum, level of productivity and competitiveness (Chang H. J., 2006). *Chaebols* who failed in paying their dues back were expelled from the market. This kind of competition under the governance of the state was harsher and even more ruthless than market competition, as the volatility in rankings of top ten *chaebols* in 1960s and 1970s reflects (chapter 5).

In addition to the economic competition among *chaebols*, it is important to understand the state's strategy to moralize the economy. After the Illicit Wealth Accumulation Charge, the state was able to force *chaebols* to serve the national interest; a new moral obligation was created. As recipients of state favoritism, *chaebols* were obligated to pay back to the country through increased exports in accordance with the principle of generalized reciprocity. Furthermore, the state established rituals such as the Order of Industrial Service Merit (産業勳章) or Trade Day as a national day of commemoration to reward and publicize business performance. Such rituals functioned to legitimate state intervention and govern the market. This meant export or market performance became not only economic but political affairs. With such display of ritual, *chaebols* were forced to participate in moral competition and internalize the norm of generalized reciprocity.

These rituals legitimated the *chaebols* at the same time. With such official ritual displays by the state, they could be treated as a pillar of the national interest, not merely greedy capitalists. Moral legitimacy drawn from competition facilitated the transformation of economic competition to moral competition, thereby conferring higher status. For them, exports led to state recognition of the devotion of *chaebols* to the development of the country. Beyond disciplining *chaebols*, the state also tried to discipline the market at large. The state imposed heavy tariffs and domestic taxes, limited domestic consumption, and even banned the import of certain luxury products (Chang H. J., 2006; Davis, 2004; Chibber, 2003). These policies are of course important for export-oriented industrialization. However, control of consumption of luxury goods has helped to create "the sense that there is a national community with a common project, whose burdens and fruits are shared by all the citizens" (Chang H. J., 2006: 28).

Park also tried to socialize *chaebols* by restructuring their corporate governance. *Chaebol* firms were initially owned by a limited number of families because they did not want "the dilution of control that equity financing would entail" (Chang H. J., 2006: 281). Park thought that *chaebol* firms should be owned not by this handful of businessmen and their families but by the people in general (Kim J.-R., 2006; Park Chung Hee Internet Memorial site). Therefore, he urged *chaebol* leaders to open their firms' governance structure by going public.[17] Undeniably behind this action lay Park's political concerns about preventing excessive concentration of economic power. However, it is also true that he believed assets and profits of *chaebols*, and, moreover, *chaebols* themselves should be public resources, not private ones. To Park, the growth of *chaebols* was due to the generalized reciprocity rendered by state and society. As such, the state, going beyond governing the market, sought to discipline the market. Park spread the idea that the market is not a space within which private or individual interests are freely pursued, but a space within which public resources are produced and appropriated.

Chaebols' participation, the third element in the state/society synergy, is also important. In some literature, *chaebols* are described as "paper tigers" docilely following instructions given by the state. However, their active role and voluntary participation in the Korean developmental path should not be neglected.[18] Once moralized as legitimate market actors by the state, they actively participated in the policy-making process through formal as well as informal channels (Davis, 2004: 149–150). In order to achieve better export performance, they even demanded further intervention of the state. Paradoxically, devices created by the state to monitor firms and hold them accountable, such as the Ministerial Meeting with Businessmen, served as a forum in which *chaebol* leaders could deliver feedback on state policies (Chibber, 2003: 168). In these meetings, business leaders were encouraged to report on the quality of state service and relevant officials were expected to respond to their suggestions. Sometimes business leaders even put pressure on politically sensitive issues, such as the normalization of relations with Japan. These incidents are not short of revealing the synergy between the strong state and strong society inspired by the norm of generalized reciprocity.

Weak State and Strong Society: The Post-Park Era

Retrenchment of the strong state started in the market sector. Since the early 1990s, the government started relaxing control over the financial sector. The inauguration of the Kim Young Sam administration in 1993 accelerated the process of liberalization, aimed at interest rate deregulation, abolition of "policy loans," greater managerial autonomy for banks, capital account liberalization, and so on (Chang H. J., 2006: 209). As we argue in the next chapter, these developments contributed to the financial crisis of 1997.

Several factors brought about financial liberalization. One internal condition was Korea's economic success. The large trade surpluses and the surge of capital inflows made state control over foreign exchange less legitimate. At the same time, domestic firms started to regard state intervention as unnecessary as the credit ratings of Korean corporations and banks in international financial markets rose. Adding to these structural pressures, continued pressure from the US government to open up the financial market and the decision of the Kim Young Sam government to apply for membership in the Organization for Economic Cooperation and Development (OECD) subjected Korea to further external demands for liberalization (Chang H. J., 2006: 211).

The practice of five-year planning, which had provided an overarching policy coordination framework since 1962, was abolished under the cloak of liberalization. At the same time, the planning ministry, the Economic Planning Board, was merged with the Ministry of Finance, which subsequently became the Ministry of Finance and Economy. These episodes symbolized the demise of "planning" in Korea (Chang H. J., 2006: 214).

In the past, industrial policies provided a coordination mechanism to check excessive investment. By the early 1990s, there was no mechanism to govern or mediate market competition. Moreover, the rise of neoliberal ideology and the growing power of the *chaebols* weakened selective industrial policies. The case of *Hanbo*, a steel venture, illustrates how the demise of industrial policy affected Korean economy. *Hanbo* collapsed in early 1997, and it was revealed that behind government support for *Hanbo* lay corruption involving the President. The story of *Hanbo* not only illustrates the perils of dismantling the investment coordination mechanism but also suggests that the relationship between state and business in Korea had changed since Park's era. The corruption surrounding the *Hanbo* case was not typical of the past developmental state.

In the past regime, the *chaebols* as a group were preferentially treated but rarely were regarded as being closer to the government than others (Lew S. C., 2000). The abolition of five-year planning and the serious weakening of industrial policy made it easier to "bend the rules" for political reasons. This meant the end of the "generalistic" state–business relationship and the rapid rise of a "particularistic" or "crony" relationship. It may be argued that "it was only after the Park Chung Hee regime that genuine 'crony capitalism' was born in Korea" (Chang H. J., 2006: 217).

Along with the retrenchment of the state, however, society remained as strong as ever and may have become even stronger. This phenomenon is a natural consequence of the weakened state, especially in providing actors with robust rules and morals in competition. One scholar, criticizing the negative effect of social capital, argues that as individuals accumulate exclusive reciprocity and personal trust created by cliquish connections, "the rules of the game" can be damaged (Lee J.-H., 1999a: 49). However, exclusive reciprocity and personal trust created by cliquish connections only increase when the rules of the game are damaged in Korea.

According to studies that adopt the rational choice theory, an individual's reliance on the affective network is his or her rationally calculated choice because it reduces uncertainty and transaction costs in a sociopolitical environment of instability and uncertainty: "when uncertainty of system is high, affective networks provide trustworthy membership with predictable behavior. Therefore, people employ networks as means to reduce uncertainty" (Kim Y.-H., 1996: 106). The preference for affective networks, then, was the result of strategic choices made by rational individuals under particular environmental constraints. Affective networks based on traditional ties can provide a sense of trust essential for the exchange of political and economic resources when other institutions are underdeveloped. During social upheaval, the cost of establishing trust can rise to such levels that the cost of official constraints is higher than that incurred by transactions based on personal trust. Accordingly, people are able to gain access to scarce resources more effectively and efficiently by conducting their transactions through affective networks.

This explanation can be applied to the post-Park Chung Hee period when robust rules created and administered by the state disappeared. As we have seen in the cases of industrial policies and the New Village Movement, the past developmental state provided robust and predictable rules for competition and rewards. These rules were applied evenly to all actors. More importantly, the state offered the conviction that these rules would not change despite economic or political resistance. After the Park era, the state no longer carried out its role of providing robust and predictable rules of the game and enforcing such rules upon social actors. This contributed to the revitalization or over-activation of social capital in the social realm to cope with increased environmental uncertainty.

This situation led to fierce competition among the private interest groups who organized their own social capital to capture the state and the market. This competition entailed a more fundamental conflict over who makes the rules. These struggles are over whether other social groups—families, clans, multinational corporations, domestic enterprises, tribes, and patron-client dyads—will be able to displace or harness state organizations and make rules against the wishes and goals of state leaders (Migdal, 1988: 31).

The fact that the liberalization process, initiated by the state in the early 1990s, changed the overall incentive structures drastically is more serious. As financial liberalization continued, firms started to seek international linkages outside the nation state. They had no reason to rely on the weakened state support and discipline (Chang H. J., 2006: 211). This situation offered domestic firms bountiful opportunities to mobilize greater financial resources. At the same time, it posed a threat to state management of the financial sector and complex new problems emerged. At the individual level, as collective rewards and resource redistribution through micro-level communities disappeared, individuals did not need to maintain commitments or obligations toward their respective communities. The decline of the state created incentives to seek extra-community linkages for a broader range of opportunities and, at the same time, created threats to intra-community integrity.

Of course, this is not to say that social capital declined in its importance. Rather, it indicates that dominant forms of social capital in Korean society shifted from the past "in-group integrity" (**c** in Table 6.2) to "out-group linkages" (**d** in Table 6.2). In the past, strong intra-community integrity provided norms for commitment and cooperation by binding private and public interest. As these norms weakened, individuals utilized social capital to maximize their individual and private interests. The effects of social capital are now focused on short-term and individual dimensions, symbolizing the coming of a liberal or atomized society. Today, the form of social capital described by Putnam (1993a) as a public good rarely exists. The form of social capital criticized by Bourdieu (1986) as a basis for social exclusion and class differentiation prevails. This transformation only exacerbates conflicts among private interests, leading to a Hobbesian struggle of self-centered individuals in a war of all against all. These conflicts contributed to the devastating financial crisis, taken up in the next chapter.

Conclusion

Park Chung Hee knew that those who want to discipline others should discipline themselves first. Without setting an example of moderation, his leadership would not work. For this reason state bureaucrats were disciplined before others during his administration and the state was able to successfully extend discipline to the rest of the society. Of course, discipline entails a measure of discomfort. This may be the reason why he is often referred to as authoritarian or dictatorial leader. However, the discipliner must follow the universally accepted rules (norms) in order to ensure compliance and gain legitimacy, as argued in chapter 5. Discipline will also fail if the rule the discipliner imposes is found to be arbitrary. The disciplinary leader is required to follow his own rules foremost.

By now we find that his discipline was not just for himself. He practiced it for the country. His dream, to bring about National Restoration (民族中興) or Modernization of the Fatherland (祖國近代化), was achieved by his discipline: diligence (勤勉), self-help (自助), and cooperation (協同). However, simultaneously, he became a scapegoat of the discipline he practiced. The strong society, nurtured by the strong state under his discipline, now claims freedom from the state. The retrenched state is no longer able to cope with a resilient strong society that has transformed itself into a modern as well as contentious civil society. In this regard his state dug its own grave, as the strong civil society and *chaebols*, the beneficiaries of discipline, claimed independence and broke free from state controls.

The irony we find in today's Korea is that the conservatives, or alternatively, the political right, who believe the liberal market to be the ultimate solution, worship his memory. On the other hand, the progressives, or alternatively, the left, who believe the state should discipline capital and govern the market, condemn him. However, the uncomfortable truth is that Park Chung Hee was never a liberal. His moral values show rather that he was a communitarian, perhaps a state communitarian, who appreciated the norms of generalized reciprocity.

Behind this irony lies the convenience of the post-Park generations' evaluation of the past. Their simple assessment of his discipline is that it was "economically good, but politically bad." However, such an idealized dichotomy cannot be applied to real history. For Park Chung Hee, authoritarian discipline and rapid industrialization represent two sides of a double-edged sword (Kim H. A., 2004). His well-known words, "Let Them Spit on My Grave,"[19] show he was already aware of the irony that his greatest beneficiaries would also be his harshest critics.

Notes

1. For example, Migdal (1988), following Max Weber's notion of the state, views the state as an institution enforcing regulation, at least partly through a monopoly of violence. According to his view, states always confront, in their quest for social control and dominance, the resistance posed by chiefs, landlords, bosses, rich peasants, clan leaders, and other strongmen through their various social organizations (Migdal, 1988: 33–35). Therefore, as shown in the following model of state–society relations, the coexistence of strong state and strong society is an anomaly in his theory.
2. In the social capital debate, two contrasting approaches define the function and the roles of social capital: the American school and the European school (Arneil, 2006: 4–10). The American school, represented by Putnam (1993a, 1993b), is focused on the macro-level and views social capital as a public good while the European school, represented by Bourdieu (1986), is a micro-level approach arguing that social capital is not a benign force working equally in the interests of each and all. Woolcock (1998) tries to synthesize insights from these two camps to advance a more unified conceptual framework for understanding social capital theory and policy.
3. While the concept of "embeddedness" was introduced by Polanyi (2001[1944]) and revived by Granovetter (1985), the concept of "autonomy" was derived from theories of the state (Evans, 1995).
4. According to Woolcock (1998: 164), autonomy at the macro-level is defined as a situation in which "senior policy makers are themselves simultaneously governed by a professional ethos committing them to negotiating and pursuing collective goals, and recruiting and rewarding colleagues on the basis of merit." From his view, autonomy at the macro-level is close to the concept of "state capacity" of state theories.
5. Korean economic development presents a distinctive social connection between urban and rural populations. Usually development and industrialization processes break up this connection. However, during compressed industrialization, the direct social connection between rural and urban continued in Korea. The urban middle class was a simple migrant of the rural middle class, and they did not have enough time to create their own distinctive identity as an urban middle class. The urban middle class maintained their rural orientation and their familial connection with the rural. The formation of the "true" urban middle class in Korea is a relatively recent phenomenon (Hattori and Funatsu, 2003).
6. It seems that "the strong state was an outcome of calculated political moves and institutional innovations as of the historical conditions and culture" (Chang H. J., 2006: 96) rather than historical inheritance or colonial legacy.

7. Institutions and policies do not sufficiently depict the whole picture. Institutions do not function in a vacuum but interact with other institutions (Chang H. J., 2007: 6). Sometimes institutions, in order to function, require un-institutional settings.
8. The importance of the social capital is widely accepted among schools of economic and institutional theory. Coleman's argument is directly linked to new institutional economics that places importance on "transaction costs" within the market (Coleman, 1988; Williamson, 1989). These authors explain that because those who do not share social capital always face problems of trust, that is, the problem of opportunistic behavior of the transaction partner, it is necessary to introduce reliable safeguards (e.g., insurance or official endorsements). However, if the trust between the two participants exists in a transaction, then safeguards merely become cumbersome formalities that increase transaction cost in accordance with the contract. Consequently, social capital is an important mechanism for reducing transaction costs (Granovetter, 1985).
9. Putnam points to the "dense social networks" of East Asian economies, such as Japan, South Korea, Taiwan, and China, and argues that "well-developed trust relationships facilitate individual actors to cooperate in a variety of productive efforts that fall outside the scope of market relations" (Putnam, 1993b: 38; Arneil, 2006: 127).
10. Similar features of generating and maintaining group cohesion among state bureaucrats—because the development and prosperity of community they belong to can be extended to every individual in the near future through affective networks—are also observed here.
11. As such, this type of reciprocity earned the label of "balanced reciprocity" (Sahlins, 1972). The norm of balanced reciprocity is usually applied to an exchange in the market. In this situation, reciprocity to whom, with what, and when, is automatically determined as a contract is agreed upon. One should reciprocate to specified partners with the same amount of value as soon as possible.
12. In particular, this concept is often applied to the analysis of the moral economy of peasants (Scott, 1976).
13. Ms. Park Geun Hye carried out the duties of the First Lady after Mrs. Park was assassinated in 1975 until the demise of the Park Chung Hee administration in 1979. After a long seclusion she returned to politics in 1998 to become a four-time elected Congresswoman, and finally she ran for the president to win the popular election in December, 2012.
14. Portes and Sensenbrenner (1993) and Portes (1998) point out four conditions to increase in-group social capital: having distinct phenoltypical or cultural characteristics, which increase prejudice toward members and thereby lowers the probability of entry and exit; engaging in strong, frequent confrontation with other groups perceived

to be more powerful; suffering a high degree of discrimination and without alternative avenues for social honor and economic opportunity; and possessing a high degree of internal communication and ability to confer unique rewards upon its members. Among these, the first and the second conditions can be applied to explain the high degree of in-group integrity in villages during the movement. The scarcity of out-group linkages lowered the probability of exit and, thereby, increased in-group integrity. In addition, competition, geared by the state, created strong and frequent confrontation among villages.

15. Herein lies the characteristic of the gift as explained by Mauss (1990[1925]). The form usually taken is that of a gift, disinterested and spontaneous, generously offered, but in fact obligatory and socially demanded. This manifests distinctive features of the moral economy of Korean peasants at the time.

16. A considerable number of "rural Koreans tend to resemble the ideal-typical image of peasants: attachment to land, familism, or family-centrism outlook, traditionalism, and superstitious orientation... confounded by moralist obligation and collective particularism chiefly embodied in strong kinship ties and familism. A calculating economic rationality and the urban and industrial experience was... far from the rural farmers' grasp.... The subordination of individual goals and satisfaction to those of the collectivity—family, lineage, neighborhood, or village—is nearly automatic, while excessive individualism stands out and is likely to be criticized.... For many small farmers family and collective betterment mattered more than individual economic success" (Davis, 2004: 124).

17. This idea is quite similar to the recent campaign to promote minority shareholder rights, which is vigorously pursued by the so-called "progressive" or "left" circles.

18. Rejecting the predominance of the state, Chibber (2003: 82–83) argues that the export-led industrialization was a "pact" between the state and bourgeoisie. According to him, it was not foisted onto business by the new regimes; on the contrary, it was pushed by the business itself.

19. This phrase became famous after a distinguished journalist, Cho Gab Je, published a biography of Park Chung Hee in 13 volumes in 2007.

Chapter 7

Did the 1997 Financial Crisis Transform the S. Korean Developmental State? Focused on the Public Fund

with Hye Suk Wang

Developmental State and the 1997 Financial Crisis

Many scholars have explained South Korea's economic development in terms of "developmental state." They point out that the success of the South Korean government intervention was mainly due to "the control of the state over the industrial capital through financial resources" and "the existence of the independent bureaucracy able to discipline the capital"[1] (Johnson, 1982; Amsden, 1989; Wade, 1990; Kim E. M., 1997; Chibber, 1999). Based on a high-level state autonomy and capacity, the South Korean developmental state was able to discipline the industrial capital to comply with the state's policies and successfully intervene in the economic market with its own characteristic resource allocation and competition mechanisms (Amsden and Euh Y. D., 1993; Chang H. J., 1998; Cherry, 2005; Lim W. H., 2003; chapters 5 and 6). They argue that the formation of a triple alliance among "the state, the financial capital, and the industrial capital" guaranteed the state's effective dominance over the domestic capital (Kim E. M., 1997; Woo-Cumings, 1999; Hahm J. H., 2003).

Why did such a successful model collapse in the crisis of 1997? The more we laud the past success of the developmental state model, the more we find the failure of the model puzzling in the late 1990s. As soon as the crisis broke out in late 1997, many scholars readily started a new industry of seeking out the causes of the crisis. The situation seemed to favor the internal causality that blamed the ineffectiveness of the developmental state model. They called for the neoliberal reforms to "get prices right" and limit state intervention (Lee Y. H., 2000).

Others, based on an outward looking viewpoint, insisted that the crisis in Korea was resulted from contagion from Southeast Asian economies and therefore, nothing was wrong with fundamentals of Korean economy itself (Radelet and Sachs, 1998).

This chapter supports that the determinant factors of a crisis should be found from the inside. However, we reject both the internal and external causes of the crisis found in the existing literature. The two strands assume that the Korean developmental state has been continued without change since the 1970s. This is far from the truth. The classical model of the developmental state during the Park Chung Hee regime has undergone gradual changes, especially in its controls over the domestic market and its relations with *chaebols*. Since 1993 when the Kim Young Sam administration started, economic liberalization and globalization accelerated this change (Shin J. S. and Chang H. J., 2003).

This contextual knowledge presents important implications for theories that explain how the crisis occurred and what has happened since. The financial crisis of 1997 triggered a fierce debate over the future validity of the South Korean developmental state model (Thurbon, 2001). Some argued that the demands of global agents would undermine the long-established developmental legacy of a strong state (Frankel, 2000). The state, faced with this crisis, could not manage without financial aid from international organizations such as the International Monetary Fund (IMF), International Bank for Reconstruction and Development (IBRD), or World Bank. These institutions in turn demanded neo-liberal economic reform that inevitably reduced the state's room to maneuver (Aoki, Kim H. K., and Okuno-Fujiwara, 1997).

Others insisted that the crisis paradoxically provided an opportunity to strengthen the state's role in both internal and external terms. The state was responsible for concluding an entente with foreign organizations and developing a strategy to exit the crisis (Shin J. S. and Chang H. J., 2003). If their claim seemed reasonable, a bailout by the IMF could serve as a chance to strengthen the state's power in the Korean economy by turning a crisis into an opportunity.

These two contrasting views raise the following question: did the financial crisis transform a developmental legacy which was already being gradually dismantled, or did it revive and strengthen the developmental state model? To answer this question we examine the changes in autonomy and capacity of the state after 1997 with a focus on "public funds" hurriedly constructed to cope with the crisis. The public fund constituted a source of financial resources the state was allowed to use under its IMF program to alleviate the insolvency of the financial sector (Bank of Korea, 2010: 222–238). The public fund was a pivotal financial measure placed in the hands of the state in order to restore the South Korean national economy. This restorative process affected not only the internal state bureaucracy but also its external relationship with financial and industrial capital. Therefore, the process of mobilizing, injecting, monitoring and recovering the public fund in South Korea is a good yardstick for evaluating the state's autonomy and capacity.

Before starting the examination, our conceptualization of the terms autonomy and capacity and this chapter's application of these concepts to the public fund should be clarified (Evans, Rueschmeyer, and Skocpol, 1985: 9). Confucian capitalism (chapters 5 and 6) was characterized by a state that had both autonomy and capacity. By "autonomy" we mean a relationship with society—and capital—that is not captured but independent, and governed by a "legitimate" exchange of benefits for performance. By "capacity" we mean the internal organizational ability to get things done.

This chapter divides state capacity further into two dimensions: the intra-state dimension of the bureaucracy and the state's external relationship with the ruling class (capital). Internal cohesiveness across governmental agencies serves as the most critical factor in enhancing intra-state capacity.[2] Internal cohesiveness is acquired by the presence of a robust and rule-following corps, disciplined with bureaucratic rationality (Chibber, 2002). Based on this intra-state capacity, the state could externally discipline and supervise industrial capital and thus exercise autonomy. In this respect, the technocracy during South Korea's economic development can be regarded as a stereotypical bureaucracy with high state capacity and autonomy (Chibber, 1999; Kim H. A., 2004). As such, the core characteristic of the Korean developmental model has been referred to as "financial support with discipline" by the autonomous and capable state.

How can these concepts be applied to public fund policy? The public fund policy process has two components: the injection of public funds into insolvent financial institutions and the recovery of public funds from these institutions following the sale of assets and business normalization. The former shows the degree of state autonomy, because it depicts the extent of financial support given by the state to domestic capital. Considering the fact that the crisis made it impossible for private capital to mobilize financial resources easily, the role of the state is surprisingly similar to that of the state 30 years ago.

In order to evaluate the internal aspects of state autonomy,[3] this chapter explores how the state acquired control over financial and industrial capital, as well as the share of the national economy occupied by the public fund. The results will show whether using the public fund in this financial restructuring changed the nature of developmental coalition among the "state-financial capital-industrial capital" after the 1997 crisis.

Recovery—the ability of the state to make a return on assets it has acquired and sold—can be seen as an index to evaluate the degree of state capacity, because it shows the state's ability to supervise and discipline domestic capital to cooperate with the state's policies. The final goal of the public fund policy is market normalization and overcoming the crisis, which means the public fund injected should ultimately be paid back to the state or recovered.

We divided state capacity into two dimensions: internal and external. In regard to the internal capacity we trace changes in the arrangement of authority and bureaucratic cohesion, which are considered to be keys to the capacity of the developmental state. If there is no cohesion or bureaucratic rationality among the agencies in charge of the public fund, this situation can be interpreted to show weakened internal capacity of the state. As for the state's external capacity, that is, discipline of the ruling class, we examine how the state governed and controlled the financial institutions that received public funds. If the state did not obtain adequate repayment from these institutions, that is, poor performance in public fund recovery, it can be interpreted as the state demonstrating weakened external capacity in disciplining capital.

Mobilization and Injection of the Public Fund: Strengthened State Autonomy

The Size of the Public Fund and Its Mobilization and Injection

The process of how the state mobilized public funds shows the autonomous role that the state played in the crisis. The public fund was raised from four financial resources. The first was "bonds issuance" that referred to money raised through bonds guaranteed by the government and issued by the Korea Asset Management Corporation (KAMCO) and the Korea Deposit Insurance Corporation (KDIC).[4] The second was the "fund redeemed" that refers to the money reused from the public fund after the recovery. The third was "government money" that was mobilized through foreign loans[5] from Asian Development Bank (ADB) or IBRD, and national property including pension fund, and other sources. The fourth consists of extra funds that did not belong to any of the above three resources. For example, the fund that KAMCO and KDIC borrowed from financial institutions and the fund that KDIC mobilized from the deposit insurance belongs to this category. Table 7.1 summarizes the composition of the four resources of the public fund.

Let us examine the detailed process of raising each source of funding. To raise the public fund through "bonds issuance," the Ministry of Finance and Economy (MOFE) was required to estimate how many bonds should be issued for the public fund, then submit the legislation to the National Assembly for approval. In this procedure, the National Assembly could have hindered the state's autonomy by using institutionalized intervention. However, considering the speed with which the public fund policy was passed, the National Assembly could only ratify an agreement on policies regarding the public fund proposed by the government. Any hindrance would mean a failure on its part in recovering the national economy.[6] Therefore, the portion of the public fund raised through bond issues is the evidence that the government could push through its own policy preferences and priorities without any resistance from the Assembly.

In the case of the "fund redeemed," the MOFE was in charge of the management and supervision with very little oversight by the National Assembly.[7] This situation meant that the government had absolute autonomy in using those funds. The third one, "government money," was also under the direction of the minister of MOFE, who was the chairman of the Government Funds Management Fund Committee.[8] The government could also use this kind of public fund at its discretion. Therefore, the government could mobilize the public fund independently without any interference, which is an explicit index to show the strength of state autonomy.

Before injecting public funds, the types of injection should be clarified. This judgment is mainly based on the degree of insolvency

Table 7.1 Mobilization of the public fund by financial resources (Nov. 1997–Jun. 2006)

	Bonds issuance	Fund redeemed	Government money	Others	Total
Amount	102.1	42.0	19.9	4.3	168.3
(%)	(60.7)	(25.0)	(11.8)	(2.6)	(100.0)

Source: Ministry of Finance and Economy and the Financial Supervisory Commission (2006: 257).
Unit: Trillion Korean *won* (billion USD, at exchange rate of 1,000 KRW, spring 2008).

of the beneficiary financial institutions and the likelihood that each business would recover after receiving the money. The public fund injection has taken five forms: equity participation, capital contribution, deposit payoff, asset purchase, and nonperforming loan (NPL) purchase. When a financial institution is at the brink of being dissolved or going bankrupt, the public fund is injected as a capital contribution or deposit payoff. If the beneficiary financial institutions can normalize their business through asset sales or their own restructuring endeavors, the public fund is injected by way of equity participation. Particularly in the case of equity participation, the government acquires an owner's share in the funded institutions as an investor. With other types of injection, the government did not take an ownership share but rather supplied temporary liquidity to depositors and financial institutions.

The decision about the type of injection directly relates to the life or death of the funded institution as well as the governance structure of beneficiary financial institutions. Then, who decides which type of injection is most appropriate? The Public Fund Oversight Committee (POFC) was in charge of these decisions.[9] As a result, the public fund was a financial resource that supported the state's autonomy over the financial market. The state had the ability to act independently without being captured by other social forces such as the capitalist class, the National Assembly, civil society groups, and so on. Thus, the public fund can be used as an explicit index that measures the extent of the increasing autonomy of the state.

How much weight did the public fund occupy both nominally and relatively in the national economy? Table 7.2 shows the amount of annually injected public fund. The total sum of public fund amounted to 168.3 trillion Korean *won* (approximately US$168 billion).[10] The annual injection varied widely but was concentrated in the first four years of intervention. The amount has decreased since 2002. If the amount of the public fund is compared with the volume of national budget (government expenditure), we can evaluate the quantitative dimension of the state's autonomy. From 1998 to 2000, the amount of the public fund was more than half of the annual national budget. Under the control of the government, this money was injected into financial institutions. The quantitative significance of the public fund shows that the state's autonomy extended over the national financial market. In the crisis, in particular, the public fund was the one and only financial resource that the financial sector could use. The credit downgrading of Korea's financial institutions by the international financial market made it difficult to access alternative financial

Table 7.2 Government expenditure and the public fund, 1998–2006

	1998	1999	2000	2001	2002	2003	2004	2005	2006	Total
Public fund (A) (%)	55.6 (33.0)	35.5 (21.1)	37.1 (22.0)	27.1 (16.1)	3.7 (2.2)	2.2 (1.3)	3.9 (2.3)	2.9 (1.7)	0.3 (0.2)	168.3 (100.0)
Govt. expenditures (B) (general account)	73.2	73.2	80.5	98.7	108.9	117.2	118.2	135.2	144.8	949.9
A/B (%)	76.0	48.5	46.1	27.5	3.4	1.9	3.3	2.1	0.2	17.7

Source: Financial Service Commission* Press Release, Dec. 28, 2012: 5.

Unit: Trillion Korean *won* (billion USD, at exchange rate of 1,000 KRW, spring 2008).

*Financial Service Commission opened in March 2008.

resources. In this situation, the public fund functioned as a means for the state to strengthen its control over the domestic financial capital.

Financial Restructuring through the Public Fund

What changes has the public fund brought to the Korean financial market? Tables 7.3 and 7.4 show "changes in number of financial institutions" and "distribution of the public fund by injection type." The detailed restructuring processes depended on the characteristics of institutions, especially between banks and nonbanking institutions.

Let us explore the restructuring process of banks first. The government started an extensive restructuring of banks in 1998 (Park K. S., 2003). As Table 7.3 shows, the number of banks decreased from 33 in 1997 to 18 in 2006. Table 7.4 shows the amount that the public fund injected into banks reached about 86.9 trillion Korean *won*, which was 51.6% of the total public fund. Consequently, the banks

Table 7.3 Changes in number of financial institutions, 1997 and 2006

Financial sector	Numbers in 1997	Restructuring				Newly established	Numbers in June 2006
		Exit	Merger	Others	Total		
Banks	33	5	11	-	16	1	18
Nonbanks	2,070	164	171	533	868	106	1,308
Merchant Banking Corp.	30	22	7	-	29	1	2
Insurance companies	50	10	6	4	20	21	51
Securities companies	36	5	7	3	15	19	40
Invest trust companies	32	7	5	-	12	28	48
Mutual savings	231	107	28	1	136	15	110
Credit unions	1,666	2	116	524	642	13	1,037
Leasing companies	25	11	2	1	14	9	20
Total	2,103	169	182	533	884	107	1,326

Source: Ministry of Finance and Economy and the Financial Supervisory Commission (2006: 360).

Table 7.4 Distribution of the public fund by injection type and financial institutions

Sector	Equity Participation	Capital Contribution	Deposit Payoff	Asset Purchase	NPL Purchase	Total (%)
Banks	34.0 (20.2)	13.9 (8.3)	-	14.4 (8.6)	24.6 (14.6)	86.9 (51.6)
Nonbanks	29.5 (17.5)	4.5 (2.7)	30.3 (18.0)	2.7 (1.7)	12.0 (7.1)	79.0 (46.9)
Merchant Banking Corp.	2.7	0.7	18.3	-	1.5	23.2
Insurance companies	15.9	3.1	-	0.3	1.8	21.2
Securities companies/ Invest Trust Companies	10.9	0.3	0.01	1.7	8.5	21.4
Mutual savings	-	0.3	7.3	0.6	0.2	8.4
Credit unions	-	-	4.8	-	-	4.8
Foreign institutions	-	-	-	-	2.4 (1.4)	2.4 (1.4)
Total (%)	63.5 (37.7)	18.4 (10.9)	30.3 (18.0)	17.1 (10.2)	39.0 (23.2)	168.3 (100.0)

Source: Ministry of Finance and Economy and the Financial Supervisory Commission (2006: 258).
Unit: Trillion Korean *won* (billion USD, at exchange rate of 1,000 KRW, spring 2008).

underwent a severe restructuring process. In regard to the public fund injection types, the restructuring process of banks was different from that of other financial institutions. In the case of the banks, the highest proportion of the public fund was provided by way of equity participation (Table 7.4). As discussed above, equity participation meant that the government took on an owner's position in relevant financial institutions, thus acquiring the right to intervene directly in the institutions' corporate governance and management.

After the injection of the public fund, the ownership structures of banks radically changed. Before the crisis, the government had stakes in only two commercial banks, *Kookmin* and *Korea Housing & Commercial Bank* (Bank of Korea, 1998: 75 and Table 7.5).[11] However, as shown in Table 7.5, in 1998 when the public fund was

Table 7.5 Government ownership change among commercial and local banks

	1996	1997	1998	1999	2000	2001	2002	2003
Commercial Banks (19)								
Woori	------	------	------	------	------	Established	KDIC (87.7)	KDIC (86.8)
Hanvit	NA	NA	Merged	KDIC (74.7)	KDIC (100.0)	KDIC (100.0)	Merged	------
Commercial Bank of Korea	NA	NA	Merged	------	------	------	------	------
Chohung	0	0	KDIC (91.1)	KDIC (80.1)	KDIC (80.1)	KDIC (80.1)	KDIC (80.0)	0
Korea First (Cheil)	0	0	MOFE(46.9) KDIC (46.9)	KDIC (96.9)	KDIC (45.9)	KDIC (45.9)	KDIC (45.9)	KDIC (48.5)
Seoul	NA	NA	NA	Govt (46.9) KDIC (46.9)	Merged	------	------	------
Korea Exchange	BOK (47.9)	BOK (47.9)	BOK (33.6)	EIBK (18.2) BOK (17.8)	EIBK (18.2) BOK (17.8)	EIBK (18.2) BOK (17.8)	EIBK (18.2) BOK (17.8)	EIBK (14.6) BOK (6.4)
Kookmin	Govt. (17.1)	Govt. (15.2)	Govt. (8.2)	Govt. (6.5)	Govt. (6.5)	Govt. (9.7)	Govt. (9.3)	0
Korea Housing & Commercial	Govt. (46.8)	Govt. (22.4)	Govt. (16.1)	Govt. (14.5)	Govt. (14.5)	Merged	------	------
Shinhan	0	0	0	0	0	0	0	0
KorAm (Hanmi)	0	0	0	0	0	0	0	0
Hana	0	MOFE (46.9)	MOFE (46.9) KDIC (46.9)	KDIC (97.8)	KDIC (100.0)	KDIC (100.0)	KDIC (27.8)	KDIC (21.7)
Peace	0	0	0	0	KDIC (100.0)	Merged	------	------
Daedong	0	0	Bankruptcy	------	------	------	------	------

Dongnam	0	0	Bankruptcy	---------	---------	---------
Dong Hwa	0	0	Bankruptcy	---------	---------	---------
Boram	0	0	Merged	---------	---------	---------
Korea Long Term Credit	0	0	Merged	---------	---------	---------
Hanil	0	0	Merged	---------	---------	---------
Local Banks (10)						
Daegu	0	0	0	0	0	0
Pusan	0	0	0	0	0	0
Kwangju	0	0	0	KDIC (100.0)	WFG* (99.0)	WFG* (99.0)
Kangwon	0	0	Merged	---------	---------	---------
Kyungki	0	Bankruptcy	---------	---------	---------	---------
Chungbuk	0	0	Merged	---------	---------	---------
Chungchong	0	Bankruptcy	---------	---------	---------	---------
Cheju	0	0	0	KDIC (97.7)	KDIC (44.7)	KDIC (32.0)
Jeonbuk	0	0	0	0	0	0
Kyongnam	0	0	0	KDIC (100.0)	WFG* (100.0)	WFG* (100.0)
Govt. Banks (6)	The Bank of Korea (BOK), Korea Development Bank, The Export-Import Bank of Korea (EIBK), Industrial Bank of Korea, National Agricultural Cooperative Federation, National Federation of Fisheries Cooperatives					

Source: Korea Listed Companies Association (www.kocoinfo.com, searched on December 1, 2006).

Note: * WFG (Woori Financial Group) is included in the Government because KDIC occupied 87.7% of its total share. NA means no data available and "---------" stands for nonexistence.
KDIC: the Korea Deposit Insurance Corporation; MOFE: The Ministry of Finance and Economy.

injected, the equity held by the government drastically increased. Considering that private stock ownership in commercial banks is limited to 4% by law, the overall ownership level by the government was substantively higher. Among the 11 banks that still ran their own business in 1998 (*Hanvit, Chohung, Korea First, Seoul, Korea Exchange, Kookmin, Korea Housing, Shinhan, KorAm, Hana,* and *Peace*), government itself (MOFE) or government agencies such as KDIC and Export-Import Bank of Korea (EIBK) held equities in eight of these banks (*Hanvit, Chohung, Korea First, Kookmin, Korea Housing,* and *Hana*). Moreover, the equity participation level was quite high in these eight banks because the stock ownership ceiling did not apply to them.

In 2003, after most of the injection of the public funds had been completed, the government's equity participation level still remained high. Government agencies still held equities in four (*Woori, Korea First, Korea Exchange,* and *Hana*) of the eight banks that were still in business. Among these four banks, a decrease in equity participation could be found in only two banks, *Hana* and *Korea Exchange*. As the public fund injection and financial restructuring continued from 1998 to 2003, private capital's participation in commercial banks fell drastically. At the same time, the government's participation in the banking sector increased. As public capital rapidly replaced private capital in the banking sector, bank privatization, which had allowed greater independence from the state since the 1980s, was completely reversed.

However, these figures do not tell the full story of how the state intervened in banks' decision-making as a majority shareholder. If the government had not participated in the management of banks through its ownership, "voluntary" restructurings of the relevant banks might have taken place. However, the following incident demonstrates that the restructuring process was begun by the government's direct intervention rather than the autonomous choices made by the banks in response to the market pressure.

For example, in July 1999 when the *Daewoo* Group, then the second largest *chaebol* in Korea in terms of asset size, was facing complete dismantlement, the government urged banks to buy *Daewoo*'s corporate bonds (Lee D. G., 2003). This forced purchase of corporate bonds dealt a serious blow to the financially vulnerable *Peace Bank*. As a result, it was absorbed into *Woori Bank* in 2000 (The Secretariat of the National Assembly, 2001: 19). In addition, during the early period of the public fund injection, many suspicions were raised that major banks including *Hana, Kookmin,* and *Chohung* had been merged by governmental coercion rather than voluntary restructuring (The Secretariat of the National Assembly, 2000).

Moreover, the government used a huge amount of the public fund to merge *Hanil Bank* and *the Commercial Bank of Korea* into a megasize state bank, the *Hanvit Bank*. According to the original restructuring plan, the nationalization of banks should have been temporary. The banks should have been privatized after their business regained stability. Nevertheless, the merger of the two large insolvent banks only made the situation worse. Since the merger increased not only the funding required but also the risk of takeover, it became more difficult to find a buyer with the desire and ability to manage the merged *Hanvit Bank* (Korea Institute of Finance, 2001: 183). This is one of unique features in Korea's restructuring process, in comparison to the other restructuring cases in which states intervene in order to wholly dismantle inefficient institutions and limit concentration of economic power.

Another unique characteristic is found in the fact that the state limited the scope of market participants in the restructuring process. The government's restructuring policy excluded any private industrial capital, especially the *chaebols*, from participation in the banks, which is the legacy of the past developmental state known as "the principle of separation of industrial and financial capital" (金産分離). This principle made the privatization of the once nationalized banks less feasible. In the midst of crisis, no other private capital but the *chaebol* was able to take over troubled banks. Thus, the restructuring process used the public fund injection only to consolidate the state's control over banks in the long run, rather than guaranteeing the independence and autonomy of banks in the near future.

How were nonbank financial institutions restructured with the public fund injection? Nonbanking financial institutions can be put into six categories: "merchant banking corporations," "securities companies," "insurance companies," "investment trust companies," "mutual savings," and "credit unions" (see Tables 7.3 and 7.4).[12] Their restructuring depended mainly on two institutional characteristics of each category: their relationship with the leading industrial capital and their function in the financial market.

Most studies of South Korean enterprises point out that the *chaebols*' expansion and diversification drives were mainly funded by the aggressive short-term borrowing (Lee Y. H., 2000; Ahn C. Y., 2001; Cherry, 2005). As Table 7.6 shows, the leading industrial firms had maintained a high level of dependency on short-term borrowing until the crisis. For corporations, short-term borrowing such as direct loans

Table 7.6 Composition of top 30 *chaebols*' borrowings by year, 1991–2000 (unit: %)

	Short-term borrowings	Current Maturities of noncurrent liabilities	Long-term borrowings	Bonds payable	Total (trillion KRW)
1991	38.0	13.7	27.8	20.6	100.0 (70.0)
1992	41.8	16.3	24.9	17.0	100.0 (84.8)
1993	42.5	14.5	23.9	19.1	100.0 (92.4)
1994	41.7	13.8	23.5	21.0	100.0 (105.3)
1995	42.8	14.7	21.2	21.4	100.0 (129.9)
1996	41.7	14.0	22.0	22.3	100.0 (166.1)
1997	41.7	13.9	22.8	21.6	100.0 (228.9)
1998	31.4	16.8	18.4	33.4	100.0 (240.9)
1999	26.5	22.6	20.6	30.4	100.0 (171.0)
2000	27.0	30.3	17.3	25.3	100.0 (144.4)

Source: Korea Investors Service Inc. (www.kisline.com searched on December 1, 2003).
Note: Trillion Korean *won* = billion USD (at exchange rate of 1,000 KRW, spring 2008).

from financial institutions or bill discounts was more convenient than long-term borrowing. Using corporate bonds or stock as collateral meant meeting complicated terms, since the size of issuance of corporate bonds or stocks was strictly limited and tightly controlled by the government. For these reasons, business corporations could not help but become subordinate to nonbanking financial institutions that supplied short-term loans.

It would be more convenient for the corporations if they owned the financial institutions in order to supply their short-term borrowings. However, under the government's principle of "the separation of industrial and financial capital," ownership of financial institutions, especially banks, by industrial capital is strictly regulated. Therefore, the corporations tried to acquire nonbanking financial institutions that had easier ownership regulations to secure a continued supply of short-term financing.

However, as the financial crisis deepened, industrial capital's aggressive short-term borrowing and participation in the nonbanking financial institutions became the target of government concern. The more connections the nonbanking financial institutions had with the industrial capital, and the more liquidity they supplied to it, the harsher the extent of restructuring imposed on them. It is merchant banking corporations that met perfectly the two conditions, short-term finance supply and eased ownership regulation, in the Korean financial capital market.

The main business of the merchant banking corporations was short-term financing. Furthermore, because access to merchant banking corporations was the least limited among the six categories of nonbanking financial institutions, the industrial capital preferred them to other financial institutions and actively participated in their governance. Not surprisingly, merchant banking corporations became the main target of financial restructuring. The number of these institutions was 30 in late 1997 but fell down to 2 as of June 2003 (Table 7.3).

How about nonbanking institutions other than merchant banking corporations? As shown in Table 7.3, the number of insurance companies remains stable, and the number of securities companies and investment trust companies has increased from 1997 to 2003. Their functions concentrated on sales of marketable securities and bonds, which are typically categorized into long-term borrowings. Therefore, they could remain away from the harsh financial restructuring that swept all the national economy.

The initial plan for financial restructuring intended to reduce the high corporate debt–equity ratio, as well as to mitigate aggressive diversification and expansion of the corporate sectors based on short-term borrowings. Its target was to minimize the financial risk in the corporate sectors. As intended, the category of merchant banking corporations, which mainly deal with short-term borrowings, had drastically decreased. This plan and result concurred with the state's intention to induce the financial market to long-term-based borrowings that the state could easily manage and control. Such a transformation of Korean financial market meant the revival of the past Korean developmental model, which rendered high level of state autonomy over the industrial capital through the control on financial capital. As such, public fund policy was utilized once again as means to re-strengthen state autonomy that has been weakened since the liberalization in 1993.

However, overall financial restructuring process brought about an important but unintended outcome to the industrial capital. Financial market transformation centered on long-term borrowings meant that corporate finances were more accessible to large-sized corporations than small- or mid-sized corporations. It is because companies had to meet complicated conditions with respect to asset size, sales volumes, and debt–equity ratios in order to issue securities or bonds for corporate finance. Small- and mid-sized corporations could not easily fulfill these conditions. In other words, the financial restructuring turned out to be more favorable to large industrial capitals. Moreover, mutual savings and credit unions, which had more relationships with the lower-income bracket and small- or mid-sized corporations, drastically shrank from 1997 to 2006 (Table 7.3). Consequently, financial restructuring through the public fund produced a financial market more favorable to the large industrial corporations. This outcome has a close relationship with the intensified concentration of economic power into *chaebols*, which are mostly large industrial corporations, after the restructuring.

Corporate Restructuring through Financial Restructuring

This section examines the restructuring process of the financial sector through the public fund provision in the corporate sector. Table 7.7 summarizes the liabilities outstanding in the corporate sector from 1997 to 2002, which shows how the corporate sector mobilized financial resources. Among the listed items, "long-term securities," "government loans," and "other equities" belong to direct financing, while "loans by financial institutions" (A) shows the outstanding of liabilities through indirect financing. This item is closely related to financial restructuring. The absolute value of the subtotal of "loans by financial institutions" remained relatively stable across the years. However, "bank loans" (B) have gradually increased from 48.0% in 1997 to 62.4% in 2002. This increase is exceptional considering that the portions of other loans by nonbanking financial institutions such as "insurance companies' loans" and "merchant banking corporation loans" have decreased.[13]

This decrease can be interpreted as an indicator that shows corporations' increased dependence on bank loans. After financial restructuring, corporations could no longer borrow short-term debt from nonbanking financial institutions. They were therefore forced to rely on banks that were under government control as discussed previously. The corporate sector also came under indirect control by the state. This situation only strengthened state autonomy over domestic capital.

These circumstances are not so different from the stereotype of the past developmental state model. The injection of public funds into the financial sector, as well as the corporations' reliance upon the financial sector, especially upon the banks, is similar to the previous coalition of "the state–financial capital (banks)–industrial capital (*chaebol*)." Ironically, the concentration of economic power, a key feature of the developmental state model, reappears as an outcome

Table 7.7 Corporate sector's financial liabilities outstanding, 1997–2002

	1997	1998	1999	2000	2001	2002
Loans by financial institutions (A) (%)	335.8 (100.0)	312.3 (100.0)	312.6 (100.0)	326.8 (100.0)	327.9 (100.0)	389.0 (100.0)
BOK (%)	0.0 (0.0)	0.4 (0.1)	0.4 (0.1)	0.4 (0.1)	0.6 (0.2)	1.0 (0.3)
Bank (B) (%)	161.1 (48.0)	156.3 (50.1)	170.7 (54.6)	185.0 (56.6)	188.8 (57.6)	242.7 (62.4)
Insurance company (%)	26.5 (7.9)	20.8 (6.6)	21.0 (6.7)	22.2 (6.8)	20.7 (6.3)	21.4 (5.5)
Merchant Banking Corp. (%)	18.3 (5.5)	12.1 (3.9)	10.8 (3.4)	4.9 (1.5)	3.9 (1.2)	2.8 (0.7)
Credit-specialized financial institution (%)	0.0 (0.0)	0.0 (0.0)	0.0 (0.0)	15.7 (4.8)	16.6 (5.1)	18.0 (4.6)
Others (%)	129.8 (38.7)	122.6 (39.3)	109.7 (35.1)	98.7 (30.2)	97.3 (29.7)	103.3 (26.6)
Long-term securities	173.9	216.4	213.1	200.4	218.5	209.9
Government loans	7.3	8.2	9.9	14.7	15.3	16.8
Other equities	25.1	26.3	28.9	33.6	39.6	42.5
Miscellaneous liabilities	390.6	375.3	409.4	458.1	490.3	538.1
Total	932.6	938.4	973.8	1033.7	1091.6	1197.3

Source: Bank of Korea (www.bok.or.kr, searched on December 1, 2003).
Unit: Trillion Korean *won* (billion USD, at exchange rate of 1,000 KRW, spring 2008).

of financial restructuring with the public fund. As Table 7.8 shows, the total assets and sales of the leading corporate groups gradually increased. This increase can be interpreted as an indirect outcome of state intervention triggered by the crisis. When comparing the assets and sales of the leading corporate groups to the grass domestic product (GDP), economic power apparently has become concentrated in a small number of large companies.

The reappearance of concentrated economic power was brought about because the government solved problems of bad corporate loans and poor assets in the financial sector with the injection of public funds. At the same time, the financial institutions, under the strong

Table 7.8 Assets and sales of top 50 and 200 companies

		1991	1996	2001	2006
Assets	Top 50	125.4 (55.5)	277.4 (61.8)	422.2 (67.9)	549.5 (64.8)
	Top 200	190.1 (84.1)	428.1 (95.4)	629.8 (101.2)	799.9 (94.3)
Sales	Top 50	86.6 (38.3)	220.3 (49.1)	338.3 (54.4)	482.7 (56.9)
	Top 200	159.2 (70.5)	352.3 (78.5)	538.0 (86.5)	703.3 (82.9)

Source: Kim, S.-J. (2008: 69).
*Numbers in parentheses are the ratios to GDP.
Unit: Trillion Korean *won* (billion USD, at exchange rate of 1,000 KRW, spring 2008).

restructuring process by the government, preferred larger companies to small- or mid-sized companies. The financial institutions realized that the latter were too risky for investments or loans because of the new criteria adopted by the financial restructuring process.

The initial plan of the public fund was the fundamental reform of the South Korean economy by resolving the problem of debt-financed expansion and high debt–equity ratio of *chaebols* and dismantling the concentration of economic power, which was once condemned as the ultimate cause of the crisis (Cherry, 2005). However, the restructuring process only revived the concentration of economic power in *chaebols*. How should we interpret this irony?

This failure can be considered a failure of restructuring, including the public fund policy. However, in another sense, it can be a corollary of the state's intention to strengthen its control over financial and industrial capital through the extended financial resources provided by the public fund. The state intervened in the market on the basis of expanded financial resources that resulted from the crisis. This intervention limited the financial beneficiaries to a relatively few large companies according to its financial policies and preferences. Allowing *chaebols* to survive, and even to concentrate economic power, can be interpreted as a sign of weakened state autonomy because *chaebols* are the dominant economic forces that possibly challenge state power. However, considering the fact that *chaebols* could not but lose most of their own independent financial institutions and gradually became subject to government-dependent banking sectors, this seeming failure can be evidence of strengthened state autonomy over *chaebols*. As far as state autonomy is concerned, it seems the past developmental state model has not been transformed at all. Instead, it was revived and strengthened during the financial crisis.

How did the state, with its re-strengthened autonomy, intervene in the market and manage the public fund? In spite of its strengthened autonomy, the state might still fail to acquire the necessary efficiency in carrying out these tasks. This argument can be proved to be the case by examining the changes in state capacity through the public fund recovery procedure: in contrast to the developmental state, the post-crisis Korean state enjoyed autonomy yet lacked capacity.

Supervision and Recovery of the Public Fund: The Weakening of State Capacity

As stated above, this chapter defines state capacity as the state's ability to discipline others through the independent bureaucracy. State capacity can be divided into internal and external dimensions. The internal dimension refers to the capacity to preside over other state economic policy agencies, whereas the external dimension refers to the capacity to discipline private capitalists and supervise their performance in pursuit of policy goals.

Internal Dimensions of State Capacity: The Absence of Bureaucratic Cohesion

The distribution of authority and bureaucratic cohesion among relevant agencies is the critical index in evaluating state capacity. Chibber (2002) argues that the hierarchical distribution of authority minimizes intra-state governmental conflicts over limited resources and enhances bureaucratic cohesion in a consistently and efficiently implementing strategic policy. To explore relationships among bureaucratic agencies related to the public fund policy, this chapter separates the period into two using the year 2000 as the point of separation. This year was when the *Public Fund Oversight Special Act* (Special Act) was enacted. Due to the enactment of the Special Act, agencies and actors assuming responsibility for the management and operation of public fund changed significantly.

Before the enactment of the Special Act, the management system of the public fund was a temporary quick fix without a long-term plan or legal support. This management style was designed just for coping with the emergent crisis. Facing an unprecedented crisis, the government established a new organization to deal with the emerging economic problems, including the public fund. In 1998, the government replaced the Economic Minister Meeting with the Economic Policy Coordination Meeting (EPCM)[14] under the President. This change allowed the President to directly control all economic policy. These meetings discussed pending economic issues with various experts and provided the road map for major economic policies.

EPCM was a consultative body, not a legally constituted committee. Therefore, it had no legal duty or responsibility to keep official minutes. However, major national issues and economic policies were decided at these unofficial meetings during the Kim Dae Jung regime. Policies decided at these informal meetings were formally submitted to a Cabinet meeting by MOFE and thereafter were sent to the National Assembly for approval. The public fund policy was not an exception.

Figure 7.1 summarizes the hierarchy of the institutional arrangement of bureaucratic agencies that were related to the public fund policy before the Special Act. As shown in the figure, EPCM, MOFE, and the Financial Supervisory Commission made decisions about the public fund policy, whereas the Financial Supervisory Service, KAMCO, and KDIC implemented the policy. As such, there was fragmentation of the administrative powers and the authorities concerned with the public fund.

The most serious problem was that there was no formal and independent agency that was charged with or responsible for the public fund policy. The most influential body, EPCM, was the subcommittee that dealt with the "comprehensive" direction of economic policies and, therefore, could not limit itself only to the public fund. In addition, laws and regulations regarding the public fund's management, such as the Depositor Protection Act and Regulation on Financial Institutions to Promote Corporate Restructuring, were pertinent to each relevant agency. However, no integrated agency existed to manage the overall operation of the public fund.

Moreover, the unofficial status of EPCM did not legitimize its right for intervention in the public fund's management. The absence of an independent and responsible agency caused many problems (Lim W. H., 2003). Confusion over the policy developed as this informal subcommittee intervened in the management of the public fund. For example, at the end of 1999, when the *Daewoo* crisis broke, the government committed an imprudent decision in dealing with the bad loans of *Daewoo* (The Secretariat of the National Assembly 2001: 19). The government followed political interests that violated market principles.

1997 FINANCIAL CRISIS AND THE PUBLIC FUND

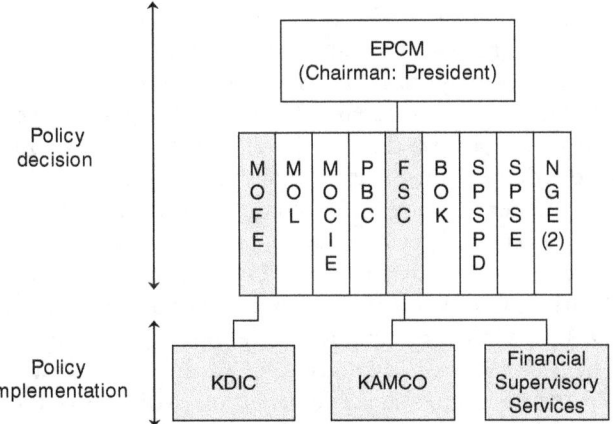

EPCM: Economic Policy Coordination Meeting
MOFE: Ministry of Finance and Economy, Minister
MOL: Ministry of Labor, Minister
MOCIE: Ministry of Commerce, Industry, and Energy, Minister
PBC: Chairman of Planning and Budget Committee, Chairman
FSC: Chairman of the Financial Supervisory Commission, Chairman
BOK: Bank of Korea, Governor
SPSPD: Senior Presidential Secretary for Policy Design
SPSE: Senior Presidential Secretary for Economy
NGE: Non-Governmental Experts (two)
KDIC: Korea Deposit Insurance Corporation
KAMCO: Korea Asset Management Corporation

Figure 7.1 Arrangement of bureaucratic agencies, before the enactment of the Public Fund Oversight Special Act, 2000

As the 2000 general election approached, the government, led by an ideological debate in political circles, injected public funds without consistent and coherent principles. The financial market passively responded to the government's restructuring due to distrust in the government's policy, which in turn caused the failure of the overall public fund policy. All these problems in the first round of the public fund naturally resulted from the fragmentation of authority and the absence of a nodal agency. It also confirmed the institutional inadequacy of government agencies in charge of the public fund.

The need to establish a public fund management system with more clearly defined rights and duties and with more structure arose. Also, some claimed that an autonomous agency, independent from the government, should supervise the operation and management of the public fund (Ministry of Finance and Economy and the Financial Supervisory Commission, 2001). To make up for the weakness in the public fund management system, the Special Act was enacted in 2000. This Special Act bestowed authority and responsibility to the newly established PFOC. Figure 7.2 summarizes the hierarchy and institutional arrangement among bureaucratic agencies related to the public fund policy after the Special Act.

This Special Act clearly defined PFOC as a nodal agency with hierarchical authority and control over other agencies. Under the Special Act, MOFE was in charge of public fund raising and overall management. The secretariat of PFOC, KAMCO, and KDIC was in charge of public fund injection and implementation (Ministry of Finance and Economy and the Financial Supervisory Commission, 2006).

However, a comparison of the arrangement before and after the Special Act enactment shows that responsibility and authority involving the public fund became increasingly horizontally fragmented. The two cochairmen, the Minister of MOFE and one nongovernment expert, were arranged horizontally in the decision-making process with equal authority and responsibility. Moreover, even though MOFE had secured the hierarchical initiative, there was no clear arrangement of authority among the relevant agencies: Ministry of Planning and Budget (MPB), Financial Supervisory Commission (FSC), the President, the National Assembly, the Supreme Court, and the five nongovernment experts. Thus, it was difficult to reach agreement on the conflicting issues.

This arrangement might have had an advantage in collecting public opinion and reflecting it on policy. At the same time, it lacked the necessary specialization and consistency in policy formulation. The participation of agencies, such as the Cheong Wa Dae (Blue House) presidential office, the Supreme Court, and the National Assembly, hindered coherent policy and bureaucratic rationality because they did not necessarily share the same policy orientation and direction in PFOC. In terms of bureaucratic cohesion, the fragmentation of authority and responsibility may have led to conflicts among agencies and inefficient policy implementation.

Above all, as KAMCO belonged to FSC and KDIC belonged to MOFE, the authorities in policy decision branches as well as policy implementation departments remained fragmented, which caused conflicts among agencies. The authority of two administrative bodies, KAMCO and KDIC, had been weakened to nothing more than implementing agencies after the passage of the Special Act. In spite

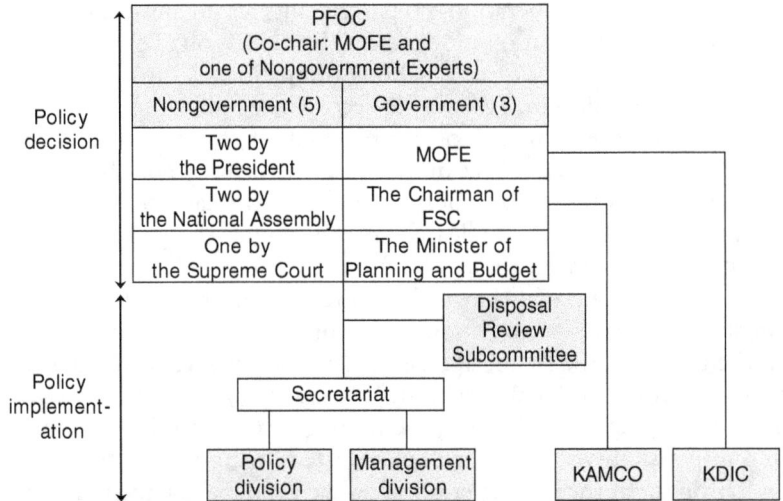

PFOC: Public Fund Oversight Committee
MOFE: Ministry of Finance and Economy, Minister
FSC: Financial Supervisory Commission
KDIC: Korea Deposit Insurance Corporation
KAMCO: Korea Asset Management Corporation

Figure 7.2 Arrangement of bureaucratic agencies, after the enactment of the Public Fund Oversight Special Act, 2000

of the establishment of a nodal agency, PFOC, the problems of fragmented authority and responsibility among the agencies could not be solved. The participation of various agencies that did not share the same policy commitment caused inefficiency in managing the public funds and also failed to specify who should take responsibility in case of any policy failure.

These problems were realized in the case of the illegal purchase of the *Korea Exchange Bank (KEB)* at a below-market price by the American private equity fund, Lone Star.[15] This case proved that an official of MOFE had artificially undervalued the bank's assets and had exaggerated its financial difficulties in order to sell it at a below-market price to an unqualified nonbanking institution. This episode disclosed the weaknesses in the institutional arrangement surrounding the public fund rather than individual corruption or moral hazard.

In the absence of agencies with administrative and bureaucratic expertise, the sale of *KEB* was decided by MOFE alone. In over five months of policy deliberation, no participants raised any questions or expressed any different opinions to MOFE's decision. They preferred easy and short-term means of selling ailing financial institutions to any buyer when deciding the way to recover the public fund. They did not favor long-term means of normalizing these institutions under their own supervision. The more urgent issue was not that financial institutions normalized business but that they avoided blame. As details of this case were released to the public, the participants in the policy decision on the public fund tried to avoid their responsibilities by insisting that they had no direct connection with the case. Most of the banks were nationalized through public fund injection in the course of the financial crisis. They were then re-privatized and revealed similar problems, including the *Chohung Bank* and the *Korea First (Cheil) Bank*. Ultimately, the fragmented structure of authority and responsibility resulted in a huge waste of national wealth.

Throughout the whole period of public fund management, including both the periods before and after the Special Act, the government failed to establish the necessary independent bureaucratic agency with responsibility and authority appropriate for this policy initiative. The establishment of such an agency would have rendered the government capable of presiding over the bureaucratic agencies. In effect, the lack of cohesion and the fragmentation of authority among the agencies connected with the public fund show the weakening of the state capacity over other intra-state agencies. Compared with developmental state model, this is a drastically contrasting feature of the restructuring process. The absence of the independent bureaucracy prohibited the government to implement policy goals against domestic capital as well as society at large, and to be able to discipline capital.

External Dimensions of State Capacity: The Absence of Discipline

The following functions are all critical for the successful implementation of the public fund policy. The state must perform an investigation on the insolvency of recipient financial institutions, decide the most rational form of support, manage the recipient institutions to implement memorandum of understandings (MOUs), and supervise the recipient institution by taking strict measures against whoever is responsible for corporate insolvency. In other words, these strategies demonstrate the state's overall ability to discipline capital. Since these strategies allowed the state to control nonstate bodies, such as financial and industrial capital, they can be used as an indicator to evaluate the external dimension of the state's capacity.

Recovery performance mainly depended on the type of injection (see Table 7.4). In cases of capital contribution and deposit payoffs, it was impossible to recover public funds injected, since these funds were injected in order to make up for the financial losses of depositors or investors of bankrupt institutions. Its recovery measure was limited to bankruptcy dividends. Capital contribution and deposit payoffs were not under the government's supervision and control. In the case of the purchase of assets and NPLs, the government recovered public fund by selling the assets acquired. The government's intervention in supervising the institutions was not needed, because the public fund could be recovered by sales of assets or corporate bonds at a cost substantially lower than the fair market value. In short, these recovery measures did not require the state to discipline financial institutions with regulation and supervision in order to enhance recovery performance.

However, recovery performance depended on enhancement of corporate efficiency in the case of equity participation. This can be achieved by the government's management and supervision of recipient financial institutions and close cooperation between these financial institutions and the government. In this sense, the recovery performance of equity participation could be used as an indicator to evaluate the government's ability to manage and supervise, that is, the state capability to discipline private capital.

Table 7.9 shows the performance of the public fund collection by recovery type. Despite the fact that 63.5 trillion Korean *won*, 37.7% of the total public fund, was injected as equity participation (Table 7.4), its collected sum amounted to only 14.5 trillion Korean *won*, 18.2% of the total collected public fund in June 2006. An absolute majority of the recovered public fund, 48.8 trillion Korean *won* (61.3% of total recovery), was collected through sales of corporate assets, including bonds and securities.

It is noteworthy that asset sales' recovery was not necessarily related to the normalization of financial institutions or the state's disciplinary capacity. Asset sales were irrelevant to operational profit and therefore cannot serve as a gauge for business normalization and the resolution of liabilities. These figures further demonstrate the failure of the government's role in managing and supervising public fund policy.

The poor performance of "equity participation collection" can be explained in two ways. The public fund was injected into financial

Table 7.9 Public fund recovery by types (Nov. 1997–Jun. 2006)

	Total injection (A)	Type of recovery				Recovery ratio (B/A, %)
		Equity participation collection[1]	Bankruptcy dividends collection[2]	Asset sales collection[3] *	Total recovery (B)	
Total (%)	168.3	14.5 (18.2)	16.3 (20.5)	48.8 (61.3)	79.6 (100)	47.3

Source: The Ministry of Finance and Economy & the Financial Supervisory Commission (2006: 266).
Unit: Trillion Korean *won* (billion US$ at exchange rate of US$1 = 1,000 KW as of 2007).
Note:
1) Equity participation collection 14.5 = 12.8 (KDIC) + 1.7 (Govt).
2) Bankruptcy dividends collection 16.3 = 16.3 (KDIC).
3) Asset sales collection 48.8 = 5.4 (KDIC) + 36.7 (KAMCO) + 6.6 (Govt).
* Asset sales collection includes share buybacks and reimbursement of loans.

institutions that showed less possibility of rehabilitation because the government failed to examine the precise extent of corporate insolvency. If the public fund was injected properly into the financial institutions with a high possibility of rehabilitation, the government's role in managing and supervising those financial institutions in order to enhance recovery performance was inadequate. Both of the two interpretations reveal the lack of discipline and the state's weak capacity.

Conclusion: The Legacy of the Developmental State

Now we are back to our initial question: "Did the 1997 Asian financial crisis transform the South Korean developmental state?" In one sense, the answer is "no." The state's intervention after the financial crisis reflected its autonomy by gaining control over financial resources and strengthening its dominance over industrial capital. Ironically, the state tried to overcome the crisis by dismantling the triple alliance among "the state, financial capital, and industrial capital." However, it turned out that the historical path dependency of the Korean developmental state defined the way it intervened in the economy and maintained this relationship.

Nevertheless, the answer is "yes" at the same time because the state after the crisis, in spite of its increased autonomy, failed to govern and discipline the market and showed a vacuum in the state's capacity. We suggest two aspects of weakening state capacity, which resulted in policy failure. Fragility in bureaucratic cohesion and the fragmented arrangement of authority among bureaucratic bodies resulted in the internal failure of policy decision-making and lack of performance in the recovery of public funds. This failure was closely related to the absence of control over domestic capital, that is, a weakened external capacity to discipline the economy.

The most distinctive characteristic of the Kim Dae Jung government's economic restructuring was the dualism in "state-led reform" aimed at the "separation of the state and the market" (Mo J. R. and Moon C. I., 2003). This dualism of the state was embodied in the fact that the government intervened strongly in the financial market with policy initiatives and financial resources, while withdrawing from the market in regards to management of supported banks and firms (Cherry, 2005). In other words, the state intervened strongly with financial support, but played a weak role in disciplining financial and the industrial capital (Lee Y. H., 2000). This can be summarized as "financial support without discipline," which contrasts to the "financial support with discipline" that characterized the developmental state.

Financial support without discipline, that is, state autonomy not accompanied with state capacity, results in the overall failure of the state intervention. Eventually it caused a financial deficit that imposed a heavy burden on the taxpayers and triggered an increase in foreign debt. This weakened state capacity also caused a decline in state autonomy. State intervention, including the public fund, garners only distrust and resistance from both society and the market.

These findings suggest many implications for the appropriate role and the ability of the nation-state in the light of globalization. Some insist the role of the nation-state is still important despite the globalized economy (Wade, 1996; Shin J. S. and Chang H. J., 2003; Shin J. S., 2005b). Others argue the nation-state should give way to the market in governing the economy (Frankel, 2000). This study champions the former, the importance of appropriate state intervention. The claim that globalization will make the nation-state powerless is only a myth (Weiss, 1998). As seen in the case of the public fund in South Korea, the financial crisis and globalization offer an opportunity to strengthen the state autonomy and show it is even necessary.

However, our analysis also warns that market-opening policies may not succeed without the internal and external capacities to support state autonomy. With the advent of globalization, many scholars have tried to choose between two alternatives. These alternatives include transformation to a regulative state or a path that depends on the developmental state (Stubbs, 2009). Today 15 years have passed since the Asian financial crisis, and globalization never shrinks the role of nation-states. Instead, it creates new demands for the intervention of the state (Lee K. and Kim B. Y., 2009) and warrants renewed appreciation of the accomplishments of the East Asian developmental state.

Notes

1. Various terms, such as "guidance," "governing," "discipline," and "patrimonialism," have been used to explain the strong market intervention of the state (Johnson, 1982; Wade, 1990; Amsden, 1989; Lew S. C., 2000).
2. This agency is conceptualized as a "nodal agency" or "pilot agency" (Wade, 1990; Chibber, 2002).
3. This approach may have a certain limitation since it highlights only the internal aspect of state autonomy. Surely, the mobilization of the public fund includes foreign loans from international economic organizations, which can affect the external aspects of state autonomy. However, the substantive sum of foreign loans was US$17 million (2 hundred million from ADB and 15 hundred million from ABRD), which made up only 0.92% of the total sum of the public fund. Therefore, it is neither feasible nor possible to evaluate changes in the external aspect of state autonomy through the public fund.
4. The Korea Asset Management Corporation (KAMCO) was established by the government based on the Korea Development Act in 1965. Its major roles were the management and operation of nonperforming assets (NPAs) fund, the acquisition and resolution of NPAs from financial institutions, and implementation of workout programs for distressed companies. The Korea Deposit Insurance Corporation (KDIC) was established by the government in 1995. Its primary goal was the protection of depositors' funds at KDIC-insured financial institutions. By providing a partial deposit protection system and by acting as the guarantor of depositors' funds, the KDIC, in cooperation with other agencies, strove to provide a vital financial safety net in order to help maintain the stability of the nation's financial system. These two agencies took the critical role in implementing public fund policy.
5. We cannot deny that the US$57 billion of foreign loans from IMF in November 1997 was critical in coping with the economic crisis. However, the bulk of IMF money was drained quickly to defend the local currency, leaving no leftover for the corporate restructuring process.
6. For example, the National Assembly's Finance and Economy Committee unanimously passed a bill on the public fund of 64 trillion Korean *won* submitted by the government on August 28, 1998, and both the ruling and opposition parties also unanimously passed this on September 2, 1998. Hence, a government-drafted bill was passed in less than a week without a detailed examination and discussion.

7. To reuse the recovered public fund, in law, the consent of the National Assembly was required. However, this principle was ignored in practice.
8. The Government Funds Management Fund (*Kong'gong cha'gŭm kwalli kigŭm*, 公共資金管理基金) Committee was established in 1993 to manage government bonds, foreign loans, public pension, and national property. This committee was composed of 15 members, including the Minister of MOFE (as chairman), the Governor of the Bank of Korea, the Minister of the Ministry of Labor, and so on.
9. For more explanation about the Public Fund Oversight Committee (PFOC), see Figure 7.2.
10. One trillion Korean *won* approximately equals one billion US Dollars, at exchange rate of 1,000 KW in spring 2008.
11. Almost half of *Korea Exchange Bank* was owned by the Bank of Korea. However, BOK ownership does not belong to the category of government ownership because BOK is supposed to be independent from the government.
12. "Leasing companies" in Table 7.3 and "foreign financial institutions" in Table 7.4 are excluded, because the amounts of public funds that they received are too small to be discussed here.
13. The exceptional increase in long-term securities since 1998 is a corollary of financial restructuring that cut off the corporations' mobilization of financial capital from short-term debt. As such, one of the alternatives left to the corporate sector was to mobilize the long-term capital by issuing corporate bonds and stocks. However, this figure did not show any further expansion after 1998 because the amount of issuance cannot exceed given ceiling limit set by the government.
14. EPCM was composed of the President (as chairman); the Minister of Economy and Finance; the Minister of Labor; the Minister of Commerce, Industry and Energy; the Chairman of the Financial Supervisory Commission; the Chairman of Planning and Budget Committee; the Governor of the Bank of Korea; the Senior Presidential Secretary for Policy Design; the Senior Presidential Secretary for Economics; and two Non-Governmental Experts.
15. Byun Yang-ho, a former official at the Ministry of Finance and Economy, and Lee Gang-won, former president of Korea Exchange Bank (KEB), allegedly acted in collusion with Lone Star Fund to artificially lower the bank's BIS ratio so that Lone Star Fund, as a nonbanking institution, would qualify to buy the KEB at a below-market price. Because Lone Star Fund was not a financial institution, according to the Bank Law, Lone Star Fund could not be the major shareholder of the KEB (*Seoul Daily*, April 25, 2006; *Kukmin Daily*, June 20, 2006; *Hankyoreh Daily*, December 11, 2006).

Conclusion

Chapter 8

Moral Economy of Growth

Wrap up of Arguments and Findings in Each Chapter

The introductory chapter 1 explains the missing links in understanding the Korean development. In particular, the embeddedness among cultural, social, and political dimensions is emphasized to suggest that the most fundamental core of Korean development was the articulated match of a strong state and a strong society. At the end of the chapter, book organization and arguments of each chapter are offered.

Chapter 2 argues for the positive role of Confucian tradition in Korea. It examines the religious significance inherent in the Confucian value of filial piety and illustrates how the value came to be a powerful economic motive among Koreans. The religious imperative of filial piety, which entails remembering and representing one's ancestors, acts as an important spiritual ethos for Koreans to become economically competitive by providing a self-sacrificing work ethic and zeal for education. Three pressures significantly influence remembering and representing ancestors in the modern context: developmental, successive, and collective. It emerges that filial piety did not stop at being merely an ethical standard; it was the fundamental basis for a macro-social dynamic closely linked to the development of capitalism in Korea.

Chapter 3 explains how affective networks contributed positively to the development of a "strong society" in Korea. It starts by offering a critical review on existing research trends regarding familial, school-based, and regional affective networks, and argues that neither affective networks are closed inner-groups nor do they necessarily lower social efficiency; they are not antagonistic with civic engagement. Further evidence is given to explain historic-cultural factors involved in the continuing proliferation of affective networks in modern Korea. Confucian worldview supporting affective networks has shown a strong tendency to condemn cronyism and corruption, and it provides ground to assert that affective networks based on human relations are a form of social capital that enriches trust and reciprocity for modern society.

Chapter 4 clarifies that affective networks, into which characteristics of Confucian culture have strongly infiltrated, are deeply rooted in the nonprofit and nongovernmental sectors in Korea. Strong attachment and devotion to affective networks among Koreans can only be understood when historic-cultural factors are taken into account. Affective networks are influential because they are able to maintain spontaneous reciprocity, particularly "generalized reciprocity" that mutually benefits members and their families in times of need. In addition, their roles and functions are extended to penetrate deeply into the state and market sectors. Finally, this chapter goes back to history to clarify that the scholar networks, especially those formed by literati outside state office, assumed the role of a check upon state power.

Chapter 5 highlights "Confucian capitalism," which exemplified state-led industrialization in East Asia, emerged from a historical context entirely different from that of the West. Civil society and free markets in the Western mode were unnecessary for the development of Confucian capitalism. Instead, state bureaucrats organized capitalism in such a way that policy decisions of state superseded decision-makings of businesses and the private sector was mobilized around the needs and plans of the state through traditional Confucian affective networks. The term "state–business collusion" describes this structural characteristic of Confucian capitalism. However, the collusion has been constantly monitored by media and intellectuals who are the heirs of the former Confucian literati. These checks and balances efficiently and effectively minimize negative consequences of the collusion.

Chapter 6 offers a challenge to the existing literature on economic development that has attributed the economic success of Korea to the role of the "strong state." It has been widely accepted that, in contrast to the state, Korean society was weak and passive and was simply mobilized by a strong state. This chapter explains how Korea during the Park era was a showcase of synergy between a strong state and a strong society. The leader's value orientation at the macro-level and the responses of villages and business groups at the micro-level are investigated to illustrate these interactions. The conclusion suggests that the problem today is that there is no longer a strong state to match the ever-strong society in Korea.

Chapter 7 aims to answer a more concrete question—"did the 1997 financial crisis transform the South Korean developmental state?"—by examining the path that the Korean developmental state took after the 1997 crisis. It focuses on the "public fund" and the critical role of the state in overcoming the financial crisis. Failures in the restructuring process were not caused by state intervention in or of itself, but by improper state intervention. In this regard, globalization does not shrink the role of the nation-state. Rather, globalization demands proper intervention by the state with more autonomy and better capacity along the developmental path the state has followed.

Theoretical Underpinning of Affective Network on Trust and Social Capital

This book overviewed the long and complicated process of how Korea achieved economic development, in which the articulation of cultural, social, and political dimensions played critical roles. However, some would be skeptical about the viability of this model in the future environment of growing globalization. The current trend seems to decrease any room for the nation-state to maneuver in the gradually internationalized or globalized economy. However, as the US under the Obama administration has learned, the market failure from the Wall Street paradoxically provides an opportunity and necessity to strengthen the state's autonomy and capacity. Contrary to the views of those who proclaim the end of the nation-state, the advance of globalization demands a strengthened and more efficient state intervention (Wade, 1996; Weiss, 1998; Shin J. S., 2005b).

Leaving aside the viability of the Korean development model, many are doubtful as to whether other countries could replicate this model. Installing a certain model without considering the original context in which the model has to work would solve nothing. As explained throughout this book, considering sociocultural context is critical in understanding development process: thus, this concluding chapter underpins theoretical argument regarding affective networks from the perspective of social capital and trust.

Affective social relations have been ubiquitous in societies for centuries and have their own positive and negative effects (Hahm C. H. and Bell, 2004). Therefore, we must consider how to make use of their positive effects in a productive and cooperative way while minimizing their negative effects. Converting these relations into social capital within historical context is a critical issue: dismantling them would end up with a waste of valuable historical and sociocultural resources.

Offe (1999: 63–64) stresses the importance of "sense of belonging" in building trust. According to him, trust can be generated from symbolic representation of communities or pseudo-communities as well as familiarity and interaction of concrete persons. Invoking the shared belonging to some community and its presumably distinctive history, identity, or spirit can develop trust relationships. Here, communities he enumerates encompass an extended family, religious groups, a location, a college, service in a military unit, a nation, and so on. These various communities are exactly what we call affective networks and it means that sense of belonging to affective networks can contribute to the development of social capital by generating trust.

As such, affective networks themselves have nothing better or worse than civic associations or interest groups of civil society. Then, what is the virtue of affective networks that differentiates them from other organizational mechanisms? First of all, family relations and kinships are considered as the most fundamental form of social capital. Uslaner (2008: 109) takes a step further and stresses the importance of experience in building trust: "the most critical determinant of trust, especially in young people, is family life" because family values and structure shape their fundamental optimism and pessimism.

Moreover, trust thrives best under conditions of nonanonymity. "The conditions that make for the maintenance of trust are best met in relatively limited ranges of social activities and interaction, such as the family or kinship groups in which social interaction is regulated according to primordial and interpersonal criteria" (Offe, 1999: 55). Family is also the most outstanding group that internalizes the norm of generalized reciprocity: practices of inter- and intra-generational transfer of resources internalize the norm of generalized reciprocity.

The problem is how to extend "the range of trust beyond the narrow minimal scope of primordial units" of affective network (Offe 1999: 55), that is, how to overcome the amoral familism and build linkage with outside groups (Woolcock 1998). Facing this problem, institutionalists rely on trust-producing institutions. Zuker (1986) explains how institutional apparatuses and devices, such as notarization or insurance, contribute to the production of trust amid a collapsing social order at the early stage of capitalistic development in America. According to Zucker (1986), risk or social uncertainty about unexpected damages from malfeasant behaviors, such as cheating or contract violation, can be eased by the institution that prepares for the worst situation. All of them emphasize that building robust and trustworthy institutions is a precondition of trust, and call this trust "institution-based" or "institution-mediated" trust.

However, can we consider the trust, produced by institutions, a real trust? As many point out, the concept of trust presupposes risk and social uncertainty (Uslaner, 2008: 102). The situation, in which one does not have to consider risk and uncertainty, does not require real trust. In other words, "what can be taken for granted does not need to be trusted" (Offe, 1999: 66). This is the so-called first paradox of trust suggested by Yamagishi (Yamagishi, Cook, and Watabe, 1998: 165–166). The larger the social uncertainty and the more difficult the establishment of trust, the more trust is required. Paradoxically, expectation beyond doubt, such as family relations and natural phenomena, cannot be encompassed in the concept of trust. Yamagishi calls this expectation as "assurance" or "a sense of security," whereas Luhmann (1979) as "confidence." Both strictly distinguished it from trust. In this perspective, it is more appropriate to conceptualize institution-mediated trust as assurance.

In addition, there is a more fundamental problem of trust that institutionalists ignore. For institutions to generate trust, everyone should have the initial trust in those institutions. Then how and where do we acquire trust in those institutions from the first place? Institution never emerges spontaneously: it is the result of cooperation among various actors who expect benefits from it. Therefore, actors participating in collaboration to produce institutions are not free from the classical collective-action problem (Demsetz, 1967; Oberschall and Leifer, 1986; Ostrom, 1990). Like public goods, once the institutions are established, even free riders can enjoy the fruits from those institutions that provide universal trust for any individuals. This situation makes it easier for individuals to behave opportunistically, and in the end leads to a failure in producing the trust-producing institutions. To solve the collective-action dilemma in production of institutions, trust among actors to build institutions is absolutely required as a prerequisite.

Moreover, the mere existence of institution *per se* never guarantees generating universal trust. Institutional arrangements such as certification of an accountant or use of escrow accounts, brokers' commissions in stock market and real estate transactions, and premiums for insurance (Zucker, 1986: 65) can operate as a trust-producing institution only when trust in those institutions already exists. If some doubt that those institutions might be manipulated more favorably to a certain group, and if some cannot guarantee trust in the quality of institution such as fairness, competence, and consistency, institutions cannot produce universal trust.

The reliance on institutions is nothing more than the classic Hobbesian problem: "third-party enforcement" and impartial institutions themselves are public goods subject to the same dilemma that they aim to solve. Therefore, institutions are the product of *ex ante* trust in government, bureaucracy, or the state that makes those institutions. In other words, any institution is a product of trust, not *vice versa*. As Cohen (1999: 218–219) points out, "trust and generalized reciprocity are presupposed for the establishment of the institutions in the first place.... Institutions are dismissed as irrelevant to social trust because its genesis already presupposes social trust."

Affective networks suggest a clue to find answers for the problem indicated above. Communities with strong positive values, including trust in others, and ties that bind people to one another have more powerful norms of generalized reciprocity. Trust allows us to participate beyond selfish individual interests. It means that we downplay bad experiences and cooperate even when we are not sure that others will oblige (Uslaner, 1999: 122). This logic can be applied to any affective networks. Especially, affective networks offer the opportunities to test and learn trust and generalized reciprocity.

People are always careful about conceding trust because trusting someone has the possibility of risks and benefits at the same time. People who trust others are vulnerable to the breakdown of the trust relation. Persons who have more resources of trust relations can survive the contingency of the trust being disappointed by switching to other alternatives. Accordingly, the rich, the powerful, and the well informed can afford to trust. In other words, the more affluent a person is, the more easily he/she can trust and benefit from the trust. Here the apparent paradox is that "those who are most in need of trust cannot afford the risk involved, while those who need it least enjoy it most" (Offe, 1999: 53).

However, as a last resort, affective relations, which are ubiquitous as well as primordial, offer moral resources, when people get damage from mislocated trust or unrewarded with generalized reciprocity. In this sense, affective networks are stepping stone on which one can make cooperative relations with others in general. This function of last resort is exactly what institutionalists try to seek in impersonal institutions or institutionalization of distrust. As such, it can be argued that generalized reciprocity stems from a particular trust among concrete interpersonal relations. Affective networks are typical relations that are built on such trust but can develop into generalized reciprocity by learning.

The paradox of trust becomes more complex if we consider a more aggressive question of "do we really need universal trust to make democracy and market work better?" Granovetter (1985: 490) argues, through the concept of "embeddedness," that the concrete and intimate personal relations can generate trust and, hence, discourage malfeasance in the market. To solve the problem of trust, "embeddedness" does not appeal to over- or under-socialized norms of individuals. It implies that concrete interpersonal relations and the social structure, which these relations create, provide selfish individuals with trust and, hence, restrain their opportunistic behaviors.

In this context, regarding the development of democracy, it is necessary to rethink about the real nature of voluntary associations in northern Italy, which Putnam (1993a) considers as the backbone of civic engagement. Putnam argues that the foundation of civic culture is laid on frequent face-to-face contacts among villagers in their daily life illustrated in sports clubs, quilting gatherings, and church choirs. In other words, Putnam's civic associations arise from the trust that is created and accumulated through continued interaction with concrete persons whom they know for a considerable period of time (Offe, 1999: 50; Yamagishi and Yamagishi, 1994).

From this, we can infer that trust or trust learning based on mutual acquaintance makes voluntary participation and cooperation active. Therefore, what makes democracy work better may be personal trust among acquaintances rather than universal trust based on institutions. Those who can trust their neighbors can trust fellow citizens, that is, "others in general." This is why Putnam (1995) laments over America's declining social capital from the fact that traditional civic associations offering face-to-face interaction are decaying as "bowling alone" represents.

To summarize, universal trust created by institutions can be categorized into assurance or confidence rather than trust that assumes risk and social uncertainty. In order to produce trust-producing institutions, trust among agents or trust in the government has to be presupposed. Even though the universal trust is not impossible, it is possible only when a personal trust extends or evolves to a generalized trust. Accordingly, what makes democracy and market work better is interpersonal trust rooted in affective networks rather than universal trust mediated and generated by institutions.

Conclusion: Moral Economy

The moral economy or premodern economy of the underdeveloped countries has been synonymous with such words as crony capitalism, patronage or clientalism, bossism, nepotism, and affective networks, putting these countries on the other spectrum of economic rationality and efficiency. Such description suggests that those words insist on deeply engraved personal and traditional relationships, unable to overcome traditional obstacles to develop an effective economic and political system. Nevertheless, such logic does not fit to Korea's miracle, which occurred without eradicating Confucian tradition and affective networks. Therefore, explaining the Korean case requires better understanding of the moral economy and its function.

The heavy reliance on the policies and strategies of economic and political institutions when making plans for development may delude us from critical assessment of the historical context in which those policies and strategies are working. The scholars who emphasize the role of institutions often neglect culture in favor of anonymous market or depersonalized civil society. However, Korea shows an alternative path for survival: fitting traditional culture to modern economic and political institutions. It turns out that Confucian values and affective networks facilitate individuals to cooperate with each other (Ringmar, 2005).

Thus, affective networks that originated from the traditional culture can serve as a third option in facing demands from the hierarchical state or the impersonal market forces. *Chaebol*, business organization based on traditional family system and the main driving force of Korea's export in the competitive world market, possibly exemplifies the best articulation of cultural tradition and modern economy. Korea's political democratization is another example of productive institutionalization of affective networks because it was achieved with the coming of regional rivalries in presidential elections. Needless to say, articulations as such are not limited to politics or economy: education and welfare are dimensions that are more sensitive to affective social relations.

Experiments are needed to explicate potential benefits from traditional culture in mending the shortcomings of institutional devices such as the market and the state. A highly individualized and atomized modern society urges us to look into affective networks as a means to tie ourselves together again. Communitarian responsibility for members of a group, moral restraint on individual selfishness, and efforts to harmonize the interests of the individual and community are present in every traditional culture.

Moral economy has been employed mainly to explain unique features of premodern societies. The setting in which Mauss (1990[1925]) observed gifts giving and Scott (1976) witnessed irrational peasants and benevolent landlords is premodern and non-Western, devoid of a democratic state or capitalistic markets (Wilk and Cliggett, 2007). As such, moral economy was invented to explain seemingly irrational activities against one's private interests at micro-level (Geertz, 1973) and traditional or charismatic authority without modern legitimacy and rationality at the macro-level (Weber, 1946).

For modern observers, these features seem irrational and inefficient. Therefore, they conclude that moral economy would soon disappear as modern institutions, that is, capitalistic market and rational bureaucracy, evolve and diffuse. However, the Korean case defies such prediction. Its success was due to utilizing rather than overcoming tradition. Korea achieved its miraculous success in industrialization and democratization through the organized manifestation of moral economy by the state and market. This process cannot merely be evaluated by the conventional state theories and liberal economics. Instead, it should be explained by moral economy: disciplinary ethos based on generalized reciprocity.

Can this explanation apply to an extended connotation, or is this only applicable under a specific context in Korea? How does moral economy appeal to the modern societies? In fact, many scholars discovered that moral values have taken a significant role in modern capitalism as they recognize Puritan rationality since Max Weber or moral sentiments since Adam Smith (Zelizer, 2005; Gintis, Bowles, Boyd, and Fehr, 2005; Zak, 2008). Moral principles have guided members of the Western society throughout the development process. Therefore, we should acknowledge that "reciprocity" based on affective relation still remains an alternative source of organizing principle (Ostrom, 1990) to "market and hierarchy" (Williamson, 1973) or "exchange and redistribution" (Polanyi, 2001[1944]).

Certainly, the character of moral economy described in this book does not apply universally. However, every underdeveloped country maintains the very feature of social relations that are in common with Korean society. Hopefully, Korean case will provide some insight for other developing countries to find their own recipes incorporated with their sociocultural and historical contexts.

References in English Language

Ahn, Chung Young. 2001. "Financial and Corporate Sector Reform in South Korea: Toward a New Development Paradigm." Unpublished paper prepared for the MDT Workshop at Tokyo University.

Ames, Roger T. 1988. "Rites as Rights: The Confucian Alternative." In Leroy Rouner (ed.), *Human Rights and the World's Religions*. Notre Dame: University of Notre Dame Press.

Amsden, Alice. 1989. *Asia's Next Giant: South Korea and Late Industrialization*. New York: Oxford University Press.

———. 2000. *The Rise of "The Rest": Challenges to West from Late-Industrializing Economies*. New York and London: Oxford University Press.

Amsden, Alice H. and Yoon Dae Euh. 1993. "South Korea's 1980s Financial Reforms: Good-Bye Financial Repression (Maybe), Hello New Institutional Restraints." *World Development* 21(3): 379–390.

Anderson, Perry. 1974. *Lineages of the Absolutist State*. London: NLB.

Aoki, Masahiko, Hyung-Ki Kim, and Masahiro Okuno-Fujiwara. 1997. *The Role of Government in East Asian Economic Development*. Oxford: Clarendon Press.

Appelbaum, Richard P. and Jeffrey Henderson (eds.). 1992. *States and Development in the Asian Pacific Rim*. London and Newbury Park: Sage Publications.

Arneil, Barbara. 2006. *Diverse Communities: The Problem with Social Capital*. New York: Cambridge University Press.

Balassa, Bela. 1981. *The Newly Industrializing Countries in the World Economy*. New York: Pergamon Press.

Bank of Korea. 2010. *The Bank of Korea: A Sixty-Year History*. Seoul: Jeon-Kwang Printing Imposition.

Barette, Richard and Martin King Whyte. 1982. "Dependency Theory and Taiwan: Analysis of a Deviant Case." *American Journal of Sociology* 87(5): 1064–1089.

Bell, Daniel A. 1996. "The East Asian Challenge to Human Rights: Reflections on an East West Dialogue." *Human Rights Quarterly* 18(3): 641–667.

———. 2008. *Confucian Political Ethics*. Princeton, NJ: Princeton University Press.
Bell, Daniel and Chaibong Hahm (eds.). 2003. *Confucianism for the Modern World*. Cambridge and New York: Cambridge University Press.
Bellah, Robert. 1957. *Tokugawa Religion: The Cultural Root of Modern Japanese Capitalism*. New York: Free Press.
Berger, Mark and Douglas Borer. 1997. *The Rise of East Asia*. London: Routeledge.
Berger, Peter. 1988. "An East Asian Development Model?" In P. Berger and H. M. Hsiao (eds.), *In Search of an East Asian Development Model*. New Brunswick, NJ: Transaction Books.
Berry, Jeffrey M. 1989. *The Interest Group Society*. Boston: Scott, Foresman/Little Brown.
Bourdieu, Pierre. 1986. "The Forms of Capital." In J. G. Richardson (ed.), *Handbook of Theory and Research for Sociology of Education*, pp. 241–258. New York: Greenwood.
Brandt, Vincent. 1971. *A Korean Village between Farm and Sea*. Cambridge, MA: Harvard University Press.
Buchanan, James, Robert Tollison, and Gordon Tullock (eds.). 1980. *Towards a Theory of the Rent-Seeking Society*. College Station: Texas A&M University Press.
Callahan, William A. 1998. "Comparing the Discourse of Popular Politics in Korea and China." *Korea Journal* 38(1): 292–322.
Castiglione, Dario, Jan W. Van Deth, and Guglielmo Wolleb (eds.). 2008. *The Handbook of Social Capital*. London: Oxford University Press.
Chan, Joseph. 1997. "An Alternative View." *Journal of Democracy* 8(2): 35–48.
———. 1999. "A Confucian Perspective on Human Rights for Contemporary China." In J. R. Bauer and D. A. Bell (eds.), *The East Asian Challenge for Human Rights*, pp. 212–237. New York: Cambridge University Press.
Chang, Ha-Joon. 1993. "The Political Economy of Industrial Policy in Korea." *Cambridge Journal of Economics* 17(2): 131–157.
———. 1994. *The Political Economy of Industrial Policy*. New York: St. Martin's Press.
———. 1998. "Korea: The Misunderstood Crisis." *World Development* 26(8): 1555–1561.
———. 2002. *Kicking Away the Ladder: Development Strategy in Historical Perspective*. London: Anthem Press.
———. 2006. *The East Asian Development Experience: The Miracle, the Crisis and the Future*. London and New York: Zed Books.
———. (ed.). 2007. *Institutional Change and Economic Development*. New York: United Nations University Press.
——— and Ilene Grabel. 2004. *Reclaiming Development: An Economic Policy Handbook for Activists and Policymakers*. London: Zed Books.

Chang, Yun-Shik. 1980. "Changing Aspects of Hamlet Solidarity." In S. J. Park, T. Shin, and K. Z. Zo (eds.), *Economic Development and Social Change in Korea*, pp. 315–336. Frankfurt: Campus Verlag.

———. 1989a. "From Filial Piety to the Love of Children." In The Korean Christian Academy (ed.), *The World Community in Post-Industrial Society: Changing Families in the World Perspective*, pp. 77–94. Seoul: Wooseok Publishing Co.

———. 1989b. "Peasants Go to Town: The Rise of Commercial Farming in Korea." *Human Organization* 48(1): 236–261.

———. 1991. "The Personal Ethic and the Market in Korea." *Comparative Studies in Society and History* 33(1): 106–129.

———. 2003. "Mutual Help and Democracy in Korea." In D. E. Bell and C. Hahm (eds.), *Confucianism for the Modern World*, pp. 90–123. Cambridge: Cambridge University Press.

Chen, Albert H. 2003. "Mediation, Litigation, and Justice: Confucian Reflections in a Modern Liberal Society." In D. Bell and C. Hahm (eds.), *Confucianism for the Modern World*, pp. 257–287. Cambridge: Cambridge University Press.

Cherry, Judith. 2005. "Big Deal or Big Disappointment? The Continuing Evolution of the South Korean Developmental State." *The Pacific Review* 18(3): 327–354.

Chibber, Vivek. 1999. "Building a Developmental State: The South Korean Case Reconsidered." *Politics and Society* 27(3): 327–354.

———. 2002. "Bureaucratic Rationality and the Developmental State." *American Journal of Sociology* 107(4): 951–989.

———. 2003. *Locked in Place: State-Building and Late Industrialization in India*. Princeton, NJ: Princeton University Press.

Ching, Julia. 1977. *Confucianism and Christianity*. Tokyo: Kodansha International Ltd.

Cho, Hein. 1997. "The Historical Origins of Civil Society in Korea." *Korea Journal* 37(2): 24–41.

Christie, Kenneth. 1997. "Liberal vs. Illiberal Democratization: The Case of Southeast Asia." *PROSEA* Occasional Paper No. 9. October.

Chung, Chullhee. 1997. "Social Movement Organizations and the June Uprising." *Korea Journal* 37(1): 81–97.

Clegg, Stewart R., Winton Higgins, and Tony Spybey. 1990. "'Post-Confucianism,' Social Democracy, and Economic Culture." In S. R. Clegg and S. G. Redding (eds.), *Capitalism in Contrasting Cultures*, pp. 79–104. New York: Walter de Gruyter.

Coase, Ronald. 1988[1937]. "The Nature of the Firm," *Economica* vol.4, reprinted in R. Coase, *The Firm, The Market, and the Law*, pp. 33–55. Chicago, IL: University of Chicago Press.

Cohen, Jean. 1999. "Trust, Voluntary Association and Workable Democracy: The Contemporary American Discourse of Civil Society." In Mark E.

Warren (ed.), *Democracy and Trust*, pp. 208–248. London: Cambridge University Press.

——— and Andrew Arato. 1992. *Civil Society and Political Theory*. Cambridge, MA: MIT Press.

Coleman, James. 1988. "Social Capital in the Creation of Human Capital." *American Journal of Sociology* 94: S95–S120.

Collins, Randall. 1980. "Weber's Last Theory of Capitalism: A Systematization." *American Sociological Review* 45(6): 925–942.

Davis, Diane. 2004. *Discipline and Development: Middle Class and Prosperity in East Asia and Latin America*. Cambridge, MA: Cambridge University Press.

de Bary, Theodore. 1998. *Asian Values and Human Rights: A Confucian Communitarian Perspective*. Cambridge, MA: Harvard University Press.

Demsetz, Harold. 1967. "Toward a Theory of Property Rights." *The American Economic Review* 57(2): 347-359.

Deuchler, Martina. 1992. *The Confucian Transformation of Korea: A Study of Society and Ideology*. Cambridge, MA: Harvard University Press.

DeVos, George A. 1998. "Confucian Family Socialization: The Religion, Morality, and Aesthetics of Propriety." In W. Slote and G. DeVos (eds.), *Confucianism and the Family*, pp. 329–380. Albany, NW: State University of New York Press.

Deyo, Frederic. 1989. *Beneath the Miracle: Labor Subordination in the New Asian Industrialism*. Berkeley, CA: University of California Press.

Duncan, John. 1998. "The Problematic Modernity of Confucianism: The Question of 'Civil Society' in *Chosôn* Dynasty Korea." Preliminary draft.

Edwards, Bob and Michael Foley. 1998. "Civil Society and Social Capital beyond Putnam." *The American Behavioral Scientist* 42(1): 124–139.

Eliade, Mircea. 1985. "Homo Faber and Homo Religious." In J. M. Kitagawa (ed.), *The History of Religions*, pp. 1–12. New York: Macmillan.

English JoongAng Daily. 2006. Editorial "Are Civic Groups Fulfilling their Role?" September 01. http://joongangdaily.joins.com/article/view.asp?aid=2807315

Evans, Peter. 1995. *Embedded Autonomy: States and Industrial Transformation*. Princeton, NJ: Princeton University Press.

———. 1996. "Government Action, Social Capital and Development: Reviewing the Evidence on Synergy." *World Development* 24(6): 1119–1132.

Evans, Peter, Dietrich Rueschmeyer, and Theda Skocpol. 1985. *Bringing the State Back In*. New York: Cambridge University Press.

Feenstra, Robert and Gary Hamilton. 2006. *Emergent Economies, Divergent Paths*. Cambridge, MA: Cambridge University Press.

Fligstein, Neil. 1996. "Markets as Politics: A Political–Cultural Approach to Market Institutions." *American Sociological Review* 61: 656–673.

———. 2001. *The Architecture of Markets: The Economic Sociology of Twenty-First-Century Capitalist Societies*. Princeton, NJ: Princeton University Press.

Frankel, Jeffrey. 2000. "The Asian Model, the Miracle, the Crisis, and the Fund." In P. Krugman (ed.), *Currency Crises*, pp. 327–337. Chicago, IL: University of Chicago Press for National Bureau of Economic Research.

Fukuyama, Francis. 1995a. *Trust: The Social Virtues and the Creation of Prosperity*. New York: Free Press.

———. 1995b. "Confucianism and Democracy." *Journal of Democracy* 6(2): 20–33.

———. 1995c. "Social Capital and the Global Economy." *Foreign Affairs* 74(5): 89–103.

Fung, Yu-lan. 1952. *A History of Chinese Philosophy*. Princeton, NJ: Princeton University Press.

Geertz, Clifford. 1973. *The Interpretation of Cultures*. New York: Basic Nooks.

Gintis, Herbert, Samuel Bowles, Robert T. Boyd, and Ernst Fehr. 2005. *Moral Sentiments and Material Interests: The Foundations of Cooperation in Economic Life (Economic Learning and Social Evolution)*. Cambridge, MA: MIT Press.

Gold, Thomas, Doug Guthrie, and Davis Wank. 2002. *Social Connections in China*. Cambridge, MA: Cambridge University Press.

Gramsci, Antonio. 1971. *Selections from the Prison Notebooks*. New York: International Publishers.

Granovetter, Mark. 1985. "Economic Action and Social Structure: The Problem of Embeddedness." *American Journal of Sociology* 91(3): 481–510.

———. 2005. "Business Groups and Social Organization." In N. Smelser and R. Swedberg (eds.), *The Handbook of Economic Sociology, the Second Edition*, pp. 429–450. Princeton, NJ: Princeton University Press.

Habermas, Jurgen. 1989. *The Structural Transformation of the Public Sphere*. Cambridge, MA: MIT Press.

Haggard, Stephan. 1990. *Pathways from the Periphery: The Political Growth in the Newly Industrializing Countries*. Ithaca, NY: Cornell University Press.

———, Won Hyuk Lim, and Euy Sung Kim. 2003. *Economic Crisis and Corporate Restructuring in Korea: Reforming the Chaebol*. Cambridge, MA: Cambridge University Press.

Hahm, Chaibong. 2000. "Cultural Challenge to Individualism." *Journal of Democracy* 11(1): 127–134.

———. 2003. "Family versus the Individual: the Politics of Marriage Laws in Korea." In D. Bell and C. Hahm (eds.), *Confucianism for the Modern World*, pp. 334–359. Cambridge, MA: Cambridge University Press.

———. 2004. "The Ironies of Confucianism." *Journal of Democracy* 15(3): 93–107.

Hahm, Chaihark and Daniel Bell. 2004. *The Politics of Affective Relations: East Asia and Beyond*. Baltimore, MD: Lexington Books.

Hahm, Joon Ho. 2003. "The Government, the *Chaebol* and Financial Institutions before the Economic Crisis." In S. Haggard, W. Lim, and E. Kim (eds.), *Economic Crisis and Corporate Restructuring in Korea: Reforming the Chaebol*, pp. 79–101. Cambridge, MA: Cambridge University Press.

Hahm, Pyung-Choon. 1986. "The Affective Society: Values and Law in Korea." In *Korean Jurisprudence, Politics, and Culture*, pp. 282–317. Seoul: Yonsei University Press.

Hahn, Sung Joe. 1981. "The Political Philosophy of the Saemaul Movement." In Man-gap Lee (ed.), *Toward a New Community*, pp. 99–131. Seoul: Seoul National University.

Hall, David and Roger Ames. 1987. *Thinking through Confucius*. Albany, NW: State University of New York Press.

Hall, John (ed). 1992. *Civil Society: Theory, History and Comparison*. Cambridge, MA: Polity Press.

Hamilton, Clive. 1986. *Capitalist Industrialization in Korea*. Boulder, CO: Westview Press.

Hamilton, Gary and Nicole W. Biggart. 1988. "Market, Culture and Authority: A Comparative Analysis of Management and Organization in the Far East." *American Journal of Sociology* 94: 52–94.

———, William Zeile, and Wan-Jin Kim. 1990. "The Network Structure of East Asian Economics." In S. Clegg and G. Redding (eds.), *Capitalism in Contrasting Cultures*, pp. 105–29. Berlin: Walters de Gruter.

Han, Sang-Jin. 1997. "The Public Sphere and Democracy in Korea." *Korea Journal* 37.4: 78–97.

Harris, Christopher. 1979. "The Sociology of the Family: New Directions for Britain." In C. Harris (ed.), *Sociological Review Monograph 28*, pp. 74–112. Chester: Bemrose Press.

Hattori, Tamio. 1989. "Japanese *Zaibatsu* and Korean *Chaebol*." In K. H. Chung and H. C. Lee (eds.), *Korean Managerial Dynamics*, pp. 79–95. New York: Prager.

———. 1997. "*Chaebol*-Style Enterprise Development in Korea." *The Developing Economies* 35: 458–477.

——— and Tsuruyo Funatsu. 2003. "The Emergence of Asian Middle Classes and Their Characteristics." *The Developing Economies* 41(2): 140–160.

Henderson, Gregory. 1968. *Korea: The Politics of the Vortex*. Cambridge, MA: Harvard University Press.

Hill, Michael. 1973. *A Sociology of Religion*. London: Heinemann.

Ho, Yu In and Byung Hee Kim. 1981. "The Economic Plight of Korean Farmers." *Korean Scope* 2/4(September): 6–30.

Hofheinz, Roy Jr. and Kent E. Calder. 1982. *The East Asia Edge*. New York: Basic Books.

Hsu, Francis. 1967. *Under the Ancestor's Shadow*. New York: Anchor Books.

Huntington, Samuel. 1993. "The Clash of Civilization?" *Foreign Affairs* 72(3): 22–49.
Jacobs, Norman. 1958. *The Origin of Modern Capitalism and Eastern Asia.* Hong Kong: University of Hong Kong Press.
———. 1985. *The Korean Road to Modernization and Development.* Urbana: University of Illinois Press.
Janelli, Roger and Dawnhee Yim Janelli. 1982. *Ancestor Worship and Korean Society.* Stanford, CA: Stanford University Press.
Janelli, Roger and Dawnhee Yim. 1993. *Making Capitalism: The Social and Cultural Construction of a South Korean Conglomerate.* Stanford, CA: Stanford University Press.
———. 2004. "The Transformation of Filial Piety in Contemporary South Korea." In C. Ikels (ed.), *Filial Piety*, pp. 128–152. Stanford, CA: Stanford University Press.
Johnson, Charlmers. 1982. *MITI and the Japanese Miracle: The Growth of Industrial Policy, 1925–75.* Stanford, CA: Stanford University Press.
———. 1985. "Political Institutions and Economic Performance: The Government–Business Relationship in Japan, South Korea, and Taiwan." In R. A. Scalapino et al. (eds.), *Asian Economic Development: Present and Future.* Berkeley, CA: Institute of East Asian Studies, University of California.
Jomo, Kwame Sundaram (ed.). 2003. *Southeast Asian Paper Tigers?: From Miracle to Debacle and Beyond.* London and New York: RoutledgeCurzon.
Kahn, Herman. 1979. *World Development: 1979 and Beyond.* Boulder, CO: Westview Press.
Kang, David. 2003. "Regional Politics and Democratic Consolidation in Korea." In S. Kim (ed.), *Korea's Democratization*, pp. 161–180. Cambridge, MA: Cambridge University Press.
Keane, John. 1988. *Democracy and Civil Society.* London: Verso.
Kim, Dae Jung. 1994. "Is Culture Destiny?: The Myth of Asia's Anti-Democratic Values." *Foreign Affairs* 73(6): 189–194.
Kim, Eun Mee. 1997. *Big Business, Strong State: Collusion and Conflict in South Korean Development, 1960–1990.* Albany, NW: State University of New York Press.
Kim, Hyung-A. 2004. *Korea's Development under Park Chung-Hee: Rapid Industrialization, 1961–79.* New York: RoutledgeCurzon.
Kim, Joon Han and Seok-Choon Lew. 1995. "Recent Regime Transition and Political Successions in South Korea: From Authoritarianism to Democracy." In K. Jung, D. Kim, W. Gumpel, and Gottfried-Kinderman (eds.), *Economic Integration in Asia and Europe*, pp. 181–212. Seoul: Institute of East and West Studies, Yonsei University.
Kim, Sun-hyuk. 1998. "Civil Society and Democratization in South Korea." *Korea Journal* 38(2): 214–236.

Koh, Byung Ik. 1996. "Confucianism in Modern Korea." In W. Tu (ed.), *Confucian Traditions in East Asian Modernity: Moral Education and Economic Culture in Japan and Four Mini-Dragon*, pp. 191–201. Cambridge, MA: Cambridge University Press.

Kohli, Atul. 2004. *State-Directed Development: Political Power and Industrialization in the Global Periphery*. New York: Cambridge University Press.

Kramer, Ralph. 1984. *Voluntary Agencies in the Welfare State*. Berkeley, CA: University of California Press.

Krugman, Paul. 1994. "The Myth of Asia's Miracle." *Foreign Affairs* 73(6): 62–78.

Lee, Dong Gull. 2003. "The Restructuring of Daewoo." In S. Haggard, W. Lim, and E. Kim (eds.), *Economic Crisis and Corporate Restructuring in Korea: Reforming the Chaebol*, pp. 150–180. Cambridge, MA: Cambridge University Press.

Lee, Jung Young (ed.). 1988. *Ancestor Worship and Christianity in Korea*. New York: Edwin Mellon Press.

Lee, Keun and Byung-Yeon Kim. 2009. "Both Institutions and Policies Matter but Differently for Different Groups of Countries: Determinants of Long-Run Economic Growth Revisited." *World Development* 37(3): 533–549.

Lee, Kwang-Kyu. 1997. *Korean Family and Kinship*. Seoul: Jipmoondang.

———. 1998. "Confucian Tradition in the Contemporary Korean Family." In W. Slote and G. DeVos (eds.), *Confucianism and the Family*, pp. 249–266. Albany, NW: State University of New York Press.

Lee, Seung-hwan. 1992. "Was There a Concept of Rights in Confucian Virtue-Based Morality." *Journal of Chinese Philosophy* 19: 241–261.

Lee, Yeon-ho. 2000. "The Failure of the Weak State in Economic Liberalization: Liberalization, Democratization and the Financial Crisis in South Korea." *The Pacific Review* 13(1): 115–131.

Lew, Seok-Choon. 1999. "An Institutional Reinterpretation of 'Confucian Capitalism' in East Asia." *Korean Social Science Journal* 26(2): 117–134.

———. 2000. "The Structure of Domination and Capital Accumulation in Modern Korea." In Yun-Shik Chang, Donald L. Baker, Hur Nam Lin, and Ross King (eds.), *Korea between Tradition and Modernity: Selected Papers from the Fourth Pacific and Asian Conference on Korean Studies*. Institute for Asian Research, University of British Columbia, Vancouver.

———, Mi-Hye Chang, and Tae-Eun Kim. 2003. "Affective Networks and Modernity: The Case of Korea." In Daniel A. Bell and Hahm Chaibong (eds.), *Confucianism for the Modern World*, pp. 201–217. Cambridge, MA: Cambridge University Press.

——— and Tae-eun Kim. 2001. "Development of Township-Village Enterprises and the Re-Institutionalization of the Family in China." *Global Economic Review* 30(4): 83–111.

———, Woo-Young Choi, and Hye Suk Wang. 2011. "Confucian Ethics and the Spirit of Capitalism in Korea: The Significance of Filial Piety." *Journal of East Asian Studies* 11(2): 171–196.

——— and Hye Suk Wang. 2010. "The Korean Development Model: Lessons for Southeast Asia." In D. Steinberg (ed.), *Korea's Changing Role in Southeast Asia: Expanding Influence and Relations*, pp. 176–204. Singapore: Institute of Southeast Asian Studies (ISEAS).

Leys, Colin. 1996. *The Rise and Fall of Developmental Theory*. Bloomington, IN: Indiana University Press.

Lim, Won Hyuk. 2003. "The Emergence of the *Chaebol* and the Origin of the Problem." In S. Haggard, W. Lim, and E. Kim (eds.), *Economic Crisis and Corporate Restructuring in Korea: Reforming the Chaebol*, pp. 35–52. Cambridge, MA: Cambridge University Press.

Lin, Justin and Ha-Joon Chang. 2009. "Should Industrial Policy in Developing Countries Conform to Comparative Advantage or Defy It? A Debate between Justin Lin and Ha-Joon Chang." *Development Policy Review* 27(5): 483–502.

Luhmann, Niklas. 1979. *Trust and Power*. New York: John Wiley and Sons.

Lynn, Hyung Gu. 2005. "Book Review: State-Directed Development: Political Power and Industrialization in the Global Periphery." *Pacific Affairs* 78(2): 277–278.

MacFarquhar, Roderick. 1980. "The Post-Confucian Challenge." *The Economist*, February 9: 67–72.

Maison, Edward, Manje Kim, Dwight Perkins, Kim Kwang Suk, and Dadid Cole (eds.). 1980. *The Economic and Social Modernization of the Republic of Korea*. Cambridge, MA: Harvard University Press.

Mauss, Marcel. 1990[1925]. *The Gift: The Form and Reason for Exchange in Archaic Societies*. Translation by W. D. Halls. London: Routledge.

Metzger, Thomas. 1977. *Escape from Predicament: Neo-Confucianism and China's Evolving Political Culture*. New York: Columbia University Press.

Migdal, Joel. 1988. *Strong States and Weak States*. Princeton, NJ: Princeton University Press.

Mo, Jong Rin and Chung In Moon. 2003. "Business–Government Relations under Kim Dae-jung." In S. Haggard, W. Lim, and E. Kim (eds.), *Economic Crisis and Corporate Restructuring in Korea: Reforming the Chaebol*, pp. 127–149. Cambridge, MA: Cambridge University Press.

Morishima, Michio. 1981. *Why Has Japan 'Succeeded'?* London: Cambridge University Press.

North, Douglas and Robert Thomas. 1973. *The Rise of the Western World*. New York: Cambridge University Press.

Oberschall, Anthony and Eric Leifer. 1986. "Efficiency and Social Institutions: Uses and Misuses of Economic Reasoning in Sociology." *Annual Review of Sociology* 12: 233–253.

Offe, Claus. 1999. "How Can We Trust Our Fellow Citizens?" In Mark E. Warren (ed.), *Democracy and Trust*, pp. 42–87. London: Cambridge University Press.

Ornatowski, Gregory K. 1996. "Confucian Ethic and Economic Development: A Study of the Adaptation of Confucian Values to Modern Japanese Economic Ideology and Institutions." *Journal of Socio-Economics* 25(5): 571–590.

Ostrom, Elinor. 1990. *Governing the Commons*. New York: Cambridge University Press.

Orru, Marco, Nicole Woolsey Biggart, and Gary Hamilton. 1991. "Organizational Isomorphism in East Asia." In W. W. Powell and P. J. DiMggio (eds.), *The New Institutionalism in Organizational Analysis*, pp. 361–389. Chicago, IL: The University of Chicago Press.

Oxburn, Phillip. 1995. "From Controlled Inclusion to Coerced Marginalization: The Struggle for Civil Society in Latin America." In J. Hall (ed.), *Civil Society: Theory, History and Comparison*, pp. 250–277. Cambridge, MA: Polity Press.

Park, Kyung Suh. 2003. "Bank-Led Corporate Restructuring." In S. Haggard, W. Lim, and E. Kim (eds.), *Economic Crisis and Corporate Restructuring in Korea: Reforming the Chaebol*, pp. 181–206. Cambridge, MA: Cambridge University Press.

Platteau, Jean-Philippe. 1994a. "Behind the Market Stage Where Real Societies Exist—Part I: The Role of Public and Private Order Institutions." *Journal of Development Studies* 30(3): 533–577.

———. 1994b. "Behind the Market Stage Where Real Societies Exist—Part II: The Role of Moral Norms." *Journal of Development Studies* 30(4): 386–422.

Polanyi, Karl. 1957. "The Economy as Instituted Process." In K. Polanyi, C. M. Arsenberg, and H. W. Pearson (eds.), *Trade and Market in the Early Empires: Economies in History and Theory*, pp. 243–270. Glencoe, IL: The Free Press.

———. 2001[1944]. *The Great Transformation: The Political and Economic Origins of Our Time*. Boston: Beacon Press.

Portes, Alejandro. 1998. "Social Capital: Its Origins and Applications in Modern Sociology." *Annual Review of Sociology* 22: 1–24.

——— and J. Sensenbrenner. 1993. "Embeddedness and Immigration: Notes on the Social Determinants of Economic Action." *American of Sociological Journal* 98(6): 1320–1350.

Putnam, Robert. 1993a. *Making Democracy Work: Civic Traditions in Modern Italy*. Princeton, NJ: Princeton University Press.

———. 1993b. "The Prosperous Community: Social Capital and Public Life," *The American Prospect* 13(spring): 35–42.

———. 1995. "Bowling Alone: America's Declining Social Capital." *Journal of Democracy* 6(1): 65–78.

Pye, Lucian W. 1985. *Asian Power and Politics: The Cultural Dimensions of Authority.* Cambridge, MA: Harvard University Press.
———. 1999. "Civility, Social Capital, and Civil Society: Three Powerful Concepts for Explaining Asia." *Journal of Interdisciplinary History* 29(4): 763–782.
———. 2000. "'Asian Values': From Dynamics to Dominoes?" In S. P. Huntington and L. E. Harrison (eds.), *Culture Matters: How Values Shape Human Progress,* pp. 244–255. New York: Basic Books.
Radelet, Steven and Jeffrey Sachs. 1998. "The Onset of the East Asian Financial Crisis." Manuscript. Harvard Institute for International Development. March.
Redding, Gordon. 1990. *The Spirit of Chinese Capitalism.* London: Walter de Gruyter.
Ringmar, Erik. 2005. *Surviving Capitalism: How We Learned to Live with the Market and Remained Almost Human.* London: Anthem Press.
Rodrik, Dani. 2007. *One Economics, Many Recipes: Globalization, Institutions, and Economic Growth.* Princeton, NJ: Princeton University Press.
Rosemont, Henry. 1988. "Why Take Rights Seriously? A Confucian Critique." In L. S. Rouner (ed.), *Human Rights and the World's Religions,* pp. 176–182. Notre Dame: University of Notre Dame Press.
Rozman, Gilbert. 1991. "The East Asian Region in Comparative Perspective." In G. Rozman (ed.), *The East Asian Region: Confucian Heritage and Its Modern Adaption,* pp. 3–42. Princeton, NJ: Princeton University Press.
———. 1992. "The Confucian Faces of Capitalism." In M. Borthwick (ed.), *Pacific Century,* pp. 310–22. Boulder, CO: Westview Press.
Sahlins, Marshall D. 1972. *Stone Age Economics.* Chicago, IL: Aldine.
Salamon, Lester M. and Helmut K. Anheier. 1996. *Social Origins of Civil Society: Explaining the Nonprofit Sector Cross-Nationally.* Working Papers of Johns Hopkins (Comparative Non-Profit Sector Project).
Schwartz, Bentzamin. 1996. *China and Other Matters.* Cambridge, MA: Harvard University Press.
Scott, James. 1976. *The Moral Economy of the Peasant: Rebellion and Subsistence in Southeast Asia.* New Haven, CT: Yale University Press.
Shim, Jae-Hoon. 1984. "Phenomenon of the Cross." *Far Eastern Economic Review* 124: 16.
Shin, Doh-Chull. 2012. *Confucianism and Democratization in East Asia.* Cambridge, MA: Cambridge University Press.
Shin, Jang-Sup and Ha-Joon Chang. 2003. *Restructuring Korea Inc.* London: RoutledgeCurzon.
Shin, Jang-Sup. 2005a. "Substituting and Complementing Models of Economic Development in East Asia." *Global Economic Review* 34(1): 99–118.
———. 2005b. "Globalization and Challenges to the Developmental State: A Comparison between South Korea and Singapore." *Global Economic Review* 34(4): 379–395.

Sorensen, Clark and Sung-Chul Kim. 2004. "Filial Piety in Contemporary Urban Southeast Korea: Practices and Discourse." In C. Ikels (ed.), *Filial Piety*, pp. 153–181. Stanford, CA: Stanford University Press.

Steinberg, David I. 1997. "Civil Society and Human Rights in Korea: On Contemporary and Classical Orthodoxy and Ideology." *Korea Journal* 37(3): 145–165.

Stubbs, Richard. 2009. "What Ever Happened to the East Asian Developmental State? The Unfolding Debate." *The Pacific Review* 22(1): 1–22.

Sung, Kyu-taik. 2005. *Care and Respect for the Elderly in Korea*. Seoul: Jimoondang.

Tai, Hung-chao (ed.). 1989. *Confucianism and Economic Development: An Oriental Alternative?* Washington, DC: Washington Institute Press.

Taylor, Rodney. 1990. *The Religious Dimensions of Confucianism*. Albany, NY: State University of New York Press.

The Bank of Korea. 2010. *A Sixty-Year History*. Seoul: Jeon-Kwang Printing.

Thurbon, Elizabeth. 2001. "Two Paths to Financial Liberalization: South Korea and Taiwan." *The Pacific Review* 14(2): 241–267.

Tocqueville, Alexis. 1969. *Democracy in America* (translated by G. Lawrence). New York: Anchor Books.

Troeltsch, Ernst. 1958[1912]. *Protestantism and Progress: A Historical Study of the Relation of Protestantism to the Modern World* (translated by W. Montgomery). Boston, MA: Beacon Press.

Tu, Wei-Ming (ed.). 1991. *The Triadic Chord: Confucian Ethics, Industrial East Asia and Max Weber*. Singapore: The Institute of East Asian Philosophies, National University of Singapore.

———. 1996. *Confucian Traditions in East Asian Modernity: Moral Education and Economic Culture in Japan and the Four Mini-Dragons*. Cambridge, MA: Harvard University Press.

Uslaner, Eric M., 1999. "Democracy and Social Capital" In Mark E. Warren (ed.), *Democracy and Trust*, pp. 121–150. London: Cambridge University Press.

———. 2008. "Trust as a Moral Value," In Dario Castiglione, Jan W. Van Deth, and Guglielmo Wolleb (eds.), *The Handbook of Social Capital*, pp. 101–121. London: Oxford University Press.

Vogel, Ezra. 1991. *The Four Little Dragons*. Cambridge, MA: Harvard University Press.

Wade, Robert. 1990. *Governing the Market: Economic Theory and the Role of Government in East Asian Industrialization*. Princeton, NJ: Princeton University Press.

———. 1996. "Globalization and Its Limits: Reports on the Death of the National Economy Are Greatly Exaggerated." In S. Berger and R. Dore (eds.), *National Diversity and Global Capitalism*. Ithaca, NY: Cornell University Press.

Wank, David. 1991. "Merchant Entrepreneurs and the Development of Civil Society: Some Social and Political Consequences of Private Sector Expansion in a Southeast Coastal City." Paper prepared for the Annual Meeting of the Association for Asian Studies, April, New Orleans.

Warren, Mark E. (ed.). 1999. *Democracy and Trust.* London: Cambridge University Press.

Warren, Mark E. 2008. "The Nature and Logic of Bad Social Capital." In D. Castiglione, J. W. Van Deth, and G. Wolleb (eds.), *The Handbook of Social Capital*, pp. 123–149. New York: Oxford University Press.

Weber, Max. 1930[1920]. *The Protestant Ethic and the Spirit of Capitalism* (translated by T. Parsons). New York: Scribner.

———. 1946. *Max Weber: Essays in Sociology* (translated, edited and with an introduction by H. H. Gerth and C. W. Mills). New York: Oxford University Press.

———. 1951[1920]. *The Religion of China* (translated by H. H. Gerth). New York: Free Press.

———.1961[1923]. *General Economic History* (translated by F. H. Knight). New York: Collier.

Weiss, Linda. 1998. *The Myth of the Powerless State.* Ithaca, NY: Cornell University Press.

Weiss, G. Thomas and Leon Gordenker. 1996. *NGOs, the UN, and Global Governance.* Boulder, CO: Lynne Rienner.

Wilk, Richard R. and Lisa C. Cliggett. 2007. *Economies and Cultures: Foundations of Economic Anthropology.* Boulder, CO: Westview Press.

Williamson, Oliver. 1973. *Markets and Hierarchies: Analysis and Antitrust Implications.* New York: Free Press.

———.1985. *The Economic Institution of Capitalism.* New York: Free Press.

———. 1989. "Transaction Cost Economics." In R. Schmalensee and R.D. Willig (eds.), *Handbook of Industrial Organization*, vol.1, pp.136–182. Amsterdam: North Holland.

Wong, Siu-Iun. 1985. "The Chinese Family Firm: A Model." *British Journal of Sociological Review* 50: 58–72.

Woo-Cumings, Meredith J.-E. (ed.). 1999. *Developmental State.* Ithaca, NY: Cornell University Press.

Woolcock, Michael. 1998. "Social Capital and Economic Development: Toward a Theoretical Synthesis and Policy Framework." *Theory and Society* 27: 151–208.

Woolcock, Michael and Deepa Narayan. 2000. "Social Capital: Implications for Development Theory, Research, and Policy." *The World Bank Research Observer* 15(2): 225–249.

World Bank. 1991. *World Development Report 1991: The Challenge of Development.* Oxford: Oxford University Press.

———. 1993. *The East Asian Miracle: Economic Growth and Public Policy.* New York: Oxford University Press.

Wuthnow, Robert. 1991. "The Voluntary Sector: Legacy of the Past, Hope for the Future?" In R. Wuthnow (ed.), *Between States and Markets: The Voluntary Sector in Comparative Perspective*, pp. 288–308. Princeton, NJ: Princeton University Press.

Yamagishi, Toshio and M. Yamagishi. 1994. "Trust and Commitment in the United States and Japan." *Motivation and Emotion* 18: 129–166.

———, Karen Cook, and Motoki Watabe. 1998. "Uncertainty, Trust, and Commitment Formation in the United States and Japan." *American Journal of Sociology* 104: 165–194.

Yao, Souchou. 2002. *Confucian Capitalism*. London: RoutledgeCurzon.

Zak, Paul J. 2008. *Moral Markets: The Critical Role of Values in the Economy*. Princeton, NJ: Princeton University Press.

Zakaria, Fareed. 1994. "Culture is Destiny: A Conversation with Lee Kuan Yew." *Foreign Affairs* 73(2): 109–126.

Zelizer, Viviana. 2005. *The Purchase of Intimacy*. Princeton, NJ: Princeton University Press.

Zuker, Lynne G. 1986. "Production of Trust: Institutional Sources of Economic Structure, 1840–1920." *Research in Organizational Behavior* 8: 53–111.

References in Korean Language

Cha, Seong-hwan (Ch'a, Sŏng-hwan). 1992. "Shinyugyo-wa sajŏk'yulli (Neo-Confucianism and Private Ethics)." In S. H. Cha (ed.), *Han'guk chonggyosasang-ui sahoehakjŏk ihae* (Sociological Understanding of Korean Religious Thoughts), pp. 44–110. Seoul: Munhakgwa Jiseongsa.
Cho, Gab Je (Cho, Kap-je). 2007. *Park Chung Hee* (Biography of Park Chung Hee). 13 Volumes. Seoul: chogabje.com
Cho, He-in (Cho, Hye-in). 1993. "Chosŏn hyangch'ŏnjilsŏ-ui t'eukjing-gwa kū chŏngch'akkwajŏng (Characteristics and Orders of Rural Village in Chosun)." In Hanguk Jeongshin Munhwa Yeonguwon (ed.), *Yugyojŏk chŏnt'ong sahoe-ui kujo-wa t'ūksŏng* (The Structure and Characteristics of Confucian Traditional Society), pp. 149–184. Sŏngnam: Hanguk chŏngshin munhwa yŏn'guwon.
Choi, Bong-young (Ch'oe, Pong-yŏng). 1999. "Sŏngrihakjŏk inkankwan-gwa inbonchu'ŭi (Neo-Confucian Perspective on Human Being and Humanism)." *Dong'yangsahoesasang* (Thoughts of Eastern Society) 2: 31–77.
Choi, Jae-seok (Ch'oe, Chae-sŏk). 1975. *Han'guk nongch'on sahoe yŏn'gu* (A Study on Korean Rural Society). Seoul: Iljisa.
———. 1983[1965]. *Han'gugin-ŭi sahoejŏk sŏngkyŏk* (Social Characterisitics of Koreans). Seoul: Kaemunsa.
Choi, Jang-jip (Ch'oe Chang-jip). 1991. *Chi'yŏk gamjŏng yŏn'gu* (A Study on Regional Sentiment). Seoul: Hakminsa.
———. 1996. *Han'guk minjuju'ŭi-ŭi chokŏn-gwa chŏnmang* (Conditions and Prospects of Korean Democracy). Seoul: Nanam.
Choi, Seok-Mann (Ch'oe Sŏk-man). 1999. "Yugyosasang-gwa minjuju'ŭi-ŭi chŏphap-ŭl wihan iron kusŏng mit pangbŏpron (Theoretical Formation and Methodology for Uniting Confucian Ideas and Democracy)." *Dong'yangsahoesasang* (Thoughts of Eastern Society) 2: 5–29.
Chosun Daily (Chosŏn ilbo). Sep 15, 2010.
Chosun Daily (Chosŏn ilbo). July 13, 2001.
Dong-A Daily (Dong'a ilbo). Feb 8, 2000.
Dong-A Daily (Dong'a ilbo). Sep 1, 2006. Headline (http://www.donga.com/fbin/output?n=200609010087).

REFERENCES IN KOREAN LANGUAGE

Financial Service Commission Press Release. December 28, 2012.
Gong, Byung-Ho (Gong, Pyŏng-ho). 1993. *Han'guk ki'ŏp hŭngmangsa* (A History of Korean Corporations). Seoul: Meoungjin Ch'ulp'an.
Hahm, Chaibong (Ham, Chae-bong). 1998. *T'algŭndae-wa yugyo* (Postmodernism and Confucianism). Seoul: Nanam.
Hankook Daily (Han'guk ilbo). June 14, 1998. 2nd page.
Hankyoreh Daily (Han'gyŏrye Shinmun), April 11, 1998.
Hankyoreh Daily (Han'gyŏrye Shinmun), December 11, 2006.
Hwang, Tae-Yun (Hwang, T'ae-yun). 1997. *Chiyŏk p'aegwon-ŭi nara* (A Country of Regional Hegemony). Moodang Media.
Jeon, Sang-in (Chŏn, Sang-in). 2008. "Chosŏn shidae-ŭi sahoejabon: Yangban-ŭi yŏndae, yŏn'gye, yŏnjul (Social Capital in Chosun Period: Solidarity, Linkages, and Networks of Two Upper Classes)." In S. C. Lew et al. (eds.), *Han'guk-ŭi sahoejabon: Yŏksa-wa hyŏnshil* (Social Capital in Korea: A Comparative Study on Traditional Society and Modern Society), pp. 75–104. Seoul: Paeksan.
Jeong, Jin-yeong (Chŏng, Chin-yŏng). 1991. "Chosŏn hugi dongsŏng ma'ŭl-ŭi hyŏngsŏng-gwa sahoejŏk kinŭng (The Formation and Social Functions of Clan Villages in Late Chosun)." In Kuksa P'yŏnch'an Wiwonhoe (ed.), *Hanguksaron 21: Chosŏn hugi-ŭi hyangch'on sahoe* (Korean Historical Debate 21: Country Village Societies in the Late Chosun), pp. 29–68. Kwacheon: Kuksa P'yŏnch'an Wiwonhoe.
Jung, Bok-Mi, Hae-Ok Jung, and Eun-Sil Kim (Chŏng, Pok-mi, Hae-ok Chŏng, and Ŭn-shil Kim). 2004. "Pusanji'yŏk-gwa chŏn'namji'yŏk chubudŭl-ŭi cherye'ŭisik chosa yŏn'gu (A Study on Ancestral Service Preparation and Sacrificial Consciousness of Housekeepers Living in Pusan and Yeosu Area)." *Han'gukjorihakhoeji* (The Korean Journal of Culinary Research) 10(3): 135–154.
Jung, Keun-Sik (Chŏng, Kŭn-shik). 1997. "Pulgyundŭng paljŏn-gwa chi'yŏkju'ŭi, gŭrigo chi'yŏk damron-ŭi pyŏnhwa (Unequal Development, Regionalism and the Change in Discourse on Regions)." In Han'guksahoesahakhoe (ed.), *Han'guk hyŏndaesa-wa sahoepyŏndong* (A History of Modern Korea and Social Change), pp. 285–315. Seoul: Munhakgwajisŏngsa.
Kang, Myong-Ku (Kang, Myŏng-gu). 1995. "Pyŏnhyŏk chihyang shimin sahoe undong-ŭi kanŭngsŏng-gwa han'gye (Possibility and Limits of Reformist Civil Movement)." In P. M. Yu and H. K. Kim (eds.), *Shimin sahoe-wa shimin undong* (Civil Society and Civil Movement), pp. 212–227. Seoul: Hanul.
Keum, Jang-tae (Kŭm, Chang-t'ae). 1992. "Yugyo-ŭi ch'ŏnsangjegwan (Gods in Confucianism)." In S. S. Yun (ed.), *Kŏngjasasang-ŭi palkyŏn* (A Discovery of Confucius' Thoughts), pp. 211–230. Seoul: Minŭmsa.
———. 2000. *Yugyo-ŭi sasang-gwa ŭirye* (Thoughts and Rituals in Confucianism). Seoul: Yemunsŏwon.

REFERENCES IN KOREAN LANGUAGE

Kim, Dae Ho (Kim, Dae-ho). 2009. "Ssangyongjadongch'a Sat'aerŭl T'ongt'anhanda (Deploring the Ssangyong Motors Incident)." http://www.goodpol.net/inquiry/statistics.board/entry/56 (searched on Nov 20, 2009).
Kim, Deok-Gyun (Kim, Deok-gyun). 2004. "Hyo-ŭi kwanjŏmesŏ barabon sinjin'yuga-ŭi saseanggwan-gwa jesa'ŭishik-ŭi shilje (Life and Death and Religious Services of Confucianism from the Perspective of Filial Piety)." *Hyohak Yŏn'gu* (Filial Piety Studies) 1: 290–303.
Kim, Dong-No (Kim, Dong-ro). 1997. "Kukga-ŭi chŏngdangsŏng kyŏlyŏ-wa saenghwal segye-ŭi waekok (Lack of Legitimacy of the State and the Distortion of Everyday Life)." *Hyŏnsang-gwa inshik* (Phenomenon and Perception) 21(1): 71–96.
Kim, Jeong-Ryum (Kim, Jŏng-ryŏm). 2006. *Ch'oebin'guk-esŏ sŏnjinguk munt'ŏkkachi* (From the Poorest Country to the Developed Country). Seoul: Random House.
Kim, Moon-Jo (Kim, Mun-cho). 1993. "Chi'yŏkju'ŭi-ŭi hyŏngsŏnggwajŏng-gwa t'ŭksŏng (Formation and Characteristics of Regionalism)." In H. S. Yim and G. S. Park (eds.), *Onŭl-ŭi Han'guksahoe* (Present Korean Society), pp. 151–168. Seoul: Nanam.
Kim, Sang-Jo (Kim, Sang-cho). 2008. "Kyŏngjeryŏk chipjung simhwa-wa han'guk kyŏngje-ŭi dainamiks II (Deepening of Economic Power Concentration and the Dynamics of the Korean Economy II)." *Kiŏp chibae kujo yŏn'gu* (Journal of Corporate Governance Studies) 10: 67–82.
Kim, Seong-Kook (Kim, Sŏng-kuk). 1999. "Han'guk shiminsahoe-ŭi kujojŏk pulanjŏngsŏng-gwa shiminkwonryŏk-ŭi hyŏngsŏng (Structural Instability of the Korean Civil Society and the Formation of Citizen Power: Focused on New Social Movement)." In I. C. Kim et al. (eds.), *Han'guksahoe-ŭi kujoronjŏk ihae* (Understanding the Korean Society with Structural View), pp. 299–343. Daewoo Academic Collection, Arche.
Kim, Sun-Up (Kim, Sŏn-ŏp). 1993. "Yŏnjulmang-gwa yŏn'goju'ŭi (Network and Affectivism)." In H. S. Yim and G. S. Park (eds.), *Onŭl-ŭi Han'guksahoe* (Present Korean Society), pp. 169–190. Seoul: Nanam.
Kim, Yong-Hak (Kim, Yong-hak). 1996. "Yŏn'gyŏlmang-gwa kŏraebiyong (Network and Transactional Cost)." *Sahoe pip'yŏng* (Social Criticism) 14: 86–118.
Kim, Yong-Rae (Kim, Yŏng-nae). 1996. *I'ik chipdan chŏngch'i-wa i'ik kaltŭng* (Politics of Interest Groups and Conflicts of Interest). Seoul: Hanul.
Koh, Byong-ik (Ko, Pyŏng-ik). 1996. *Dong'asia-ŭi chŏnt'ong-gwa pyŏnyong* (Tradition and Transformation of East Asian History). Seoul: Munhakgwa chisŏngsa.
Korea Institute of Finance (Han'gŭk kŭmyung yŏn'guwon). 2001. *Han'guk kŭmyung sanŏp-ŭi kwagŏ, hyŏnchae, mirae* (The Past, Present and Future of Korea's Finances). Seoul: Korea Institute of Finance.
Korea Investors Service Inc. www.kisline.com, searched on December 1, 2003.

Korea Listed Companies Association. www.kocoinfo.com, searched on December 1, 2006.
Korea National Statistical Office (Han'gŭk tonggyech'ŏng). 2008. *Han'guk-ŭi sahoe chip'yo* (Social Indicators in Korea). Seoul: Korea National Statistical Office.
Kukmin Daily (Kukmin ilbo). June 20, 2006.
Kuk, Min-ho (Kuk, Min-ho). 1999. *Dong'asia-ŭi Kukgajudo sanŏphwa-wa yugyo* (State-Initiated Industrialization in East Asia and Confucianism). Gwangju: Jeonnam daehakgyo ch'ulp'anbu.
Lee, Hae-jun (Yi, Hae-chun) 1991. "Chosŏnhugi sahoe yŏn'gu-wa hyangch'onsahoesa (Studies on Confucian Academy and Rural Village in Late Chosun)." In Guksa P'yŏnch'an Wiwonhoe (ed.), *Han'guksaron 21: Chosŏn Hugi-ŭi Hyangch'on Sahoe* (Korean Historical Debate 21: Country Village Societies in the Late Chosun), pp. 3–28. Gwacheon: Guksa p'yŏnch'an wiwonhoe.
Lee, Jae-Hyuk (Yi, Chae-hyŏk). 1999a. "Tongt'aejŏk kujo'iron-ŭi kanŭngsŏng: Haeng'wi-wa kujo-ŭi doemŏgim (Possibility of Dynamic Structural Theory: a Feedback Mechanism between Action and Structure)." In I. C. Kim et al. (eds.), *Han'guk-ŭi sahoegujo-wa chi'yŏksahoe* (Social Structure of Korea and Local Society), pp. 17–64. Seoul: Seoul National University Press.
———. 1999b. "Sahoejŏk t'ongche-ŭi chŏngch'ikyŏngchehak: Kyubŏm-gwa kwansŭp, gŭrigo kyohwan (Political Economy of Social Control: Norms, Customs and Exchange)." In I. C. Kim et al. (eds.), *Han'guksahoe-ŭi Gujoronjŏk ihae* (Understanding the Korean Society with Structural View), pp. 199–251. Daewoo Academic Collection, Arche.
Lee, Jae-Yeol (Yi, Chae-yŏl). 1998. "Minjuju'ŭi, sahoejŏk shinroe, sahoejŏk chabon." *Sasang* (Ideas) 37: 65–93.
Lee, Kap-Yun (Yi, Kap-yŭn). 1998. *Han'guk-ŭi sŏn'gŏ-wa chi'yŏkju'ŭi* (Elections in Korea and Regionalism). Seoul: Orŭm.
Lee, Seung-Hwan (Yi, Sŭng-hwan). 1998. "Yuga-e kwŏlli kaenyŏm-i innŭn'ga? (Does Confucianism have the Concept of Rights?)." In *Yuga sasang-ŭi sahoe ch'ŏlhakjŏk chaejomyŏng* (Rethinking Confucianism as a Social Philosophy), pp. 203–231. Seoul: Koryŏ daehakkyo Ch'ulp'anbu.
Lee, Seung-Yeon (Yi, Sŭng-yŏn). 2008. "Ch'ochungdŭnghakgyo chŏnt'ong'yejŏl kyo'yuk-e kwanhan sogo (A Review on Traditional Propriety Education in Elementary and Middle School)." *Ch'odŭngdodŏkkyo'yuk* (Journal of Moral Education in Primary Schools) 28: 216–238.
Lew, Seok Choon (Lyu, Sŏk-c'hun) et al. 2008. *Han'guk-ŭi sahoejabon: Yŏksa-wa hyŏnshil* (Social Capital in Korea: A Comparative Study on Traditional Society and Modern Society). Seoul: Paeksan.
——— and Yong-Min Kim (Lyu, Sŏk-c'hun and Yong-min Kim). 2000. "Han'gukshimindanch'e-ŭi mokjŏkjŏnch'i: Kyŏngshillyŏn-gwa ch'amyŏyŏndae-rŭl chungshim-ŭro (Goal Displacement of Civil Organizations in Korea: with special reference to 'Citizen's Coalition for

Economic Justice' and 'People's Solidarity for Participatory Democracy')." *Dongsŏyŏn'gu* (East And West Studies) 12(2): 5–38.
——— and Jae-Bum Shim (Lyu, Sŏk-c'hun and Chae-bŏm Shim). 1990. "Han'guksahoe Pyŏnhyŏk-ŭi tu kaji kiban: chi'yŏkch'abyŏlŭishikgwa kyegŭp'ŭishik (Two Bases of Reform Movement in the Korean Society: Class Consciousness and Regional Discrimination)." In Han'guksahoehakhoe (ed.), *Han'guk-ŭi chi'yŏkju'ŭi-wa chi'yŏkgaldŭng* (Regionalism and Regional Conflict in Korea), pp. 217–252. Seoul: Sungwonsa.
——— and Hye Suk Wang (Lyu, Sŏk-c'hun and Hye-suk Wang). 2006. *Ch'amyŏyŏndae pogosŏ* (A Report on the 'People's Solidarity for Participatory Democracy'). Seoul: Center for Free Enterprise.
Lim, Hyun-Jin (Im, Hyŏn-chin). 1999. "Kukga-wa chibaegujo: chungshimjihyangjŏk sahoe-ŭi se (The State and Ruling Structure: Center-Oriented Power)." In I. C. Kim et al., *Han'guksahoe-ŭi gujoronjŏk ihae* (Understanding the Korean Society with Structural View). Daewoo Academic Collection, Arche.
Miyajima, Hiroshi (宮島博史). 1996. *Yangban: yŏksajŏk shilch'e-rŭl ch'ajasŏ* (Two Upper Classes of Korea: In Search of Historical Substances. Seoul: Gang.
Ministry of Finance and Economy and the Financial Supervisory Commission (2001) *Kongjŏk chagŭm kwalli paeksŏ* (White Paper on Management of Public Fund). Seoul: The Ministry of Finance and Economy.
———. 2006. *Kongjŏk chagŭm kwalli paeksŏ* (White Paper on the Management of the Public Fund). Seoul: The Ministry of Finance and Economy.
Ministry of Home Affairs (Naemubu). 1980. *Saemaŭl undong shipnyŏnsa: charyo* (Ten Years of Saemaul Movement: Data). Seoul: Naemubu.
Nam, Young-Shin (Nam, Yŏng-shin). 1992. *Chi'yŏk p'aekwonju'ŭi yŏn'gu* (A Study on Regional Hegemony). Seoul: Hakminsa.
Park Chung Hee Internet Memorial Site (Pak Chŭng-hi Internet Kinyŏmgwan). http://www.516.co.kr/board/bookboard/boardread.as p?idx=60&boardtype=A&curpage=1&imgtype=a (searched on December 10, 2007).
Park, Guen-Hye (Pak, Kŭn-hye). 2006. "Han'guk saemaŭl'undong-ŭi kyŏnghŏm-gwa hanjung gong'yŏng-ŭi kwaje (Experience of Korean 'New Village Movement' and Tasks for Co-prosperity between Korea and China," Speech Delivered at the Central Academy of the Communist Party of China, Beijing, November 27, 2006.
Park, Hee (Pak, Hi). 1992. Han'guk taekiŏp-ŭi chojikgwanri-wa nosakwan'gye-e kwanhan yŏn'gu (Organizational Operation and Labor Relations in Big Korean Corporations: A Study on the Effects of Familism). PhD Dissertation, Department of Sociology, Yonsei University.
Park, Seong-hwan (Pak, Sŭng-hwan) 1994. "Han'guk-ŭi chonggyobaljŏn-gwa munhwajŏk pyŏnyong: maksŭbebŏ-ŭi han'guk'yŏn'gu-rŭl chungshimŭro

(Religion Development and Acculturation in Korea: Focused on Max Weber's Studies)." *Hanguk sahoehak* (Journal of Korean Sociology) 28: 53–84.
Park, Tae-gyu (Pak, Tae-gyu). 1995. "Kong'ikchaedan kwallyŏn chŏngbu-ŭi kyuje hwankyŏng (Korean Government Regulation on Public Foundation)." In Institute of East and West Studies (ed.), *Han'guk kong'ikchaedan-ŭi hwankyŏng pyŏnhwa-wa paljŏn panghyang* (Environmental Changes and Prospects in Korean Public Foundations), pp. 3–34. Seoul: Yonsei University Press.
Park, Young-shin (Pak, Yŏng-shin). 1983. "Han'guksahoe-ŭi kujojŏk inshik (Structural Perception on Korean Traditional Society)." In *Hyŏndaesahoe-ŭi kujo-wa inshik* (Structure and Theory on Modern Society), pp. 119–146. Seoul: Iljisa.
Seoul Daily (Seoul Shinmun). April 25, 2006.
Shin, Kwang-Yeong (Shin, Kwang-yŏng) et al., "Minjuju'ŭi-wa chŏnt'ongjŏk kach'i-e kwanhan ŭishikchosa (Survey on Democracy and Traditional Beliefs)." Korea Social Science Data Archive (KOSSDA, data # A1-2000-0003), http://www.kossda.or.kr (accessed on Sep 24, 2010).
Shin, Yu-Keun (Shin, Yu-gŭn). 1993. "Han'guk kiŏp-ŭi sahoe ch'amyŏ-wa kiŏp chaedan-ŭi yŏkhal (Social Participation of Korean Companies and the Roles of Welfare Foundation)." In Chŏn'guk kyŏngchein yŏnhaphoe (FKI: Federation of Korean Industry) (ed.), *Han'guk kiŏp chaedan ch'ongram* (Bibliography on Korean Corporations), pp. 5–21. Seoul: Chŏn'guk kyŏngjein yŏnhaphoe.
Son, Ho-chul (Son, Ho-ch'ŏl). 1993. *Chŏnhwangi-ŭi han'gukchŏngch'i* (Korean Politics in Transitional Era). Seoul: Changjak-gwa pip'yŏngsa.
———. 1995. "Kukka shimin sahoeron: han'guk chŏngch'i-ŭi taean-in'ga? (State-Civil Society: Alternative of Korean Politics?)." In *Haebang 50nyŏn-ŭi han'guk chŏngch'i* (Korean Politics in 50 Years of Independence), pp. 19–50. Seoul: Saegil.
Song, Bok (Song, Bok). 1997. *Han'guksahoe-ŭi Kaldŭlgujo* (Conflict Structure of the Korean Society). Seoul: Kyungmoonsa.
The Bank of Korea. 1998. *Urinara-ŭi kŭmyung chedo* (The financial system in the Republic of Korea). Seoul: The Bank of Korea.
———. 1999. *Urinara-ŭi kŭmyung chedo* (The Financial System in the Republic of Korea). Seoul: the Bank of Korea.
———. www.bok.or.kr, searched on December 1, 2003.
The Secretariat of the National Assembly. 2000. *Che 216 hoe kukhoe kongjŏk chagŭm-ŭi unyŏngsilt'ae kyumyŏng-ŭl wihan kukchŏngamsa t'ŭkpyŏl wiwŏnhoe'ŭirok* (The 216th Special Committee's Minutes of Parliamentary Inquiries on the Management of the Public Fund). Seoul: The National Assembly.
———. 2001. *Che217 hoe Kukhoe Kongjŏk chagŭm-ŭi unyŏngsilt'ae kyumyŏng-ŭl wihan kukchŏnggamsa t'ŭkpyŏl wiwŏnhoe'ŭirok* (The 217th Special Committee's Minutes of Parliamentary Inquiries on the Management of the Public Fund). Seoul: The National Assembly.

Um, Tae-Seok (Ŏm, Tae-sŏk). 1997. "P'uriga itnŭn han'gugin-ŭi chŏngch'iŭishik (Rooted Political Consciousness of Korean People)." *Forum 21* Fall Issue: 91–118.

Yang, Sang-Woo and Sung-Kon Cho (Yang, Sang-wu and Sŏng-gwon Cho). 1999. "Shimindanch'e sŏlmunjosa: t'ohodŭl-i ch'umch'unda (A Survey on NGOs: 'Toho (local power elites) are Present Everywhere)." *Hankyorye 21*, May 27, pp. 12–23.

Yi, Hye-kyung (Yi, Hye-gyŏng). 1995. *Konggong pumun-gwa min'gan pumun-ŭi yŏn'gye: Han'gukjŏk pokchi mohyŏng-ŭi chŏngnip-kwa chŏngch'aek panghyang* (Linkage of Public Sector and Private Sector: Korean Welfare Model and Policy). Seoul: Han'guk Pogŏnsahoe Yŏn'guwŏn (Korean Institute for Health and Social Affairs).

Yu, Pal-mu and Ho-ki Kim (Yu, P'al-mu and Ho-gi Kim). 1995. *Shimin sahoe-wa shimin undong* (Civil Society and Civil Movement). Seoul: Hanul.

Index

affective networks
  alternative views on, 62–6
  civil society and, 15, 19–20
  Confucianism and, 57–60
  functions and roles of, 86–8
  institutionalization of, 54
  modern manifestations of, 54–7
  nongovernmental sector and, 79–81
  overview, 49–50, 70–2
  previous studies on, 60–2
  sarim, 19, 85–6
  social capital and, 51–4
  social development and, 88–91
Ahn, Chung Young, 153
Ames, Roger, 83, 97
Amsden, Alice, 3, 5–6, 8–9, 35, 100, 120, 131, 141, 168
ancestors
  representation and, 18, 26, 29–40, 173
  ritual and, 30–2, 40, 42–3
  worship of, 29, 126
  see also family; filial piety
Anderson, Perry, 75, 91, 96
Aoki, Masahiko, 5, 142
Appelbaum, Richard, 9
Arneil, Barbara, 138, 139
Asian Development Bank (ADB), 144, 168
"Asian values", 96–7

Balassa, Bela, 5
Barette, Richard, 95
Bell, Daniel, 14, 34–5, 70, 72, 89, 96
Bellah, Robert, 25, 98, 175
Berger, Mark, 96
Berger, Peter, 9, 35
blood ties, 54, 70, 84
Bourdieu, Pierre, 53, 69, 136, 138
"Bowling Alone", 71, 72, 179
Brandt, Vincent, 128
Buchanan, James, 103

Callahan, William A., 88
capitalism
  Christianity and, 28
  democracy and, 70–1
  development and, 37
  family and, 61
  legitimacy of, 103–8
  Korean developmental model and, 5
  moral economy and, 180–1
  1997 financial crisis and, 49
  nongovernmental sector and, 75
  Park Chung Hee and, 11–12
  social capital and, 13, 54
  state and, 9, 143, 146, 159
  Weber's theory of, 25–6, 98–9
  see also Confucian capitalism
ceremonies, 30–1, 42–3

chaebols, 7–8, 10, 16, 54, 86,
102–6, 110, 114, 120,
131–4, 137, 142, 152–4, 156,
158, 180
see also family
Chan, Joseph, 40, 82, 89, 96
Chang, Ha-Joon, 4–8, 10–11, 35,
105–6, 108, 120, 124, 131–6,
138–9, 141–2, 167, 184
Chang Yun-Shik, 38, 71, 84
Chen, Albert, 84
Cheong Wa Dae, 162
Cherry, Judith, 141, 153, 158, 167
Chibber, Vivek, 8–10, 12, 22,
106, 121, 125, 132–3, 140,
143, 159
Ching, Julia, 28
Cho Hein, 31, 85
Chohung Bank, 152, 164
Chosŏn dynasty, 19, 33, 39, 45, 58,
60, 70, 108–9
Christie, Kenneth, 96
Chun Doo Hwan, 56, 103, 114
Chung, Chullhee, 84
civil society
  affective networks and, 15,
  19–20, 63, 86, 176
  Confucian capitalism and, 101–2,
  104, 107–10, 174
  Confucianism and, 59–60
  family and, 63
  history of, 84–6
  moral economy and, 180
  nongovernmental sector in Korea
  and, 77–9, 84–6
  social capital and, 125
  state and, 13, 65, 146
  strong society and, 125, 127
  Western culture and, 104
Clegg, Stewart, 9, 95
Coase, Ronald, 34
Cohen, Jean, 63, 89, 178
Coleman, James, 14, 53–4,
67–9, 139
Collins, Randall, 26, 98

colonialism, 9, 100, 112, 138
Confucian capitalism
  "Asian values" and, 96–7
  checks and balances in, 108–11
  civil society and, 101–2, 104,
  107–10
  history of state-business
  collaboration, 100–3
  legitimacy in, 103–8
  modernization theory and, 98–9
  overview, 114–16
  possibilities and limits of, 111–14
  rise of, 95–6
Confucianism
  affective networks and, 57–60
  continuities and changes in
  familism, 39–43
  economic motives in filial
  piety, 30–2
  family in, 32–4
  filial piety as religion, 26–30
  modern pressures for better
  representation, 34–9
  nongovernmental sector
  and, 81–4
  overview, 25–6
connection-oriented society, 62–3
corruption, 7, 11, 19, 27, 60, 88,
103–4, 107–8, 110, 121, 124,
131, 134, 163, 174
credit unions, 153, 156

Daewoo crisis, 160
Daewoo Group, 152
Davis, Diane, 5, 7–8, 10–12, 35,
106, 108, 119, 124–5, 128,
131–3, 140
de Bary, Theodore, 28
democracy
  affective networks and, 19, 21,
  50, 62, 66, 84, 87–90, 180–1
  capitalism and, 15, 54
  Confucianism and, 60,
  109–10, 112
  industrialization and, 70–1, 115

nongovernmental sector and,
  76–8, 82, 84
regionalism and, 17, 56–7, 60
social capital and, 13
trust and, 179
Demsetz, Harold, 177
dependency theory, 66
Depositor Protection Act, 160
Deuchler, Martina, 34, 109
developmental synergy, 14, 120–3,
  127–8
DeVos, George, 33
Deyo, Frederic, 113
Duncan, John, 58

Economic Planning Board (EPB),
  9–10, 21–2
Economic Policy Coordination
  Meeting (EPCM), 160–1, 169
Eliade, Mircea, 27
embeddedness, 11, 17, 20, 53,
  69–70, 116, 119–20, 122, 124,
  128, 138, 173, 179
Evans, Peter, 4, 9, 11–12, 119, 121,
  124, 143

family
  affective networks and, 15–16,
    19, 54–5, 57–61, 63–4
  business and, 53, 180
  civil society and, 102, 176
  Confucian capitalism and, 103,
    109, 111, 114–16
  Confucianism and, 26, 32–4,
    39–44, 70
  cultural importance of, 58, 70,
    76–7, 83, 97
  economy and, 15–16
  generalized reciprocity and,
    81, 174
  identity and, 58
  nongovernmental sector and,
    83–4
  public sphere and, 58–60
  representation and, 34–6

sarim groups and, 85
state and, 123, 125–6, 133, 136
trust and, 177
virtue and, 89
see also *chaebols*
Feenstra, Robert, 186
filial piety
  Confucian familism and, 32–4,
    39, 58
  economic development
    and, 16, 18
  economic motives in, 30–2
  overview, 25–6
  as religion, 26–30, 126
  representation and, 35–6
  rituals and, 42–3
  see also family
financial crisis (1997)
  arrangement of bureaucratic
    agencies, 161, 163
  external dimensions of state
    capacity, 164–6
  internal dimensions of state
    capacity, 159–64
  corporate restructuring through
    financial restructuring, 156–9
  developmental state and, 141–4
  financial restructuring through
    public fund, 148–56
  legacy of developmental state,
    166–8
  public fund and mobilization,
    144–8
  public fund recovery by types, 166
Financial Supervisory
  Committee (FSC), 161–3
Five Cardinal Relationships, 29–30,
  35, 58
Five Year Economic Development
  Plans, 10, 134
Fligstein, Neil, 5
Frankel, Jeffrey, 142, 167
Fukuyama, Francis, 35, 111,
  113, 116
Fung Yu-Lan, 45

Geertz, Clifford, 181
generalized reciprocity, 4, 18–20, 53, 69, 81, 120, 123, 126–7, 129, 132–3, 137, 174, 176–9, 181
Gintis, Herbert, 181
globalization, 21, 86, 142, 167–8, 175
Gold, Thomas, 102, 116
Gramsci, Antonio, 113
Granovetter, Mark, 14, 16, 69, 116, 138–9, 179

Habermas, Jurgen, 75
Haggard, Stephan, 95
Hahm, Chaibong, 14, 19, 28, 33–5, 44, 64, 70–2, 82, 84, 113, 141, 175
Hahn, Sung Joe, 128
Hall, David, 97
Hall, John, 75
Hamilton, Clive, 9
Hamilton, Gary, 4, 35, 53, 86, 102
Hanbo Steel scandal, 103–4, 107, 116, 134
Harris, Christopher, 193
Hattori, Tamio, 102
Henderson, Gregory, 9, 65, 112
Hill, Michael, 29
Hobbes, Thomas, 83, 136, 178
Hofheinz, Roy Jr., 35
Honam, 56, 60–1
Hsu, Francis, 30, 32
Huntington, Samuel, 112
Hwang, Tae-Yun, 73

illegitimate collusion," 108
Illicit Wealth Accumulation Charges, 10, 131–2
Indonesia, 3
industrialization, 12, 14–16, 19–20, 36–7, 44, 50, 57, 61–2, 70–1, 76–7, 98, 101, 104, 106, 115, 127, 132, 137, 174, 181

International Bank for Reconstruction and Development (IBRD), 142, 144
International Monetary Fund (IMF), 96, 114–16, 142, 168

Jacobs, Norman, 34, 102, 113
Janelli, Roger, 39, 43, 45, 54
Japan, 3–4, 25, 34, 53–4, 67, 95, 98–9, 101–2, 111–12, 133, 139
Jeon, Sang-in, 31
Johnson, Charlmers, 3, 5, 9, 95, 100, 119–20, 141
Jomo, Kwame Sundaram, 3, 7

Kahn, Herman, 35, 95
Kang, David, 117
Kang, Myong-Ku, 78
Keane, John, 75
Kim Dae Jung, 17, 56, 60, 66, 103, 110, 114–15, 160, 167
Kim Hyung A, 189
Kim Jong Pil, 56
Kim Young Sam, 56, 103, 114, 136, 142
Koh, Byong-Ik, 39, 82
Kohli, Atul, 9
Korea Asset Management Corporation (KAMCO), 144–5, 160, 162, 168
Korea Deposit Insurance Corporation (KDIC), 144–5, 152, 160, 162, 168
Korea First Bank, 152, 164
Korean Miracle, 125
Korea Trade Agency (KOTRA), 6, 131
Kramer, Ralph, 76
Krugman, Paul, 111

labor unions, 63, 108–10
Lee, Dong Gull, 152
Lee, Hae-jun, 33

INDEX

Lee, Jae-Hyuk, 14, 62–5
Lee, Jae-Yeol, 39, 69, 71
Lee, Jung Young, 46
Lee, Keun, 168
Lee, Kwang-Kyu, 28, 30, 35, 57
Lee, Seung-Yeon, 40
Lee Gang-won, 169
Lee Myung Bak, 116
Leys, Colin, 13, 125
Luhman, Niklas, 177
Lynn, Hung Gu, 9

MacFarquhar, Roderick, 35, 113
Maison, Edward, 35
Malaysia, 3
Marxism, 66, 77
Mauss, Marcel, 127, 140
Meiji Restoration, 101
memorandum of understandings (MOUs), 164
Metzger, Thomas, 28, 99
Migdal, Joel, 13, 119, 121, 136, 138
Ministry of Finance and Economy (MOFE), 145, 152, 160, 162–4
mistrust, 64, 71
Mo, Jong Rin, 167
mobilization
 affective networks and, 62, 69, 81, 126
 Confucian capitalism and, 100–1, 107, 111–12
 development and, 127–9
 familism and, 35–6, 44
 market, 20–1, 136, 143
 NGOs and, 78
 Public Fund and, 144–8, 168
 resources, 10, 17, 35–6, 44
modernization theory, 14, 62, 66, 98–9
monopolization, 10, 66, 76, 100, 104, 107, 138
moral economy, 21, 180–1
Morishima, Michio, 95

Naeari, 43
New Village Movement, 120, 123, 127–31, 135
nongovernmental organizations (NGOs), 77–81, 84, 109–10
nongovernmental sector
 affective networks and, 79–81
 Confucianism and, 81–4
 existing studies on, 77–9
 overview, 75–7
nonperforming loans (NPLs), 146, 165
North, Douglas, 104, 113
North Korea, 100

Obama, Barack, 175
Oberschall, Anthony, 177
Offe, Claus, 176–9
Organization for Economic Cooperation and Development (OECD), 134
Ornatowski, Gregory, 101
Orru, Marco, 86
Ostrom, Elinor, 177
Oxburn, Phillip, 76

Park Chung Hee
 chaebols and, 104, 106, 133, 142
 Confucian Capitalism and, 95–6, 101, 104–5, 108
 corruption and, 131, 134–5
 developmental synergy and, 127
 industrial policies, 131–3
 military coup, 104
 New Village Movement and, 127–9
 political institutionalization and, 10
 regionalism and, 60
 rural middle class and, 11–12
 state discipline and, 12, 120, 137
 strong state and, 119–21, 123–5
Park Geun Hye, 139
Platteau, Jean-Philippe, 4, 13, 125
Pohang Steel (POSCO), 104, 107

Polanyi, Karl, 5, 97, 120, 138, 181
policy loans, 134
Portes, Alejandro, 13, 120, 125, 139
postmodernism, 19, 71–2
property rights, 75, 104, 113–15
public fund
    arrangement of bureaucratic agencies and, 159–64
    corporate sector and, 156–9
    financial restructuring through, 148–56
    1997 financial crisis and, 12, 141–4
    recovery, 164–7
    size of, mobilization, and injection, 144–8
    supervision and recovery of, 159–66
Public Fund Oversight Committee (PFOC), 162–3
Public Fund Oversight Special Act, *see* Special Act
Putnam, Robert, 4, 11, 13, 45, 52–4, 68–9, 71, 72, 122, 125, 136, 138, 139, 179
Pye, Lucian W., 35, 73

Radelet, Steven, 142
Redding, Gordon, 46, 102
regionalism, 17, 52, 54, 56–7, 60–1, 73, 75, 77, 86, 88
remembrance, 26, 29–37, 42–3
representation, 26, 29–39, 43–4, 86
Rhee, Syngman, 9–11, 21, 108, 124, 131
Ringmar, Erik, 39, 58, 81, 87, 180
Rodrik, Dani, 4
Roh Tae Woo, 56, 103, 112, 114
Rosemont, Henry, 34, 82
Rozman, Gilbert, 96, 113

Sahlins, Marshall D., 81, 120, 127, 139
Salamon, Lester, 78–80

Samsung, 16, 54, 106
sarim, 19, 85–6
school ties, 14, 16, 51–2, 54–6, 88, 120, 126
Schwartz, Bentzamin, 76, 97
Scott, James, 139, 181
Shim, Jae Bum, 57
Shim, Jae Hoon, 39
Singapore, 3–4, 7, 95, 101, 111
social capital, 11, 13–14, 17–19, 21
    affective networks and, 51–4, 60, 136
    Asian Values and, 71–2
    defined, 122
    forms of, 122
    market and, 66–71
    negative effects of, 135–6
    strong society and, 125–6
social capital theory, 123, 138
social development
    affective networks and, 88–91
Sorensen, Clark, 37, 42, 45
Special Act, 159–64
Steinberg, David, 21, 85
strong state, 122, 124
    chaebols, 131–3
    developmental synergy and, 127
    New Village Movement, 127–30
    overview, 119–20, 137
    social capital and, 125–6
    strong society and, 124–5
    trust and, 71, 111, 174–9
    weak society and, 120–3
    weak state and strong society, 133–6
    see also Park Chung Hee
Stubbs, Richard, 167
subsidies, 6–7, 76, 104, 131

Tai, Hung-chao, 35, 96
Taiwan, 3, 7, 53–4, 95, 101, 111–12, 139
Taylor, Rodney, 26, 45
Thailand, 3–4, 67
Thurbon, Elizabeth, 142

Tocqueville, Alexis de, 52, 72
traditional ties, 15, 135
Troeltsch, Ernst, 27
trust, 13–15, 17, 19, 21, 37, 53, 58, 61–4, 67–9, 71, 102, 111–13, 122, 126, 135, 153, 155, 161, 167, 174–9
Tu, Wei-Ming, 25, 35, 96–7

Uslaner, Eric, 176–8

virtue, 25, 45, 59, 85, 87, 89, 176
virtuosi, 29, 44
Vogel, Ezra, 35

Wade, Robert, 5, 21, 35, 100, 120, 141, 167, 175
Wank, David, 49, 76, 102, 116
Warren, Mark, 126
Weber, Max, 18, 25–8, 33, 45, 97–9, 138, 181
Weiss, G. Thomas, 79
Weiss, Linda, 167, 175

Wilk, Richard, 181
Williamson, Oliver, 14, 34, 54, 67, 73, 102, 113, 116, 139
Wong, Siu-lun, 102
Woolcock, Michael, 4, 11, 13–14, 122, 125, 129, 138, 176
World Bank, 3–5, 8, 131, 142
world-system theory, 66
Wu-Cumings, Meredith, 5, 10, 22, 120, 141
Wuthnow, Robert, 75

xing-li-xue, 58

Yamagishi, Toshio, 177, 179
Yao, Souchou, 46, 102, 116

Zak, Paul, 181
Zakaria, Fareed, 96
Zelizer, Viviana, 181
Zhu Xi, 58
Zuker, Lynne G., 176

GPSR Compliance

The European Union's (EU) General Product Safety Regulation (GPSR) is a set of rules that requires consumer products to be safe and our obligations to ensure this.

If you have any concerns about our products, you can contact us on

ProductSafety@springernature.com

In case Publisher is established outside the EU, the EU authorized representative is:

Springer Nature Customer Service Center GmbH
Europaplatz 3
69115 Heidelberg, Germany

www.ingramcontent.com/pod-product-compliance
Lightning Source LLC
LaVergne TN
LVHW051913060526
838200LV00004B/117